AFTER THE LAST SNAP

WHEN THE GAME ENDS, LIFE BEGINS

BY
ANDRE WILLIAMS

After the Last Snap: When the Game Ends, Life Begins

© Copyright 2024 Andre Williams

DreWill.com

ISBN: 978-1629672755

All rights reserved. No part of this book may be reproduced in any form or by any electronic or mechanical means, including information storage and retrieval systems, without written permission from the author, except in the case of a reviewer, who may quote brief passages embodied in critical articles or in a review.

Trademarked names may appear throughout this book. Rather than use a trademark symbol with every occurrence of a trademarked name, names are used in an editorial fashion, with no intention of infringement of the respective owner's trademark.

The information in this book is distributed on an "as is" basis, without warranty. Although every precaution has been taken in the preparation of this work, neither the author nor the publisher shall have any liability to any person or entity with respect to any loss or damage caused or alleged to be caused directly or indirectly by the information contained in this book.

Many of the names and locations in the story have been changed to protect the privacy of the individuals involved. My only intent is to tell my story, not expose other people.

Interior Layout: Brian Schwartz
Cover Design: Tatiana Villa

r24-0904

Table of Contents

INTRODUCTION 7
CHAPTER 1: FIRST MEMORY 9
CHAPTER 2: FIRST SPORT 11
CHAPTER 3: MOVING SOUTH 13
CHAPTER 4: THINGS GO SOUTH 16
CHAPTER 5: FROM SOUTHERN TO COUNTRY 20
CHAPTER 6: FRIENDS & FRIENDS YOU CAN DEPEND ON 22
CHAPTER 7: BONFIRE 24
CHAPTER 8: PARKLAND TROJANS 27
CHAPTER 9: THE CARNAL SELF 30
CHAPTER 10: RATTY SNITCH 33
CHAPTER 11: SWEETHEART, HEARTBREAK 35
CHAPTER 12: PHS ENDNOTES 38
CHAPTER 13: FOR BOSTON 41
CHAPTER 14: CHESTNUT (HILL) ROASTING 45
CHAPTER 15: GOLDEN EAGLE 47
CHAPTER 16: MR. WILLIAMS, THE MAN-HORSE 56
CHAPTER 17: ENTANGLEMENT 58
CHAPTER 18: ANDRE THE GIANT 64
CHAPTER 19: I DO 68
CHAPTER 20: I DON'T 71
CHAPTER 21: ROOKIE 74
CHAPTER 22: REAL EYES 77
CHAPTER 23: DESCENT 80
CHAPTER 24: HER 23RD 83
CHAPTER 25: FINE PRINT 86
CHAPTER 26: BABY ON THE WAY 89
CHAPTER 27: GIANTS LOSE BY ONE 94
CHAPTER 28: ROY THE MAKER 97
CHAPTER 29: BZW 103
CHAPTER 30: FAMILY (UN)TIES 106

CHAPTER 31: ZAVIER 109
CHAPTER 32: GROWING PAINS 111
CHAPTER 33: BEFORE THE STORM 113
CHAPTER 34: COLD SUMMER 115
CHAPTER 35: FITNESS QUEST ONE 117
CHAPTER 36: A BIG BREAK 121
CHAPTER 37: MOVE OF GOD, ACT OF MAN 127
CHAPTER 38: W.I.N.O. 129
CHAPTER 39: THE SKULL & THE WOLF 132
CHAPTER 40: BEAUJOLAIS 137
CHAPTER 41: EDGE OF MIND 140
CHAPTER 42: A LOVE LETTER 144
CHAPTER 43: ENTER HADES 147
CHAPTER 44: SECRET BABY 151
CHAPTER 45: ATTRITION 153
CHAPTER 46: ONE LAST DANCE 160
CHAPTER 47: MERE FORMALITIES 166
CHAPTER 48: AFTERMATH 173
CHAPTER 49: LIBERTY FAIRS 176
CHAPTER 50: ROUGHNECKING 182
CHAPTER 51: CONTAGION 192
CHAPTER 52: VALLEY OF THE SHADOW 196
CHAPTER 53: IN THE MEANTIME 199
CHAPTER 54: DREAM CHASER 205
CHAPTER 55: TEST EVERYBODY 210
CHAPTER 56: DICEROLL 216
CHAPTER 57: GRAND OPENING 223
CHAPTER 58: NFL ON FOX 225
CHAPTER 59: DIGITAL DEMONS & THE ANGEL OF DEATH 228
CHAPTER 60: FAMINE 236
CHAPTER 61: FAMILY FEUD 242
CHAPTER 62: COLD SWEAT 245
CHAPTER 63: A TIME TO MEND DEFERRED 258
CHAPTER 64: NEW YEAR, NEW ME 263
CHAPTER 65: CLOSING REMARKS 273

Misfortune finds a good man that leads an unrighteous life because he gives his enemies the legal right to steal the things he's earned, kill his dreams, and destroy the foundation he's built.

Introduction

What's in a name? Have you ever dug deep to uncover its meaning? My full name is Andre-Rishard Williams. Break it down, and you get (Andre) Manly, (Rishard) Powerful Ruler, (Williams) Faithful Defender. Growing up, Andre Rishard Williams felt like just any ordinary name. But when I took the time to explore its roots, I was struck by its significance.

Names carry weight. They can be a prophecy, whispering hints about our destiny. The meanings embedded in a name can set a path for what life has in store. This memoir isn't just about a football player named Andre Rishard Williams. It's about the journey of my life—rising to the pinnacle of my career, plummeting into the depths, and clawing my way back wearing a pair of worn, selvedge jeans.

This tale chronicles my growth and the evolution of my spirit. It's a reflection on life's lessons, hard-earned and deeply felt. One truth I've come to know. We always have a choice. The choices I've made, both good and bad, are mine to own. They shaped my opportunities and my misfortunes alike.

This book is an addendum to my legacy, a testament for my children and for young people everywhere who dream of following the path I trod into the world of professional sport. It's both a cautionary tale and a beacon of hope. My aim is to help you avoid my missteps and soar higher than I ever did. The journey I share here is raw and real, penned with heartfelt passion and unwavering conviction. Some parts may shake you to your core, as there's an undeniable spiritual element woven through these pages.

In writing this memoir, my goal is to capture the pivotal moments and experiences that defined my life. My hope is that, whether you're a sports enthusiast or not, you'll find value in my story. Yes, football is the backdrop, but this is a narrative about self-discovery, power struggles, sex & sin, misguided idealism, triumph

& tragedy, family ties, marriage & divorce, loss & hate, faith & forgiveness, heartache & long-suffering, homelessness & happiness. It touches on the vices that nearly consumed me and the profound search for the meaning of life itself.

If even one person reading this book avoids the darkness I stumbled into during my twenties, then every word was worth writing. I wouldn't wish that hell on anyone. Conversely, if my words help a single soul find deeper meaning and achieve their dreams, then this endeavor has fulfilled its purpose. I hope that person pays it forward, extending their newfound strength to someone else in need, just as I needed support to find and understand myself.

I dedicate this book to my firstborn son, Barron. My hope is that one day you'll read these words and grasp the wisdom I'm leaving behind. May it help you understand yourself more fully, making sense of your circumstances and our shared history. Choices of my past keep me from being there for you as I wish I could be. So instead, I pour my heart into these pages, a treasure for you to discover when you're ready, BZW. My first piece of advice to you, my beloved son, is this: Research the meaning of your name. Unearth its depth, then ponder, "What does it take to lead a good life in this world?"

3 Things

A brain, think for yourself.
Take courage, follow your conviction.
And finally, always think positively.

I love you man,
Your Dad

Chapter 1: First Memory

From a young age, it was clear to everyone around me that I had a boundless love for running. I was just two years old when I first experienced one of life's harsh lessons. That lesson came in the form of a car-sized lump. It all happened during a routine grocery shopping trip with my mother and my ten-year-old brother in Plainfield, New Jersey. My playful spirit often led me into trouble, and despite my brother's best efforts to keep me close, my stubborn curiosity got the better of me.

I managed to wriggle free from his grasp and let my adventurous nature take over. I started darting around, hiding behind anything that caught my eye. But what began as innocent play quickly turned dangerous. In one of my youthful spurts, I dashed into the street right in the path of an oncoming car. It was a hit-and-run, a nightmare scenario for any parent.

The impact launched me into the air, a story my parents have recounted countless times. I landed and rolled under a parked car. A good Samaritan, who had witnessed the entire ordeal, sprang into action. They lifted the vehicle off its wheels, allowing another bystander to pull me out from beneath it. I was unconscious, my forehead bone exposed, my heart had stopped. The paramedics arrived swiftly, used an AED to bring me back, and rushed me to the nearest hospital.

My earliest memory stems from this traumatic event. I remember being strapped to a stretcher, immobilized, gazing up at the sky. Across the street, I saw a red helicopter landing on a school's grassy field. And then, I blacked out again. The next thing I remember, I was in a caged stretcher being wheeled into the hospital, a tube painfully inserted into my urethra. I recall waking up in the middle of the night, lying in a hospital bed surrounded by a murmuring crowd.

The morning after is etched vividly in my mind. I woke up to the sound of 'Chip 'n' Dale' on the TV and the taste of butterscotch pudding for breakfast. My mother often recounts how the doctors warned her about potential changes in me due to the trauma. They told her, "He may not be the same." They were right. It took seven stitches to close the gash on my forehead, and my behavior did change.

Despite the ordeal, I was discharged the next day. My boundless energy returned, and I remember running around the hospital premises, much to the astonishment of the staff. My mother called me her "miracle child." Yet, despite surviving that car accident, my family noticed a shift in me. I started behaving like a "little old man," carrying an air of seriousness that belied my young age.

Chapter 2: First Sport

Karate became my first sport, thanks to my mom's belief that it was a safer choice than football. The car accident had left a deep scar, not just on my forehead, but on her psyche as well. She worried that another blow to my head on the football field could have devastating consequences. My perspective, however, was quite different. I was convinced that if a car couldn't take me down, then no little boy stood a chance. But despite my protests, my mother's concerns won out, and I reluctantly agreed to give karate a try.

I dominated those karate classes. Sparring quickly became my favorite part, though I did get into trouble once for accidentally kicking my partner's nose bloody. Even with all the protective gear, there was no nose guard, and I found myself reprimanded by the stern instructor. Despite the reprimands, I advanced through four belts, though I started to feel an itch for more physicality and competition.

I remember one conversation with my older brother after a particularly tough karate class. Feeling proud, I sought his approval, but he dismissed my efforts, saying that my one-hour karate class couldn't compare to his two-and-a-half-hour football practice. His words struck a chord, and my interest in karate waned.

The following year, my younger brother started playing flag football, and I couldn't help but find it unfair. I pestered my mom relentlessly until she finally relented. During my sixth-grade year, I eagerly joined the local peewee football program in South Plainfield, NJ.

My first season of football was far from stellar. I can barely recall a single victory. My brother's words echoed in my mind as I struggled to maneuver through the grass, weighed down by all the equipment. Yet, despite the challenges, I loved every moment and discovered a natural talent for the sport. The coach's encouraging words left an indelible mark on me that year. "Dre," he said,

☆ After the Last Snap ☆

"you've got a lot of raw talent. Stick with it because someday it will take you places." It was the first genuine compliment I ever received from a coach, and it fueled my passion for the sport even further.

But old habits die hard, and my mom fell back into her routine the following season, forbidding me from playing football again. Instead, I found myself reluctantly joining the soccer team in seventh grade. I excelled at soccer too, but nothing compared to the thrill of charging forward with a football in my hands, clad in my athletic armor, with opponents in hot pursuit. I was hooked.

By eighth grade, I began to notice my physique growing more robust compared to my peers. Motivated by this change, I asked my mom to let me play football again, highlighting that playing for the school wouldn't require a significant financial commitment. She finally agreed, and that year turned out to be exhilarating. Our team won several games, and I shone as a running back, linebacker, and even as the kicker on the kickoff team. Towards the end of the season, my performance caught the eye of the high school team, who had big plans for me. But little did I know, my parents had even bigger plans in store.

Chapter 3: Moving South

Just before I was meant to start 9th grade, my family and I moved to Georgia. It was a period filled with unexpected and perplexing turns.

When I talk about my family, it was just my mother, my younger brother, and me. My older brother was already 21 at the time, off chasing his own dreams. My sister had just left for Cornell. My father, however, stayed behind in New Jersey to tend to his business.

Growing up, we often take for granted that our parents know best, or we overlook the possibility that they, too, can make mistakes. In hindsight, moving to Georgia stands out as one of my parents' biggest missteps. It set into motion a chain of events that eventually led to the unraveling of their marriage.

The exact reasons for my mother's sudden decision to leave New Jersey are still a mystery to me. Perhaps it was her friend Jeane, who had recently moved to Georgia, who enticed her. I struggle to understand why she was comfortable being separated from my dad or why she was in such a hurry to relocate. It might have been one of her flaws—to act first and think later, leaving my dad to deal with the fallout of her decisions.

Regardless of their reasons, she was ready to move, and he was not. My father had built up his HVAC business over a decade in New Jersey. He couldn't just uproot and leave while expecting to maintain his financial stability. Still, I can't fathom why he didn't assert himself and fight to keep the family together until a solid plan was in place. But success sometimes clouds judgment, and I think his booming business fed his ego. He made the decision to buy a house in Georgia simply because he could afford it—a $500,000 home in an upscale neighborhood. So, he sold our house in New Jersey and bought a new one in Acworth, Georgia. He

☆ After the Last Snap ☆

would come down every couple of months for the weekend and then head back to work.

It was an incredibly strange time in my life. I had just turned 13 that summer, and the throes of teenage angst hit me hard. I found myself alone in a foreign land, trying to stay connected with my best friends through World of Warcraft. Being a dedicated gamer, I had my moments of fun, but my subpar computer created unbearable lag, ruining the excitement and keeping me from engaging in high-level content. Frustrated, I would retreat to my closet, gaze out the window, and eagerly await the start of school. My room, situated on the second floor above the garage, overlooked our unfinished cul-de-sac. Ah, 2006, what a year it was.

When school finally started, I quickly realized I was in a new world. For starters, Sperry's had replaced Air Force 1's as the go-to footwear (though I never owned a pair of either). The Southern belles and gallant boys of Georgia were a stark contrast to the boisterous, quick-witted kids from the Northeast. Good manners genuinely impressed the ladies, and anything less could spell disaster.

On my first day of ninth grade, during Geography class, I found myself sitting across from a stunning brunette named Shelby Gacetta. She had bright eyes and a beautiful smile. I was intrigued, and I made it my mission to talk to her. When the teacher gave us group work, I seized the opportunity. I would look up at her, furrow my brows, and tilt my head, pretending to notice something on her face. Eventually, she caught on and asked me what I was looking at. With a mischievous grin, I replied, "Shelby... is that a chin hair?" To my shock, she gasped and burst into tears. It was not the reaction I had anticipated. Her friend glared at me and demanded to know why I would say such a thing. Mortified, I quickly apologized, assuring Shelby that it was just a joke, and she absolutely did not have any chin hair. Unfortunately, my ill-conceived attempt at humor had completely ruined my chances with her.

That interaction struck me deep, and I realized I would need to recalibrate my social skills if I wanted to survive here. Things were different down south, but one constant remained--football. That stayed the same whether I was in the North or South, and I knew exactly how to thrive and excel in that environment. Having talent

☆ Andre Williams ☆

in football in a place like Georgia was a tremendous blessing. There was a level of prestige surrounding the sport. The football program at Harrison High was exceptional, partly because football was not just an after-school activity; it was a way of life. It was almost like a combination of church and college. Sports and academics were completely intertwined, and if you were a football player, your schedule was entirely different from that of an average student. For instance, every football player had to take the "high-level lifting class," which was exclusively for football players and taught by the o-line coach.

Despite feeling alone in a new place, I felt right at home on the football field. I quickly fit in and began to establish myself. Ultimately, I had a fantastic freshman football season, and despite proving too uncouth for Shelby, all felt right in the world.

Chapter 4:
Things Go South

My second year in Georgia turned out to be my final one. Just when I began to settle down and acclimate to my new environment, everything fell apart in a disastrous manner. A mentor of mine once remarked that every choice we make takes six months to a year for the consequences to manifest, and in retrospect, this timeline was perfectly accurate in this particular case. My parent's decision to separate was made in error, and its repercussions caught up with them during my sophomore year of high school.

My dad's visit in the summer before school was a complete surprise when he brought a puppy with him. We had never had a dog before. In Jamaica, there are not many stray cats, but there are a lot of stray dogs. My grandma did have a dog in the backyard, but he was more of an outside animal than a pet, not the cuddly type at all. However, the puppy my dad brought was a soft-coated wheaten terrier. He was golden with black ears, beautiful, smart, and extremely playful. I named him Ziggy Marley Williams. He was a wonderful dog.

By that time, I had also made a new friend. His name was Alphonso, and he was two years ahead of me. Despite the age gap, we spent a lot of time together through sports. He was a running back on the football team and a sprinter on the track team, just like me. In fact, he was the fastest kid in the school. I was a close second. This summer, I didn't waste time playing World of Warcraft or staring out the window into the cul-de-sac. Instead, I was walking Ziggy and riding around with Alphonso in his burgundy Ford F-150. Our outings often led us to McDonald's. This was back when the dollar menu was still a dollar. My go-to item was the McDouble. I'd get two of them with a side of fries and an apple pie. That was until I got sick and yakked it all up and realized McDonald's wasn't real food. I haven't been back for a burger since that time. But Zo introduced me to Waffle House, and from then on, life was good. Breakfast has always been my favorite meal of the day.

School started, and everything felt perfect—or at least, that's what I thought initially. It was my first year playing varsity football, and I quickly fell in love with the deep connection between football and spirituality at Harrison High. Each practice would begin with a special ritual. We would gather around the Hoya mascot outside of the fieldhouse, placing our hands on each other and forming a large circle. Then, our coach would lead us in a prayer that never failed to ignite our spirits. It set the tone for an incredible practice session every time.

After practice, I used to catch a ride home with Alphonso and his girlfriend Shea. They were inseparable and it was cool to see. I admired their young love. I wanted to find someone special too. I ended up looking in the wrong place. That season I started dating Hillary, one of the team trainers. She was older than me, which was quickly becoming a pattern of mine. To this day, I tend to spend more time with the older crowd. Hillary had a passion for photography and had a deep appreciation for the talented Colbie Caillat. As for me, I was on a different journey—I wanted to experience the body of a woman for the first time and lose my virginity. There was a moment when I almost achieved that goal. Hillary would often invite me over to her house, where we would connect over her latest photographs and discuss our next exploration in nature—be it an old rustic barn or a serene forest clearing. Occasionally, I would indulge in some PlayStation gaming with her younger brother. Her parents were always gracious enough to give us space and freedom to be ourselves.

One time, Hillary invited me into her bedroom, and for a moment, I thought luck was on my side. She gently took my hand and directed me to sit on the bed. Our eyes met, and in that intimate moment, she leaned in and pressed her lips against mine before lying back against the bed. "Game time," I thought. Overwhelmed with excitement, I began to undress her, but we didn't get far before we were interrupted by a knock at the door. Surprisingly, it was her father who stood on the other side. Despite his advanced age, his

☆ After the Last Snap ☆

instincts were sharp as ever. Hot passion turned to cold fear. We quickly jumped to our feet upon hearing him call her name. Fortunately, Hillary reacted swiftly. She'd somehow managed to get her shirt back on before her father walked in and discovered us. His eyes were bulging, and I could see the blood pounding in his veins. He sternly instructed us to leave the room, and we obeyed without hesitation. From that moment on, I knew our time together was limited. Hillary kindly escorted me back home, but our relationship ultimately fizzled out not long after that incident. Hillary's dad hadn't laid a hand on us, but he still managed to kill all the fun. It was on a day when she dropped me off at my driveway after school that I summoned the courage to end things between us. Tears streamed down her face as she clung onto me tightly, and although I was patient, deep down, I yearned for her to leave. Our connection wasn't as profound as she imagined it, and my faithful companion Ziggy was eagerly awaiting his walk.

Winter break arrived, and my sister returned home from school. My mom decided that it was the perfect time to plan a surprise visit to my dad up north for the holidays. In hindsight, it may have been a risky idea, but little did we know what was in store. After a long drive, we finally reached my dad's high-rise apartment building in New Jersey. While everyone was eager to go up and surprise my father, I volunteered to stay behind and give Ziggy a chance to stretch his legs. It turns out, the real surprise was waiting for us when we least expected it—my father had something in store for all of us.

When Ziggy and I finally arrived at my father's place, I was puzzled by the scene before me. It was like I'd entered an alternate reality where everything was strange. My mother sat hunched in the corner on the floor, like a fallen picture frame. The room was filled with an eerie silence, hanging over everything like a grimy blanket. This silence brought discomfort and unease, making it hard to comprehend what had transpired. The details of how the day concluded or how we managed to return to Georgia escape my memory. All I know is that my father had made a grave mistake, and things took a turn for the worse. As my sophomore year came to an end, my mother had had enough of Georgia and yearned to go back up north. However, she vehemently rejected the idea of returning to New Jersey. The mere thought of going back there to live was out of the question. Instead, she decided to move to the neighboring state of Pennsylvania.

Chapter 5: From Southern to Country

I was furious with my parents when I realized we would be moving again. I was worried too because I needed a scholarship to attend University. My sister chose to continue her studies at Cornell University, and I knew an Ivy league education wasn't cheap. And now, my parents were getting ready to acquire their second home in just two years. I knew they were stretching themselves financially.

I considered the possibility of being overlooked by college recruiters. I feared that I would be lost in the shuffle when the time came for them to find me because I didn't stay in one place and build up my reputation.

Georgia was a football factory, and there was a huge opportunity for me there. Now, just when I was getting comfortable, it was time to go? I was dismayed. However, my perspective changed when real estate agents informed my parents about the thriving football scene in the Lehigh Valley. It turned out that Parkland High's football team had just lost the state championship the previous year. It was inevitable that recruiters would be flocking to Parkland. If we were to relocate, I hoped it would be to the Parkland school district. I expressed my wishes to my parents as passionately as I could and although my parents still had their differences, they were in agreement with me when they made the bold decision to move to the Lehigh Valley.

In the summer of 2008, we relocated to a charming ranch house perched on a hill in Schnecksville, PA. My parents drove back down to Georgia to go get the rest of the furniture out of the house in Acworth, Georgia and instead of trusting me to take care of Ziggy while they were gone, they took the dog with them. I'd never see Ziggy again after that. They came back without him. Their excuse was, he ran away during his bathroom time and he could not be recovered before it was time for them to head back. I was hurt. Ziggy was a great dog. He definitely needed a leash outside but he was incredible nonetheless.

Now, in a new town and without my dog Ziggy, there wasn't much left to do but go play football. I'd be going from Southern to Country. The flavor of football was a little different but the meal was the same.

At this point, I have to give credit where credit is due. Football can be a very political game. Those players that make it onto the field on game day are there because of 1 of 3 reasons: Tenure, talent, or election albeit fair or paid. These reasons can often conflict with one another, but there are rare instances in which a coach's decisions are exclusively based on what is best for the team and most conducive to winning. In my case, Coach Morgans did just that. He saw a player coming in from a great program with experience in the wing-t offense, a RB with talent and character. Coach did what he thought was best and he inserted me into the starting line up at the fullback position even though this same senior group had just been to the big show just last year. This caused some discontent in the locker room but I don't think Coach Morgans cared too much about that and neither did I. Coach Morgans cared about winning the right way. I have a ton of respect for this man. He invited me into his football family and he gave me a chance when he had no real obligation to do so.

Chapter 6: Friends & Friends You Can Depend On

I always gravitated towards an older crowd. In Georgia, I had Alphonso, and when I moved back up north to Pennsylvania, I met Diab. He lived nearby and would often give me rides home in his big black Toyota Sequoia. We connected through our shared love for football and our similar ethnic backgrounds—he was Syrian and I was Jamaican. Despite our different origins and playing on opposite sides of the ball, we bonded over the fact that our families were not from here. We both grew up with customs and beliefs that weren't strictly American. So, when I was around his family, it felt natural. We found common ground on many issues, and our deep, intellectual conversations set us apart from most people our age. He shared my passion for gaming and was an introvert like me.

We spent a lot of time together during his senior year before he went on to study and play ball at Moravian University. Diab was a true friend to me then, and our bond remains strong to this day. He has been there for me in countless challenging situations over the years. I stood by his side as a groomsman at his wedding, and I consider him the godfather of my child; his mom is like a second mother to me. I hold a deep affection for that man.

I'll admit, I wasn't always the best friend to him. There was a time when I was going through a rough patch, and I isolated myself from everyone, including Diab, because I didn't know how to talk about what I was dealing with. I struggled to admit that I had made a mistake and didn't know how to handle it. This went on for almost a year before I realized I needed help. When I finally called Diab, he showed up and demonstrated his love and support as if nothing had ever happened. More on that later.

☆ Andre Williams ☆

Now in my junior year, I fell in with a new group of friends, and with them came new habits. There's a saying that goes, "Show me your friends, and I'll show you your future," and I quickly realized the truth behind it. I discovered that Pennsylvanians have a deep affection for bonfires, and in high school, it was more than just a cozy gathering around the fire. "We were eating grilled food. We were drinking cold beverages, and the firewood was not the only thing smoking."

It was during this time that I started experimenting with weed and alcohol. I was a mere 16-year-old. I don't recall my first drink, but I do know that one of my most profound regrets happened that same year while I was under the influence of alcohol. More on that later.

Chapter 7: Bonfire

Junior year of high school marked a series of significant firsts for me. The first time I tried cannabis, I was cruising with Diab and some of his friends. They had a joint rolled up, and I decided to take a few hits out of curiosity. Not knowing what to expect, I found that, as often happens, not much happened the first time. However, the second time I tried cannabis, it was an entirely different experience.

Marcus hosted a large bonfire at his place, bringing together a large portion of the junior class. While he was occupied with his hosting duties, James and his older brother Derek accompanied me to a green jeep parked by the road, concealed in the darkness of the night. This time, James assured me that things would be different. With Derek at the wheel and James in the passenger seat, I embarked on my second cannabis experience.

I settled back comfortably in the backseat and began to inquire about the tree while Derek assembled the bowl for us to enjoy together. Derek mentioned that these particular buds had been imported from the tropical island of Hawaii. James then proceeded to explain, in simpler terms suitable for cannabis enthusiasts, how to use the bowl. "If the bud is cherried, you don't even need to light it. Just keep the shotty closed, inhale, and then release." By the second rotation of the bowl, I was starting to grasp the concept, although I still didn't feel any effects.

Derek cleared the ash from the bowl and packed it with fresh bud once more. We indulged in another round, and I could tell that Derek and James were already feeling the effects. I, on the other hand, had yet to experience anything.

James asked, with genuine surprise, "Dre, seriously, you still don't feel anything, dude?" I responded, "Nah, bro, maybe I'm just immune." He chuckled and said, "Yeah, man, maybe you're immune, but that's a bummer." We completed the round and prepared ourselves to return to the bonfire.

☆ Andre Williams ☆

A strange thing occurred as I exited Derek's green jeep. As I set foot on the ground, I sensed the Earth tilt and tremble so much, I had to catch myself. "Did you feel that, James?" I asked incredulously. With a smirk, he replied, "Feel what, Dre?" How did he miss the quake? "Bro, you didn't feel that tremor just now?" I asked. James and Derek exchanged glances and burst into laughter. "Dre, you're high right now, bro," Derek exclaimed. "Really? I can't really tell. It's kinda lame," I admitted. James reassured me, "Don't worry, Dre, it gets better."

We sat down in front of the fire Marcus had built in his backyard. As I gazed at the flames and basked in their comforting warmth, it struck me as amusing that despite living just over an hour east of here, I'd never heard of eating and drinking around a fire for fun. I watched the flames eat at the timber in the heart of the fire and, as I stared at the huge blaze, my mind began to travel through the darkness until it reached far into outer space. Suddenly, in my mind's eye, the bonfire was the sun. I watched the sun burning in the darkness of outer space from my mental spaceship. The sun became an animation, like a flipbook comic; and as I turned the pages, the sun flickered and flared one frame at a time.

There was definitely something going on now. I started to feel the most soothing sensation wherever the light of the flame touched my skin, like a thousand lovely fingertips brushing across my face and neck. I couldn't help but smile. I looked at James sitting next to me, staring intently at the fire. I said to him, "James, you were right. It got better, bro." He smiled back at me and said, "I know, Dre, I know... you wanna try some food?" The hotdogs I ate at that bonfire were the best hot dogs I'd ever eaten. The bottled water was the coolest, crispest drink to ever quench my thirst. Musical notes were hitting my ear so deeply I could feel them.

Needless to say, I had an amazing time that night. When it was over, I found myself reflecting deeply on the potential downsides of smoking weed. I knew there had to be some, but I couldn't see them at that moment. All I could focus on was the sensation of a thousand lovely fingertips caressing my skin. I knew it wouldn't be my last time smoking weed. For me, it was simply tremendous fun. Not to mention, I felt better the day after smoking than I did after having a few drinks. It occurred to me that marijuana must be the

☆ After the Last Snap ☆

athlete's drug of choice. Many things in life start out innocently before taking an unforeseen turn, and my relationship with marijuana certainly falls into that category. But more on that later.

Chapter 8: Parkland Trojans

The leader of the offensive line during my first year at Parkland was an amiable guy. Let's call him Macho. Macho didn't treat me like an outsider, unlike some of the salty seniors on the squad. One thing I firmly believe is that a running back must gain the trust of his offensive linemen to succeed. I never criticized my o-line outwardly, even when it was deserved. Instead, I saved candid discussions for the film room. The running back and the o-line must trust and align with one another; synergy is vital. This synergy might be exhibited on the field, but it's built off it—in the locker room, film meetings, and beyond. Success arises from success, but good energy nurtures success.

Having Macho as the o-line leader provided ample opportunities to nurture crucial synergy. Macho had suave, especially for an offensive lineman. He went the extra mile. Whether it was his parents' generosity in letting us host team parties at their place or their blissful ignorance of our gatherings, I got numerous opportunities to understand Macho's intricate character and form deep bonds with my teammates, on and off the field. Among countless unforgettable memories, one party particularly stands out—a memory Macho and I will take to our graves.

As I mentioned earlier, Pennsylvanians love a good bonfire party. Macho decided to throw one for the upperclassmen on the team after a Friday night home game. I was invited, and despite feeling like a bit of an outsider at the time, this party was a golden chance to bond with my teammates. The other running backs on the team were seniors and given that I was a threat to their final year of high school football, their initial skepticism of me was understandable. Instead of leaving room for awkward encounters, I decided to bring a girl, Joanna, to the party. That way, I could hang back, enjoy the party, and observe the team dynamic without being in the mix. As an added bonus, Joanna was a senior. She knew everyone on the team, and I learned something new about all of them without having to ask.

Showing up to the social event with a girl on your arm is a great way to leave a positive first impression because eye candy is a great gift, even if the candy doesn't belong to you. Joanna might not have been a perfect ten, but she was an athlete with a thick, curvy body, mesmerizing eyes, and a seductive "just-woke-up" voice. She was attracted to chocolate-skinned men—lucky me.

Throughout the night, we enjoyed drinks and engaging conversations. As the night evolved and inhibitions lowered, a delightful chemistry began to develop between us. Joanna confessed to me what I already knew: she wanted to know me intimately. I asked Macho for a private place.

Unexpectedly, he offered his own bedroom where Joanna and I found ourselves alone and wanting the same thing. I was still a virgin at this point, but I put on like I'd been here before. We slipped out of our clothes and our bodies met each other. We were there for a long time that night. I don't know if Joanna got tired or if she had a curfew to keep, but eventually she tapped out and told me she had to make it back home. I don't know if she reached climax, but I did not. The thrill of the moment had me overwhelmed.

After she left, Macho went to inspect his room. He returned with his bedsheets to display to the overnighters. They were stained with Joanna's virgin blood. Rather than being upset, Macho had a look of triumph on his face. It was as if the soiled sheets were evidence of the wild party he'd thrown. Thus, Macho, the Parkland Trojan team's leader, and I, the new running back from the Dirty South, had forged a sick, amusing, and bizarre piece of shared history. Synergy secured.

That season under Coach Morgans' guidance, I started at fullback in the wing-t offense, and we secured a decent 7-4 record. Despite a remarkable 40-10 win over Whitehall to end the regular season, we bowed out of the playoffs with a disappointing loss to Liberty. As the football season closed, I found myself being pursued by both D1A and D1AA programs. Some schools made immediate scholarship offers sent via mail. Other schools sent their scouts to meet me first and then extended offers later by phone. I was charmed by both approaches.

☆ Andre Williams ☆

However, the recruiting process was taxing. Once, a coach from Pitt University pulled me out of class for over an hour just to sell me on the school. There was no mention of an offer, just an invite to camp. I had no interest in traveling five hours for camp with no scholarship in hand. The first D1A program to make an offer was Vanderbilt University, followed by Rutgers, then Temple, and Boston College. It didn't take me long to make my choice on a school. Once I am convinced, I tend to make a decision on the spot, and I won't think twice.

I took only one official visit before deciding to attend Boston College to play football and further my studies. I committed to BC before my senior year even started. My recruiting process was over, and I was happy to conclude my senior season worry-free.

Chapter 9: The Carnal Self

I found my high school sweetheart in the spring semester of my first year at Parkland. We shared an English class, and she sat right across from me. A field hockey player who I'll refer to as Ayla. Something about her tan skin and her little hands & feet was so cute to me. Even if she may not have found me intriguing initially, I made sure to sprinkle our classroom interactions with my southern charm and New Jersey suave. Eventually, Ayla warmed up to me and we began engaging in deep conversations, by high school junior standards—texting all day, walking each other to our next classes.

Around the time Ayla and I started getting close, I began distancing myself from Joanna. Joanna and I were hookup partners but never official, a seasonal item at best, and that season was now over. The fact still stood that we'd lost our innocence to each other; my body was comfortable exploring hers, and she, mine. I didn't realize how much this meant until the significance was put to the test.

Joanna threw a graduation party in the early summer of that year, precisely the time that Ayla and I had made our relationship official. To this day, going to that party stands out as one of my life's top regrets. I was foolish enough to believe I could go to Joanna's party, drink, and hang out with no strings attached. I didn't want to mess up my budding relationship with Ayla, but for some reason, I couldn't tell Joanna no. Carson had also been invited to the party. He was a cornerback on the football team. I hitched a ride with him.

"We should have a few drinks, relax, and leave when it starts getting late," I implored as we made our way to the party. Carson gave an ambivalent response, and we soon arrived at Joanna's house. I knew my plan was doomed the moment we arrived.

☆ Andre Williams ☆

The party was in full swing when we arrived. To our surprise, we were the only males present. *We were the party favors.* Joanna had clear expectations for the night and didn't hold back. She whispered her intentions in my ear and made sure I always had a drink in hand. I had wanted Carson to pull me out of the situation, but it seemed more and more unlikely as time went by. Two hours turned into four hours, and one drink turned into five. By this time, Carson had found a partner for himself too—a girl we'll call Alana, and as the night wore on the party thinned out until there were just us four left. Now, in our heavily inebriated state, leaving would be irresponsible and dangerous.

Joanna led me into her parent's home gym in the basement for some privacy. There, on the thin carpet between the treadmill and the VersaClimber, we undressed. My mind wailed, "This is wrong!" but my body had no problem responding to hers. It was far too late to turn back now anyway. We proceeded in our drunken intimacy and a funny new thing happened as we went along. Somewhere between the hard ground and the hard liquor, I found Joanna's spot, and she found her climax. I knew because she was the type to show you the proof. She washed away the last of my inhibition and I, swept up in the passion of the moment, finally relaxed and enjoyed myself.

It is peculiar how the devilish things we enjoy come with intense color and sweet heat, but the aftermath often leads us down a road of bitter regret and cold fear. We did not kiss when we said our goodbyes. At least there was a mutual understanding of the finality of the moment. Carson drove me home. He assured me that nothing would come of the night. He said I should forget it even happened because it wasn't a big deal.

But when I laid in my bed that night, I couldn't forget it happened. I was torn between the intensity of my moment with Joanna and an intense fear that Ayla would find out what I'd done. I could still smell Joanna all over my body and I was ashamed… but I enjoyed the aroma too much to wash it off. The smell took me back to the moment and allowed me to relive its sweetness. I was wrong, but I knew that tonight, there would be no one to scold me for what I had done. I turned out the lights and slept.

☆ After the Last Snap ☆

When I awoke the next day, I was ready to shower away the physical evidence of our encounter. Overnight, the fear and the shame had soured into guilt. I needed to sweep the memories under the rug of my mind. *Last night didn't happen,* I told myself. *Joanna doesn't even go to this school anymore, and I never have to see her again,* I exclaimed. As I metaphorically swept away the images of the previous night and murmured my affirmations of denial, a sense of calm washed over me. My reality was cleansed, albeit artificially, but it was guilt-free, at least for a while.

Chapter 10: Ratty Snitch

As it turned out, Ayla's best girlfriends were all dating Parkland's popular junior class football players. Donald was stepping up as our QB, with Asher and Martin slotted to start as our linebackers. In our junior year, we were still getting to know each other, but once I started dating Ayla, we quickly grew close. By our senior year, our tight-knit, exclusive clique was formed.

As summer rolled on, my relationship with Ayla deepened, and our group became closer. Summer football camp was on the horizon, school preparations were in full swing, and from the outside, everything seemed perfect.

I had secured a football scholarship from Boston College and was committed to attending there the following fall. I took the SATs cold and scored a 1760. I was set. My only task was to stay fit and enjoy my final year. I was gearing up to fill the spotlight as the clear starter, moving from fullback to halfback, a change that I welcomed as a growth opportunity.

But beneath all these positives, I was uneasy. A shadow loomed over me, constantly whispering a secret truth that I was battling to suppress. The harsh reality was that I was deliberately deceiving Ayla, the girl who I was falling for.

A constant question spurred on by an absurd ambivalence ran endless laps in my mind. Was it best to confess or continue the charade? Deep down, I knew honesty would set me free. But I tricked myself into believing that fear of losing her was what held me back, a belief that was far from the truth. In fact, my self-centered ambition fed my dishonesty. Early summer's secret was a thick fog in my mind, but I convinced myself that in time, we could love our way right through it. I believed that if our bond strengthened enough, the pain I was hiding from her would become insignificant.

☆ After the Last Snap ☆

I struggled with that painful deceit all summer, like the dull headache from a never-ending hangover. The only respite came from the thrills of the field; those moments when the game, practice, opponent, and run consumed my every thought.

Then, on a blistering day in late August, I got a message from Ayla, a question that sent my world crashing down. "Did you hook up with Joanna earlier this summer?" My heart sank. My greatest fear had come true, and I couldn't face it. Selfishly, I wanted to keep a good relationship going. I really liked Ayla. I didn't want a dumb mistake to ruin everything, so I lied. I told her it didn't happen, and I faked anger that someone would spread such an ugly rumor. Ayla accepted my lie, and I wished hard that this initial cover-up would be the last. The buried memories, the shame, and the guilt I tried so hard to hide were now front and center in my mind. When I looked in the mirror, I could see it all on my face.

There was another worrisome thing. How did Ayla find out? Someone was the rat. It wasn't Carson; he was my friend, my teammate, and I was positive he wasn't gossiping about who I was messing with. It wasn't Joanna either; we had an understanding. It had to be Alana. She had spilled the beans. I texted her, confronting her about it, but she pushed back, saying I was the one who should be ashamed. And she was right.

So much for a carefree senior year; my inner peace was gone. I wore a mask for Ayla, to give her the smiles and positivity she expected, but beneath that, my real face was ridden with guilt and shame.

I blamed Alana, the ratty snitch, for all my troubles. But truthfully, it was all my own doing. I could only blame myself.

Chapter 11: Sweetheart, Heartbreak

She'd fallen for me, a dirty, lying dog, and she was innocent, a sweetheart. I felt bad. Even worse, the secret I had swept under the rug had reached Ayla's ears. She knew what was hidden, yet she still wanted to dive deeper. I felt terrible.

The peak of guilt and shame hit when Ayla decided she loved me enough to lose her virginity to me. Maybe I was soft, but I couldn't bring myself to inflict the damage she was unknowingly asking for. I cheated on Ayla in the worst way possible, giving my whole body to someone else, and now she wanted to give her body to me. Something about that felt intensely wrong.

It drove me mad knowing I had just lost my virginity while actively dating her, and now here I was, expected to take hers. At the very least, she should know the truth first, I reasoned. Yet, I was terrified of the consequences if I retreated from my lie. I had already told her it never happened. That was my story, and I was sticking to it. I did not heed the voice of reason.

Looking back now, the only way I can describe my behavior is... I was being a coward. It's not a word I usually say. I generally don't swear, but at that point in my life, I did, and in this case, I fit the definition perfectly. Too scared to admit that I'd breached my own principles, I was ready to abandon even more just to shield my fears.

The real issue was that Alana, the proverbial rat, continued to wreak havoc. There was nothing I could do—she wasn't the kind of rat you could simply eliminate with a cheese trap. I could only hope that she'd grow tired of stirring the pot.

Ayla approached me about the rumors at least four times. Each time, I would vehemently deny them. She would accept the falsehood, and we'd move on, but something inside was slowly decaying. The rug was smoldering, betraying the heat of the

☆ After the Last Snap ☆

growing darkness beneath. I maintained my two-faced behavior. Lying became easier over time, but it never felt right.

Eventually, I resolved to stop the deception. I had lied to Ayla too many times. I promised that if the issue arose again, I'd tell the truth. I was done with lying, almost. Of course, the chance to come clean arrived at the worst possible moment.

The day came when Ayla told me she was ready to take the next step with me. As uneasy as I was about crossing this bridge, I didn't want to disappoint her, and I wasn't ready to tell the truth. Donning my false bravado, we planned for her to come over. This was an honor I knew would eventually come if I was patient, and here it was.

We chose a day when we were assured privacy, and Ayla drove to my house. I led her to my room, and, boy, was I sweating bullets. I was sick with guilt—real feverish guilt. I tried to muster excitement, but inside, I was a corpse & rigor mortis would not take.

Sitting there, bent-kneed, with my two heads of shame under the blanket, I looked down at both her and myself, utterly will-less. After a few minutes, I caved and told her I didn't think things would work out that day. At first, she was puzzled, but Ayla, being the good and innocent girl that she was, assumed I was nervous because it was also my first time. I played along with her assumption.

In time, I did fulfill Ayla's wish, but it required me to draw on my darkest energies. It happened at a late-night house party. We went shot for shot with Bankers Club Vodka—five for five—throwing them back before we snuck off into the darkness to know each other.

I was happy that I could finally perform for her. Thanks to the alcohol, I even managed to overperform, and Ayla got more than she bargained for. However, it wasn't pride I felt, just a numb relief, along with the grim realization that I'd descended to a dark new low. We'd crossed the threshold now, and I was only more pressed to continue lying to her.

The act of sex triggered something else in me. I wanted more of it than I could get. I turned to other forms of momentary gratification. Amazed at how accessible pornography had become,

☆ Andre Williams ☆

I indulged in it alone, feeding my desires and instantly recognizing what I liked. I was chasing the high of that first encounter at the graduation party, seeking to relive it again and again.

I soon discovered it was possible to exhaust myself because the next time Ayla and I had an opportunity for intimacy, I had nothing left to offer. Confused as she was, I decided to confess right there and then. I admitted to squandering my strength over digital fantasies. For some reason, she didn't make a big deal about it. It was a relief to be honest for once, but despite the confession, I had already sown too many deceitful seeds. The shadowy space beneath the rug was sprouting very peculiar weeds.

Chapter 12: PHS Endnotes

Honestly, I can't recall much about my senior year of high school in terms of football. It seems I was overly preoccupied with my personal life. Nevertheless, there are a few significant moments that still stand out, especially when it comes to the lead-up to the season and the playoffs.

It all began with the game against Allentown Central Catholic High School. At that point, I was playing both halfback positions and sometimes fullback as well. Coach Lane's run of choice that game was a play known as the speed sweep halfback toss. Remarkably, it was the only run we called the entire night, and I managed to score on four consecutive sweeps.

Now, that may be an exaggeration, but that's how I remember it, and regardless of whether I am or not, it wouldn't affect the score or the tremendous impact this play had on Allentown Central Catholic football. I distinctly remember the Head Coach's quote in the newspaper after the game. He said, and I quote, "...I can definitely see why that young man is destined for D1 level football."

I remember our remarkable victory against Wallenpaupack in the opening round of the playoffs. We displayed an outstanding performance, triumphing with a score of 49-6. Our excitement in the locker room was palpable. However, amidst the jubilation, Asher approached me with solemn news. It turns out that during the game, Alana bluntly confronted Ayla, affirming that the rumors were indeed true—I had cheated on her the previous summer. Alana told Ayla that she knew it was true because she was there in the other room. The revelation left Ayla in tears, and she left before the game was over. Asher's news brought an abrupt end to my celebration that night. It was a wake-up call for me to confront the truth and put an end to the deceit that had drained my energy all year.

☆ Andre Williams ☆

Similarly, the East Stroudsburg South game remains etched in my memory. The treacherously slippery turf and my ill-fitted cleats posed a challenge in the first half, making it easy for the defense to contain me. Fortunately, Rob Dvorchek's formidable performance at fullback ensured that we remained in the game. However, at halftime, I made a strategic decision to switch to my trusty DYNACLAWS. This decision proved to be a game-changer, allowing me to dominate the field in the second half. This victory was indeed significant, solidifying our triumph in emphatic fashion.

I remember the district championship game against Easton. We played on cold, rainy grass at night. It was a brutal dogfight, but we ended up losing. It's one of the few times I recall shedding tears after a football game, not because I was in pain (I was) but because my high school football career was over.

The night after the Wallenpaupack game, I fulfilled the promise I made to myself and told Ayla the truth about Joanna's graduation party. I called her and confessed that it was true, I had hooked up with Joanna last summer at her grad party. I made it clear that it was a mistake, it only happened once, and that there was no one else. I told her that I was sorry and that I loved her. It was a short phone call; she hung up the moment I stopped talking.

The following day, she had cleared her things out of our locker. We were done. Yet somehow, my devious plan had actually worked. Our puppy love survived the betrayal. After a few weeks of time apart, she forgave me. She even returned to the locker. Was all the deceit and heartache in vain?

That winter, we experienced some of the most extraordinary snowstorms I can recall, with snow reaching up past our waists. With our parents' permission, I intentionally got snowed in at Ayla's place, not once, but twice. Ayla had become my most serious girlfriend ever. We were in love. It was the kind of love that impulsive, passionate teenagers experience—like two lively puppies, eagerly licking faces and playfully nibbling on toes and fingers.

We successfully navigated high school together, but then came the moment of decision. Ayla chose to pursue her education and continue her field hockey career at Central Michigan University,

☆ After the Last Snap ☆

while I was headed to BC. Despite the distance, we were determined, as two young pups could be, to make our relationship thrive.

Chapter 13: For Boston

The summer of 2010 was scorching. No air conditioning in the freshman dorms at Boston College made the heat feel even more oppressive. But not to complain... as I was there on a scholarship.

As one of the early arrivals, my fellow freshman football players and I had the chance to familiarize ourselves with the campus and bond with our teammates before the rest of the student body arrived. In addition to these team-building experiences, we were tasked with completing two summer courses and commencing training with the team.

I haven't visited Boston College in a long time, and I can't recall the specific buildings I stayed in. I believe I had a double in Fitzpatrick, but I can't be certain as it's the only freshman dorm that comes to mind right now. However, I do remember my roommate clearly. His name was Alex Amidon. He was a local, a talented wide receiver, and incredibly fast. When I first met him, he was standing barefoot and shirtless, casually eating tuna from a can. I immediately thought, "Damn, this dude is a savage. Respect." Despite his reserved nature, we bonded over our love for *Call of Duty*. As we settled into our cramped double in Fitzpatrick, we realized just how small our room was. It was going to be a hot, cramped summer. To complicate things, Alex turned out to be quite messy. Our small space made it difficult to establish boundaries, and our freshman year together was uncomfortable. We slept in a small, messy, and sweltering room—I despised that part.

At our first workout as a freshman class, Coach Loco, the head trainer, shared an intriguing piece of wisdom. With a knowing gleam in his eye, he implored us to "Look to your left and look to your right. One out of four people won't be here by the end of your time here."

Astonishingly, his statement struck an undeniable chord of truth. Each passing year witnessed the departure of one or more athletes from our team as they embarked on alternative paths or were forced to leave.

Naturally, my college teammates were the first friends I made. Aside from Alex, I formed friendships with Tahj Kimble, Shakim Phillips, Kasim Edebali, Dominique Williams, Kevin Pierre-Louis, and Colin Larmond Jr. Years later, KPL invited me to his wedding, and I can confidently say it was the best wedding celebration I've ever attended. Despite not talking frequently or regularly, I still consider Kasim, Dominique, and Kevin to be great friends. Interestingly, the turnover at the coaching level was even worse. I witnessed a complete change in my coaching staff during my time at BC. I had the unfortunate opportunity to play under two head coaches and five different offensive coordinators in just four seasons. However, we were fortunate to have Ryan Day as our last OC, who is, at the time of this writing, the head coach at Ohio State. He was the brilliant mind behind my Heisman season during my senior year. It truly is a shame that Boston College missed the chance to have him as their head coach.

My football career started late freshman year. It was game 11 against UVA. That 17-13 win made us bowl eligible, but it came at a cost. Our starting running back, Montel Harris, left the game with a knee injury. I was next up. My first run was a counter. It hit big, and we kept going back to it. Amidon caught a ball that set Nate Freese up for a game-winning field goal, and we won the game.

I made my first college start in the regular-season finale against Syracuse and delivered an impressive performance, running the ball 42 times for 185 yards and scoring a crucial touchdown, propelling us to victory. That final win paved the way for our team's journey to the Kraft Fight Hunger Bowl in San Francisco, where we faced Colin Kaepernick and the formidable Nevada Wolfpack. It was the thrilling climax of a remarkable season, and I was proud to have played a significant role in our team's success.

While San Francisco was an incredible experience, apart from a 30-yard TD run early in the game, their defense contained me on the run, and we didn't make many plays through the air. Unfortunately, Nevada secured the victory with a 20-13 win. This brought our season to a close, finishing at 7-6.

☆ Andre Williams ☆

In my freshman year, I made the decision to prioritize my core classes. I anticipated that they would be the easiest, as they are mandatory for everyone. I managed to achieve A's and B's, resulting in a 3.7 GPA by the end of the year. This high cumulative average provided me with a solid foundation for the future.

It is interesting to note that in my freshman year, I met both of the women I would marry, Marilyn and De'shonia. I would later discover that marrying a woman does not make her a wife, and so, even though I married Marilyn first, it was De'shonia who ultimately became my wife, life partner, and better half.

It was at the beginning of the school year when I first crossed paths with De'shonia. She was seated at a table in the upper campus cafeteria, engaged in conversation with a few of my fellow teammates. One of them was Tahj Kimble, a fellow freshman running back hailing from Florida. Tahj was engrossed in a discussion with Heather, a close friend of De'Shonia. Interestingly enough, both Dee and Heather had ventured onto campus together that day courtesy of an Uber ride.

I sat down at the table with my meal and saw her sitting there with her smooth brown skin, her bright eyes, and her pretty mouth. She had a smile that could put you in a trance, but when she opened her mouth, and I saw her tongue ring, I just knew that she was the finest, freakiest woman I'd ever laid eyes on. I knew if she ever touched me with that mouth I'd be instantly smitten. She was a dangerous sort of beautiful.

At that time, I was still in a long-distance puppy love relationship with Ayla. We were making it work, and I was committed to our journey. I didn't actively pursue De'shonia, and she ended up dating my roommate Derrick. She remained a constant presence throughout my college years. As time went on, I discovered that she was actually a kind-hearted girl, a true southern belle. My admiration for her grew, especially because of her unwavering loyalty to Derrick, even though he did not reciprocate it. When he injured his knee playing football and couldn't even make it to the bathroom, she was there to support him, even going as far as to change his bedpan. We developed a strong friendship, sharing our deepest secrets and confiding in one another, things we couldn't reveal to our respective partners.

☆ After the Last Snap ☆

And then there was Marilyn. I can't recall exactly what part of the year we met, but it was at nighttime, on the street. We talked a bit and took a picture together. I thought she was cute, but I didn't see much of anything beyond her "rich girl" conceit.

Something strange was happening with Ayla. We were still in constant communication, exchanging texts and talking on the phone. She seemed to be getting along really well with her field hockey teammates. The stories she shared with me initially seemed harmless, but then they took a more explicit turn. Her friends were engaging in wild behavior. There was one particular story that deeply disturbed me. Ayla confided in me that one of her teammates had resorted to consuming hard liquor as a means to induce an abortion when she discovered she was pregnant. She described how something black and ominous eventually expelled from her and her pregnancy came to an end.

It wasn't so much that this thing happened, but how Ayla rationalized it, that had me shaken up. It occurred to me that Ayla could be a different person at Central Michigan if she wasn't with me. If this was the type of person she chose to spend her weekends with, then wasn't that the kind of person she truly was? I needed to put the question to the test. So, right before the end of the first semester, I decided to end things with Ayla to see how she would react and what choices she would make with her newfound freedom.

During a school break, we reunited as friends back home, and I vividly recall sitting with her in the living room of my parents' house. We engaged in a lengthy conversation, pouring our hearts out. Though I missed her, I needed to ascertain if my time and energy weren't being wasted on someone who surrounded herself with such unsavory individuals.

At that moment, in the comfort of my parents' living room, Ayla confessed to me that she had not just hooked up with one, but three basketball players at school since we had broken up. It was not devastation or shock that washed over me, but rather a deep sense of disgust. I'd been right about her all along, but that didn't save me from feeling let down. We never spoke again afterward.

Chapter 14: Chestnut (Hill) Roasting

Things took a turn for the worse during my sophomore season. We only managed to win four games all year. Coach Spaz shuffled the offensive coaching staff, leading to a lot of confusion and inconsistency. Among the changes, Coach Ben Sirmans, our running back coach, stood out as exceptional at his job.

There was one moment on the field during practice that I'll never forget. I had just finished a run and was heading back to the huddle when I felt a firm grip on the collar of my shoulder pads. Coach Sirmans was pulling me towards the end zone. "RUN, ANDRE, RUN! STOP HOLDING BACK AND GO SCORE THE TOUCHDOWN!" he roared in my ear.

He was like an angry father, and I felt like a scared child, suddenly spurred into action. Without thinking, I picked up my pace and sprinted as fast as my legs would carry me into the end zone. From that moment on, whenever I had the ball, I made sure to finish my run with everything I had. I learned not to save anything for the next play because I knew if Coach Sirmans caught me slacking again, there wouldn't be a next play.

After my sophomore year, Coach Sirmans accepted a job with the St. Louis Rams. In his place, they brought in a new coach named Sean Desai. It was clear from the beginning that he was unqualified for the position, which created a lot of discomfort within our running back group.

To be honest, my memories of my sophomore and junior seasons blur together. What I can say for certain is that my junior year was even worse than my sophomore year. We only secured two wins that season.

☆ After the Last Snap ☆

Despite the hardship, there was a crucial difference between those two years. After my sophomore campaign, I began to question whether Boston College was the right place for me. Was coming here a mistake? Could there be a better opportunity waiting for me elsewhere? I wondered about the possibilities of playing down south or in the Midwest, where I kept hearing rumors of "under the table" money that I never saw. Could I transfer to a school with less academic rigor, allowing me to dedicate more time to the game?

In search of answers, I turned to the only thing I knew how to do: I got down on my knees and prayed, asking God for guidance and direction.

God told me that if I truly believed in myself, I could achieve success anywhere. The only catch was that leaving would only delay the process, resulting in a year off. I was determined not to postpone my progress, take a year off, or spend an extra year in school. So, I heeded God's advice and stayed, and as a result, we won two games.

Chapter 15: Golden Eagle

Some of us had a sense that 2013 would be an exceptional year. One summer day, after practice, my teammate Juice and I were talking about the kind of season I was going to have in the fall.

"Dre, after that practice, you seem like you're ready to skip for a thousand!" he exclaimed.

I looked him in the eyes and responded firmly, "Juice, I have to run for a thousand." I didn't flinch. His eyes widened as we locked eyes.

"When you say it with your chest like that, it sounds like you're ready to run for two thousand!" he remarked. I nodded in agreement, "Juice, I have to run for two thousand!" Together, we merged our belief and determination, releasing it into the air. It became more than a mere intention—it was a promise.

We were coming off a two-win season in 2012, but the Boston College Eagles were facing a turning point. The arrival of a new Athletic Director, Brad Bates, brought new opportunities. Ryan Day returned to the Heights seeking the Head Coaching position. BC foolishly passed on him, but he became the Offensive Coordinator nonetheless, a position of power that would serve us well that year.

Coach Day was no newcomer to the team. He'd been on staff before as the wide receiver coach, and he easily identified the team's individual talent and effectively communicated its value to the coaching staff, who in turn conveyed this value to the players. In 2013, our foundation as a team would be set on player value.

Despite the shortcomings of the bald, hard-headed man that Brad Bates chose as head coach, the staff understood we had more than enough talent in the locker room to win games. Coach Day let everyone know we had a horse, and if we played our cards right, we could all ride that horse to a bowl game. I was the horse.

☆ After the Last Snap ☆

I'll never forget the first time the Tight End coach lashed out at us in the film room over a careless play that led to a player on the ground in the trenches. It was a wonder that a gross injury did not occur. The coach's intense demeanor was well-known. He exclaimed in stronger terms than I care to write here, "You guys need to stay on your feet! This running back is NFL-bound! If any of you roll up on his ankle, you'll be riding the bench so fast you won't know what hit you!"

It seemed like the private discussions Juice and I had in the dorm had become public knowledge. Everyone was on board with the fact that Andre Williams was going to run wild this year.

I exploded on the field that season. Mentally, something clicked inside me. I woke up every day truly believing that my time had arrived. Physically, I had finally grown into my body, and I could feel it—this was my moment. The people around me felt it too, and their support only fueled my belief. I faced each day with unwavering faith that I stood at destiny's door and behind it was professional football. Nothing was standing in my way.

Many young athletes have asked me about that period in my life, wondering how I dealt with the pressure. My answer to them is this: everything in your environment will tell you who you are. Your teammates, your coaches, your opponents—they all have their opinions about who you are. But ultimately, it's up to you to truly know yourself.

The way I see it, the pressure within me was greater than any external force. My relentless determination to succeed became a supernatural force, driving me to be exceptional. Both my teammates and coaches recognized my strength of will was special, and even my opponents acknowledged it. I heard it come out of their mouths in various forms of exasperation, the moment our suits would collide. The impact of my sheer determination was evident in the pain it inflicted on my opponents and with each passing week, it became more widely known that encountering me came at a cost.

After the game, the truly exceptional individuals always make direct eye contact, firmly shake your hand, and offer words of encouragement such as, "Good luck next year, I'll see you again." In these moments, the power of your determination becomes your

☆ Andre Williams ☆

greatest asset. All I needed to do was unleash that power on the field, and remarkable feats became inevitable. When I donned my super suit and saw the number 44 emblazoned on my chest, I truly believed I was extraordinary. The last thing I did to seal myself in glory was to turn to prayer. I entreated Yahweh to send His angels down to the field, and hedge us all in a protective shield, allowing us to play to our fullest potential without fear or malice. In this mental environment, pressure simply ceases to exist.

In 2013, I rushed for 2,177 yards in football, a performance worthy of the Heisman. I became only the fifth player in NCAA history to achieve over 2,000 yards in a single season.

I must confess, as a running back, my game was lacking in one area—I had zero receptions throughout the year. However, few could stop me from running the football. Win or lose, I always had the drive to push through. I embraced my strength, and Coach Day ingeniously constructed an offense that maximized my potential.

My prowess as a pure runner, combined with the coaching staff's ingenuity in tailoring the offense to my strengths, propelled me to the professional level. I was fortunate to be in an environment where my true value was recognized. When the opportunity arose at Boston College, I was fully prepared, both physically and mentally, to seize it.

We kicked off the season against Villanova. Before the game, Juice challenged me, saying, "I bet you won't run for 100." "Alright, bet," I replied. I ended up with 114 yards on 23 attempts. After the game, Juice came up to me and exclaimed, "Man, I told you that you were going to run for over a hundred! But I bet you won't run for 200 next week!" I dapped him up and said, "Alright, bet!" The following week against Wake Forest, I rushed for 204 yards on 35 attempts. After the game, Juice approached me once again. "Damn, bro, impressive! I don't want to bet anymore, but can you rush for 300?" I looked at him and replied, "Juice, the way I'm feeling, I can do anything I set my mind to, bro." When my body was completely healthy, my mind was clear and incredibly sharp, able to pierce through any goal I set it to. In fact, my mind was so quiet and calm that it became hard to relate to my peers, but I really didn't mind. In my mind I only saw destiny's shining door and I was getting closer every day.

☆ After the Last Snap ☆

We faced the Tar Heels once during my four seasons at BC, and honestly, I don't recall much about the game besides the fact that we suffered a loss. However, one vivid memory that remains is being forcefully taken down on my shoulder by Tre Boston after a solid run. The sensation of pain was far from ordinary. Despite this setback, I still managed to accumulate an impressive 172 rushing yards. Nonetheless, a subsequent medical examination confirmed that I had sprained my AC joint. This injury plagued me throughout the season and ultimately forced me to sit out the season finale against Syracuse.

In week 11 against NC State, I pulled off a masterful performance where I concluded the game with 339 yards on 42 rush attempts. This marked the fourth game in a remarkable five-week series in which the Boston College Eagles displayed absolute run dominance. In those five weeks, I ran for an impressive 1,235 rushing yards, solidifying my place as the NCAA rush leader.

Following the triumphant victory over NC State, my name began to grace the discussions of the esteemed ESPN personalities in relation to the highly coveted Heisman race. Initially, I regarded this attention with a grain of skepticism. However, as I continued to showcase my violent rush style, leaving a remarkable impression with two touchdowns and 263 yards on 32 attempts against NM State, it soon transcended mere discussion. In a whirlwind of events, the confirmation soon arrived: I was to venture to the illustrious city of New York to join the ranks of incredible talents such as Jameis Winston, Johnny Manziel, Tre Mason, AJ McCarron, and Jordan Lynch in the remarkable realm of the Heisman.

The Maryland game will be remembered as one of my all-time favorite college football memories. We were tied 26-26 in the fourth quarter, with only a few moments left on the clock. In true BC fashion, we initiated our two-minute drive by running power, but this time we unleashed a special wrinkle that we hadn't shown all year. When our guard, Harris Williams, pulled to the right, the defensive line thought they knew what was coming and overplayed their hand, revealing a hole in the backside A gap that I was happy to burst through. I made it all the way to the Maryland 22-yard line

☆ Andre Williams ☆

before being dragged down on a badly aching AC joint separation in the right shoulder.

Although I had to leave the field to recover from the pain, my effort was enough to create an opportunity for Nate Freese to secure an easy game-winning kick. Leading up to this point in the season, Nate had been perfect. But just as Nate let the ball fly and it sailed towards the uprights, the referee blew the whistle to signal a timeout called by Maryland. Apparently, the Maryland coach believed it would be a smart move to try to freeze Mr. Freese. Surprisingly, it was a huge break for us, as Nate finally missed, and the ball went wide right. After the timeout, Freese prepared for another kick, and this time he sent the ball through the uprights, securing a victory for BC. Despite the pain in my shoulder, the moment of wonder and excitement at such an incredible win overwhelmed us. We all went wild on the sidelines.

One game that stands out as a strong contender for my all-time favorite college football games was our match against New Mexico State. The head coach at NM State had just previously served as an offensive coordinator at BC. It was an awkward situation for our offense because he had in-depth knowledge of our strengths and weaknesses. However, New Mexico State's true advantage was the location. None of us were prepared for the desert-like environment we encountered there. It felt similar to playing at high altitudes, but the conditions were exacerbated by the abundance of dust in the air.

After two or three plays, I found myself gasping for air, my muscles burning, and my throat parched. Looking around the field, I could see that every Eagle out there was experiencing the same symptoms. Of course, the Aggies were accustomed to their environment and relishing in their home field advantage. They started off quickly, scoring touchdowns through the air. We responded with a quick slant to Amidon for a touchdown. We attempted to control the flow of the game by running the ball as usual, but the environment was draining our energy. It was now fourth and one, and we needed to convert to keep the ball in our hands for the rest of the second quarter. We ran power to the left. The defense anticipated our move, as they always did. There was no opening to exploit or edges to push, so I jumped. Somehow the

☆ After the Last Snap ☆

jump turned into a tumble and a flip over the entire offensive and defensive line. I even landed on my feet. I was just as surprised as everyone else and managed to rush for a few extra yards before getting tackled. Coach Washington went wild when he witnessed that play. And so did I. It's fascinating how energy works, how a source of visual inspiration can be just as invigorating as a cheeseburger and a coffee.

By halftime, most of us had grown accustomed to the dry climate, and Coach Day decided to intensify our ground attack. He fed me the ball, and I devoured the opportunity.

Although we hadn't utilized the inside zone much in this game, we incorporated it strategically, causing the opposing defense to collapse. I burst through the middle of the field, racing for a scorching 80-yard touchdown. On the very next possession, we ran power to the right, resulting in a dominant 47-yard score. Amidon displayed his exceptional blocking skills, driving his man into the end zone. Victory was ours.

As we arrived in Syracuse for the season finale, I had already amassed well over 2,000 rushing yards. However, my AC joint sprain had progressed from level one to level two. The consistent ache, especially at night as I tried to sleep, was a constant reminder of my injury. I was relieved that this would be our last game of the season, and I brimmed with excitement. I knew that my performance so far had more than earned me the opportunity to transition from amateur to professional play.

It felt fitting that we returned to Syracuse to conclude the season, as it was there that my collegiate career began during my freshman year. I was determined to deliver an exceptional performance and end the season on a high note.

We chose to take a bus to Syracuse due to the relatively short distance from BC and as we approached the Carrier Dome, a light snow gracefully descended from the sky, setting the stage for the upcoming event. I can remember strolling through the locker room in my leggings, listening to my favorite pregame jam, which was "Know the Ledge" by Rakim and Eric B. Amidst the melodic backdrop, my thoughts gravitated towards my ailing shoulder. Its relentless pain had reached a powerful crescendo, forcefully wielding its power to sideline me from the game. I thought about the Maryland game: we did enough to win but I'd finished the game on the sideline. Determined to confront the challenge head-on, I reached for two aspirins, firmly affixed a protective donut pad onto my shoulder joint and set out to the field to commence my warm-up routine.

In my mind, it was time to play, to conquer adversity, and leave a final, indelible mark on the game. In retrospect, it would have been a wise decision to sit the game out. We would have made it to the bowl game with a win at Syracuse or loss, and I would have been a healthier, less damaged running back. Maybe it wasn't so much about facing the adversity of playing the game injured as it was avoiding the adversity of bumping heads with the coaching staff for sitting out. Maybe I chose the greater evil only because it was the evil I was used to dealing with. Looking back now, I wish I had the same courage off the field as I did when I was on it.

The Syracuse defense meant business. They were well aware of what they needed to do in order to stand a chance against us. I managed to score once on a sweep to the left before things took a turn. During our next offensive drive, Rettig handed me the ball. However, there was a breakdown upfront that I couldn't avoid. I was engulfed by the defense, and they knew just what to do. They dumped me right on my shoulder. That was the end for me. I had to leave the game. This time, the pain and weakness were too much to recover from. My regular season was over. Watching my teammates give their all for the following two and a half quarters was inspiring. Chase Rettig played like never before and although we came close, it simply wasn't enough. When it was all over, tears streamed down my face. Whether it was from the pain, the loss, or the end of a remarkable journey, I could not tell.

With only seven wins, our options for a bowl game were limited. We could have gone back to San Francisco as we did in my freshman year, but instead, we made the decision to face Arizona in the Advocare bowl in Shreveport, Louisiana on New Year's Eve. The headline of the nation's top running back, Andre Williams, going against the second-best running back in the country, Ka'Deem Carey, was too enticing to resist.

We arrived in Shreveport in the afternoon, a week before the game. It would have been better to come the night before like we did in the regular season. Shreveport was nothing to look at. I took the time to settle in and make myself comfortable at the hotel. Later that night, Juice suggested we explore and find dinner. As we left the hotel in our small group, we were struck by the quietness of the town at night, with only a few passing cars and no one on the streets.

We soon realized that finding food wouldn't be easy without walking for miles or taking an Uber. Somehow, we ended up at a strip club, and my first per diem dollars went towards the cover charge rather than a meal. It was an unfortunate choice for my first experience in a strip club, with the dim orange lighting accentuating the tired appearance of the women. We ordered drinks in the hope of brightening the atmosphere, but it did little to improve the scene. Nevertheless, we managed to have a good time and shared some laughter. As time passed, more sketchy-looking individuals entered, and after 40 minutes, we decided it was time to leave.

Shreveport was the worst possible location for a bowl game. I couldn't find a single good meal during my time there. I do recall receiving warnings to stay away from certain dodgy establishments, but in hindsight, that's probably where the good food was. The combination of the location, the defeat, and the state of my body all worked together to taint my memory of the end of college and college football.

Before the first practice, Coach Adazzio accompanied me to the locker room with the purpose of assuring me that my shoulder was in perfect condition and that the medical staff had given him their assurance that I had enough time to recover. I simply nodded in agreement. I was already present. There was no running now, but Adazzio and the medical staff were mistaken. We were all mistaken. My shoulder was not fine. It throbbed incessantly, and I should not have been there. I had already exceeded my limits. I needed rest and recovery, but I was not willing to assert myself and walk away from the bowl game. I allowed Adazzio to continue to manipulate me with his words.

Our game against Arizona was humiliating. Arizona's offense dominated our defense. Our strategy remained the same: contain their offense, exert pressure on the defense, keep the game close, and wait for the defense to falter against my shoulder in the second half. However, we failed at the first step. We couldn't contain Ka'Deem and the Wildcats at all. Arizona was scoring relentlessly.

Meanwhile, it was my own shoulders that were crumbling. Normally, I would be the one delivering blows to the defenders, but I simply didn't have it in me that New Year's Eve. Injury didn't remove me from the game this time, but it didn't matter. I was hurting myself by being there. At times, I could feel my shoulder bones and joints grinding underneath my pads with each hit. By the end of our pitiful performance, I was in agonizing pain. It was the kind that gave me chills when it rang out across my body.

Chapter 16: Mr. Williams, the Man-Horse

As I mentioned before, it was my impressive 300+ yard performance against NC State that year that secured my spot in the Heisman race. After three years of relative obscurity on campus, I suddenly became Andre "The Man-Horse," or just Mr. Williams for short. Sometimes, if I lingered too long at the food court, a small crowd would form around me. It was then that I realized, "So this is celebrity, huh... this is strange." I had fought, sweated, and bled simply to win the game. That was always my focus. I didn't play for fame or for the love of the game. Don't ask me about stats or football lore. I just played to win, and I was a damn good player. I ran through everything. I was the juggernaut in 2013.

Don't misunderstand me, our season wasn't the greatest. We ended up with a record of 7-8, more losses than wins. However, the way we played, both in victories and defeats, was remarkable. I firmly believe that we were the best power football team in the NCAA that year. Our violent, relentless performance caught people's attention, and eventually, they wanted to hear from me.

I was used to keeping a low profile, focusing on my studies amidst the constant changes in coaching staff and the negativity surrounding our football program. I wasn't prepared to handle the attention that my performance would bring. When it arrived, I felt uncomfortable. All I wanted was to win and be left alone. Looking back, I realize that this was a sign of my immaturity. I wanted the results and the rewards but not the responsibilities and the consequences. It was an illogical desire that I couldn't grasp at the time.

As time went on, the BC media approached me for an appearance on ESPN. I was a top contender for the Doak Walker

☆ Andre Williams ☆

Award, recognizing the best running back in the NCAA. Now, I had to make a case for myself and prove why I deserved to be considered for the Heisman. I was diving headfirst into a completely new world, unaware of the responsibilities that came with it.

Fast forward to December. The season had come to an end, and things were picking up speed. In that very same month, I was scheduled to travel to Orlando, Florida, for the College Football Awards. It turned out that I would miss my graduation due to the timing of the award show and my early completion of the semester. The winter ceremony clashed with the event in Orlando, but that was a small price to pay as long as I could still obtain my degree. At the College Football Awards, I ended up winning the Doak Walker, and I was recognized as the nation's best running back of 2013. Later that night, I hopped on a charter plane to fly back to New York for the Heisman ceremony.

Jameis Winston was the recipient of the award that year. I had the honor of being a finalist alongside Johnny Manziel, Tre Mason, AJ McCarron, and Jordan Lynch.

Amidst all the media attention, I had the opportunity to unwind with former winners at a private bar meet-and-greet. I shared drinks and laughter with legend running back, Mike Rozier for the first time. We run into each other once a year now for celebrity golf, and my admiration for his physique at his age continues to grow. During the ceremony, I sat to the right of Houston Oilers running back Earl Campbell. His team reached out to me for a jersey exchange as he admired my running style. Many people drew comparisons between us at the time. It was an incredible honor to be in the company of those extraordinary individuals, and after the ceremony, the weight of my achievement began to sink in. I was the top running back in college football in 2013.

I never returned to school after that unforgettable night. It marked the end of an era. With unwavering determination, I embarked on a journey to seek treatment for my bruised and battered body, fully committed to preparing for the highly anticipated NFL draft.

Chapter 17: Entanglement

If I had to pinpoint the most significant character flaw I had developed by 2013, it was twofold. Subconsciously, it manifested as a reluctance to confront things I found challenging. I was troubled by the transformation of campus life as the excitement around the Heisman Trophy intensified. I felt entitled to maintain a low profile while competing for the highest honor in college football. Consciously, my weakness manifested as an addiction to entanglement. Once I removed the football pads, my rapidly changing environment brought me discomfort, and I sought relief from that discomfort in a romantic partner. I was constantly seeking the perfect companion to fill my time. I never wanted to be alone. These flaws led me down a perilous path.

It's amusing to reflect on it. In a football game, I thrived on confrontation. More often than not, I found myself better equipped than my opponents to overcome it. With persistence, I could almost always make them yield. However, I didn't apply the same principles when it came to my social life. I was the one who yielded. I ran away. It wasn't that I was antisocial; I simply chose what was comfortable for me and ignored the rest. I believed I had that right. To avoid campus life as much as possible, I sought ways to spend my nights off-campus. This desire was heightened by the fact that most of my roommates had been expelled from campus for scandalous reasons. My immediate roommate was either training to become a Navy SEAL or living with his girlfriend at the time. My dorm room often stood empty. I needed a hobby.

Nighttime life on campus had become something I viewed as awkward. People would stare, ask for pictures, inquire with foolish questions, and suddenly everyone wanted to be friends. Having been an introvert for so long, I didn't know how to handle this new environment.

☆ Andre Williams ☆

During that time, I made the mistake of nurturing my own shortcomings and seeking validation from women. Sage was one such woman. Physically, she was nearly flawless. An All-American Ice Hockey beauty with a light chocolate complexion, natural curls, and a strong, athletic build. Though her physical allure was undeniable, it was her emotional disposition that truly frustrated me. I'm no psychologist but it seemed obvious that she had some deep-seated issues with her biological father that prevented her from nurturing a healthy relationship with a strong-willed man like myself. We attempted a relationship the year before, but after spending a weekend at her stepfather's place in Cleveland, things took a turn. A trivial incident during a shared shower convinced me that we were mentally and emotionally incompatible. She became irate and ruined our sensual shower because I "washed my hair too fast" with her expensive shampoo. She was a cutie, but I lost my taste for her that night. I broke it off with her the next day when I'd landed safely back in Pennsylvania.

She graduated that year and was then chosen to play professionally for the NWHL Boston Pride the following season. After settling in Boston, not far from BC's campus, she expressed her hope that we could give our relationship another chance. The offer was hard to resist-she'd chauffer me off campus in her Jeep Patriot and do her best to win me over with late night dinners and passion. However, despite the allure, I knew I had to resist the goal of her advances. I have a personal rule not to reopen closed doors; I've never dated the same girl twice. There are plenty of other opportunities out there, and I prefer to leave the past behind. Nonetheless, I did enjoy the escape from campus life.

One morning, Marilyn approached my breakfast table as I was recovering from my morning workout. We hadn't seen each other in years, but she'd begun attending the games when her brother walked on to the team as a wide receiver that year. There was something intriguing about her. It wasn't her physique or her appearance. Physically, she was a poor substitute for Sage. But I knew that giving in to Sage's allure one more night would lead to trouble.

I had gathered enough about Marilyn from our freshman year encounter to realize that I didn't particularly like her. She carried herself with an air of superiority, but when I found out that Marilyn also lived off campus, I became curious to learn more about her. We began spending time together at my place on campus after our days were over.

At that time, I was wrestling with some dark thoughts. I pondered the significance of the fact that if things progressed, she would be the seventh girl I had ever been intimate with. I saw this as a kind of taboo because seven is the biblical number of completion. I didn't want to risk committing to her by being intimate because deep down, I knew she wasn't what I truly desired in a life partner. Looking back, I realize how foolish I was to discern the gravity of such heavy spiritual principles and still ignore them to gratify shallow, carnal desires. It's no surprise to me that I ended up spiraling down such a dark path with her.

Marilyn borrowed a sleek black Honda, a vehicle she affectionately named Lafonda, from her friend, Donna. Whenever she needed transportation, she would borrow Lafonda from Donna and graciously offer to pick me up and drive me to her off-campus apartment.

It was during one of those rides that I first noticed a troubling sign. That sign took the form of a person residing in Marilyn's apartment, occupying her living room couch. This person was none other than Gary, Boston College's friendly neighborhood weed dealer. Surprisingly, Marilyn seemed unfazed by his presence, as if it were perfectly normal. In fact, Gary had taken up residence in Marilyn's living room, paying his rent in the form of cannabis. Astonishingly, Marilyn found this arrangement perfectly acceptable.

Their relationship seemed platonic, so I didn't think much of it at the time. I didn't ask questions; I just assumed he would be gone soon enough if I was going to spend any time there. He was gone the next month, and I did begin to spend time with her.

Should I have asked myself, "What kind of girl shares a one-bedroom apartment with another man whom she wasn't intimate with in exchange for weed?" Yes, I should have. Instead, I dismissed it. It was college, and I had seen many people doing extraordinarily questionable things. Being young and naive, I joined the party. I enjoyed her company, the smoke, the escape.

☆ Andre Williams ☆

Marilyn had successfully lured me in, preying on my weakness, my tendency to distract myself from the uncomfortable. I struggled to handle the small talk, the eyes, the expectations, the invasion of space. On the field, it was easy. Off the field, I was not acclimated to it. But it was too late. I had become Mr. Williams, the Man-Horse. I focused on what came easy: finishing my last semester of school, completing the rest of the season. My body was bruised, but I was headed to New York for the Heisman. I was the Man-Horse now. I couldn't avoid my destiny. Instead of embracing the uncomfortable truth of public life on campus, I ran away to the comfort of Marilyn's smoky retreat. I made these trips off-campus daily, burning the trees that numbed the pain in my shoulders and wondering about the future in relative peace.

Marilyn eventually proved she had some value beyond an off-campus retreat. The accolades I had received that year had opened doors to exclusive circles. As I had learned, walking into a room with an attractive woman on your arm is an automatic icebreaker. Marilyn handled these events with confident familiarity that left me impressed. That's when I realized what truly set her apart—her affluent background. Although she had mentioned it before, I only grasped the extent of it when I brought her into those privileged circles. She seemed to effortlessly fit in.

I was invited to the Walter Camp Gala at Yale University, an event put on by the Walter Camp Award foundation for NCAA football All-Americans. The gala spanned an entire weekend, and attendees had the option to stay the weekend. Marilyn accompanied me to the Walter Camp Gala. She was my arm candy for the weekend. Her family's opulent mansion was conveniently located in Stamford, CT, close to the university. She effortlessly navigated the event with confidence and grace.

She exuded warmth and greeted everyone with a smile, making small talk to ease the pressure of performance. Despite her unremarkable appearance, Marilyn's superficial yet effective social methods impressed me. She thrived in the company of the nation's athletic elite. Having just arrived, it was a world I had not yet fully grown accustomed to. Perhaps attending the Walter Camp retreat alone would have fostered the growth I needed in that moment. It may have been awkward at times but through introspection and networking, I would have quickly adjusted to my environment on my own. Instead, I leaned on familiarity and played my crutch, missing the opportunity for personal development.

Marilyn and I stayed together before the draft, maintaining a long-distance relationship. As I departed for Georgia from the bowl game in Shreveport, she returned to finish her last semester at BC. Taking up residence with my older brother Danique and his wife Shekayla, I commuted from Marietta to Norcross for NFL Combine training at Chip Smith's center. His outstanding program and unique methods set the stage for my NFL journey.

Before beginning my training, I needed to choose an agent who would cover the expenses for the training and all my pre-draft needs. I remember my first option was Joe Linta. We invited him for dinner, and he was representing Joe Flacco at the time. He didn't hesitate to highlight his extensive experience in the game, presenting himself as a special figure. However, I didn't find him impressive. He didn't establish a genuine connection with me, which I felt was vital. Despite this, Joe might not have been a bad choice. The signing bonus would have been modest, but it would have been mine to keep.

In the end, I signed with Erik Burkhardt of Select Sports Group after meeting him and his partner, Steve Mudder, at an Atlanta Hawks game. Our conversation was genuine and engaging. Erik was representing Johnny Manziel at the time, which I found cool as I knew Johnny from the Heisman. He provided me with insights into the game from his perspective and assured me that he could secure better deals for me, leveraging the strength of Johnny and the other players on his team.

He was approachable, young, experienced, and made me feel like we would become real friends. Additionally, he offered to loan me $50,000 if I signed with him. I was convinced. My urgent need to start rehab, coupled with my trust in him, made it an effortless decision. Erik promptly arranged my training and rehab, setting me on the path to recovery.

I was dealing with a great deal of uncertainty at this time. I was honest with Erik about the condition of my shoulders after he signed me. He didn't seem overly concerned but that didn't put my mind to rest because I'd been invited to the Reese's Senior Bowl.

☆ Andre Williams ☆

The pain in my shoulders prevented me from sleeping comfortably at night. I began to question if I had made it this far just to arrive in the big leagues with a broken body. I expressed this to him, and he agreed that it might not be a good idea, as it could further expose me to injuries or unnecessary medical examinations before the combine.

He suggested that I respectfully contact the commissioner of the Reese's Senior Bowl and withdraw from the event in order to focus on rehabilitation and training. Perhaps I should have still made the trip to Mobile just to make an appearance, but that decision is now in the past.

I stayed away from the bench press at Chip's spot because it was not helping my shoulders; it was only causing more pain. I knew that my upper body needed rest if I wanted to have a chance during the season. Therefore, I chose to abstain from the bench press at the combine. I knew that my numbers there wouldn't impress anyone, but the tape didn't lie. My greatest assets were explosiveness, incredible strength, and durability. I would stand on those qualities. I focused on working my explosiveness and catching the football.

After the completion of my training period, I decided to treat Marilyn and myself to a trip to Chicago in April, just before the draft. We indulged in a week filled with city exploration and good eating. Little did I know that this small decision would later prove to be a colossal error.

Chapter 18:
Andre The Giant

I was projected to go in the second or third round as a Heisman finalist, but my end-of-season decisions ended up costing me. Opting out of the Senior Bowl and the bench press at the combine raised red flags for some teams, and as a result, I dropped to the fourth round. I was selected by the Giants with the 113th pick in the draft on May 10th, 2014. Sitting on the couch with Marilyn, I received the call from Coach Coughlin that changed everything. No one was paying attention any longer, but I was calmly watching the draft ticker countdown when my phone rang.

I responded, "Hello?"

"Yes, how are you doing? Is this Andre? This is Coach Coughlin with the New York Giants."

"Yes, sir. This is Andre. How are you doing, coach?"

"Good. Listen, we are about to call your name with our next pick. How are your shoulders? Are you healthy?"

"Yes, sir. My shoulders are in good shape."

"Are you ready to play some football for the New York Giants?"

"Yessir, I'm ready, let's go!"

"Congratulations! Someone else will come on the phone for you, stand by. I'll see you soon."

Marilyn was thrilled that I finally got the call and that I was going to New York. I'd only be a short drive from Connecticut. Her dreams were coming true. I asked my dad to take Marilyn to the airport the following morning. The Giants were sending a car to pick me up for the journey to New Jersey. The door of destiny was wide open, and it was time to embrace the next phase of my life.

The following morning, the team arranged for a limo to pick me up and take me to my new home in East Rutherford, New Jersey. They had all the rookies staying at an extended stay hotel that was less than ten minutes from the training facility. We would be there for the duration of the rookie minicamp. My roommate for camp was first-round pick, Odell Beckham Jr. I can't say that we hit it off right away; we had different interests. He'd brought his PlayStation with him and challenged me to a game of FIFA. That was around the time it was just getting popular. I had never learned to play or appreciate FIFA, and I didn't even try, in an attempt to bond with my teammate. I was more of an RPG type of guy, but I hadn't even thought about bringing my PlayStation. I was too nervous, worried about whether my shoulder would hold up this next season. Now that I had officially made it, the real work was about to begin. The interview was over. Now it was time to perform.

    I wonder if by now, it is clear to all who are reading this memoir that I am a very cerebral individual. I often indulge in deep contemplation and introspection, as I naturally lean towards introversion. Give me some solitude, and I can amuse myself all day long with my own thoughts. I spend a good portion of my day engaged in conversation with myself. Adjusting to this new situation in the pros wasn't at all what concerned me, as I was accustomed to being on the move and growing with a team. My two main concerns were this: did I have enough time for my shoulders to recover and regain strength before the season commenced? Secondly, 2177 rush yards, 0 receptions, and 0 receiving yards. My stat line was two kinds of incredible. I spoke to myself with urgency as I paced about the hotel drinking water and juggling racquetballs: "Dre, you need to be ready to catch Mr. Eli's ball. It's time to step up your game."

    Simply put, the first day of the rookie minicamp was a nerve-wracking and embarrassing experience. I found myself practicing alongside some of the best wide receivers in the world, as well as one of the greatest quarterbacks to ever play the game. Meanwhile, I had just finished a season at Boston College without a single reception. I knew that one training season with Chip Smith wouldn't magically change my situation, and unfortunately, the reality of my lack of skill at catching the football was evident that day. Even though the statistics might not reflect it, it felt like I dropped every pass. It was a terrible feeling.

☆ After the Last Snap ☆

I wasn't accustomed to the 7v7 style practices. Physically, it was a great blessing that my body desperately needed but mentally, I got beat. As I left the field, I thought about how steep the learning curve to become a well-rounded running back in the pros could be. I had a great challenge ahead of me. We headed to the film study to review our practice and begin learning some of the basics of offensive strategies. It was during this session that my running back coach, Craig Johnson, pointed out what was already painfully clear: I needed to learn how to catch the football, and I needed to learn it quickly. Otherwise, someone else would be taking my position. The pressure was mounting, but I had no intention of backing down.

Fortunately, Coach Johnson wasn't just tough; he was cool and smooth. I connected with him on a personal level, and while Coach Coughlin may be portrayed as stern and old-school, I believe he truly understood the importance of player development. He knew what to do when he chose me for this New York team. I believe he understood who I was as a player and believed in my potential.

In the running back room, we had a talented group: David Wilson, Peyton Hillis, Rashad Jennings, Michael Cox, and our newest addition, Andre Williams. However, amidst this distinguished lineup, I was no longer Mr. Williams the Heisman finalist man-horse. I was just the new guy, #34, dropping balls in rookie minicamp.

As part of the quest to reclaim my identity, I made a bold move. I offered Peyton Hillis a sum of $15,000 to relinquish his cherished number, #44. (He initially requested $25,000 for the number, but I worked him down.) It may have seemed excessive to some, but to me, it was the price I was willing to pay because that #44 connected me to my true abilities. It was a physical reminder to everyone who saw it, including myself, of the player I was built to be.

But there were still four months in front of me before I'd be reminding anyone of anything, and I was thankful for them. I knew better than anyone that I needed rest from the banging, and I needed the jugs machine. I needed to develop a new part of my game.

"Catch the ball, Dre!" These words echoed in my mind. I heard it from others, I heard it from myself. Each new catch was an accumulation of experience and of course I did become better and better, but the day-to-day was a grind. I got on the jugs most days after practice to log some catches but some days I was so discouraged, I just felt like going inside. That was the immature, silly kid in me. If I could go back and slap my neck for taking even one opportunity to get better for granted, I'd gladly take the trip back in time, and I'd slap hard.

All in all, I was not a quitter when it came to sport. Some days were tough, but I would not allow myself to falter now, after coming so far, no matter how hard it got. I was determined to overcome my obstacles to success.

I made it through minicamp. We had some free time before reporting for the preseason to settle into our housing and get organized. That's when Marilyn dropped the bomb on me – she was pregnant. Me, being the green, idealistic donkey that I was... I decided that I wanted to "do the right thing" by Marilyn for the sake of the child and our family. I decided that it was time to move in together and get married. Marilyn wholeheartedly agreed. Fresh out of BC, it was the perfect transition to adulthood for her – marrying her college sweetheart, a professional football player and continuing her privileged life.

I secured a suite in a nice apartment in Secaucus, just seven minutes from the training facility in East Rutherford. Then, I began the process of announcing to everyone that I was going to be a father and that Marilyn and I were planning to get married. I cringe as I write these words now, but in the moment, I felt convinced that I was doing the right thing.

Barely a man, with little guidance and life experience, I found myself facing the daunting responsibilities of fatherhood and braving the path of self-discovery in a high-pressure environment, without any prior preparation or discussion. As a 21-year-old, I had to rely on my own judgment to navigate the uncharted waters of parenthood and personal identity. All the time I had spent avoiding discomfort and seeking temporary distractions had not prepared me for this life-altering moment.

Chapter 19: I Do

Here we were, in the summer of 2014, on the brink of every athlete's dream: my debut season playing professional football with the New York Giants. I was on a high. However, there was one small complication: Marilyn was pregnant. It seemed that it had happened during our week-long trip to Chicago, which I had planned as a post-training treat for myself before the draft. I had taken her along, to explore the city, savor the city's best food, and enjoy each other in the Langham Hotel.

Now, the threat of fatherhood was at the door because I wanted to go on vacation with my girlfriend before the NFL Draft. I didn't know what would happen next, but I had a responsibility to address it. Was Marilyn the woman I had envisioned as my wife or possibly the mother of my child? Absolutely not. Was I in love with her? No. We were just barely getting to know each other. Nevertheless, here we were, because of my own choices. I resolved to adopt an optimistic approach. In my youthful and idealistic mind, Marilyn and I both wanted the same thing, which was to do what was right for the family we were creating and get married. Marilyn supported this decision. I reasoned that it was in the best interest of the child to grow up in a nurturing two-parent household. I thought:

- √ I had fun with Marilyn, she could be a good wife.
- √ She took decent care of her dog, she'd probably be fine with a baby.
- √ She's a trust fund baby. She's not after my money.

I think back now on how damn stupid I was. I was getting ready to learn some hard, painful lessons.

I recall when I first shared my plans with my family, and they all rejected the idea. Even Marilyn's own parents were against it. I remember sitting down with them one afternoon in the backyard of their Stamford home, and it took a hardy form of idiocy to ask for a woman's hand in marriage only to be denied, and then still go through with it anyway. Everyone had reservations about me marrying Marilyn, except me. It was the last red flag I missed before we were married.

My sister asked me over the phone, "Do you love her?" I responded, "No, but I believe we can cultivate that love with time. Love will blossom over time if we both are sincere and authentic about the relationship." Genuinely sincere intentions are great, but nothing can grow in bad soil.

I thought about my parents. They had three children before they decided to marry. I was the third child. Growing up, I never knew my parents to be separate. That was normal for me—to have both of my parents in the house and of one accord—and I wanted that for my kid too. I was content to chase an ideal for the sake of my child. I knew that my intentions were good, and so I felt I couldn't go wrong.

We had made the decision to set a date for our marriage ceremony at the town hall in Secaucus, NJ. It was the most efficient way to ensure it was done before the season began. We'd plan an actual wedding later on after the season, we thought. However, little did I know...

Mayor Gonelli of Secaucus, New Jersey, officially married us on August 29th, 2014, the day after my birthday, when I turned 22. It was also the day after the final preseason game of the year, in which we defeated the Patriots 16-13. Our lives seemed to be going well, but almost immediately after the marriage ceremony, strange things started happening, as if the very fabric of reality was beginning to unravel.

At the time, Marilyn was eight weeks pregnant. We eagerly awaited our first doctor's appointment to monitor the baby's progress. Sadly, the news we received was devastating. The baby was not developing properly, with a cyst growing on the body. The doctor's prognosis was grim, warning of serious complications for both Marilyn and the baby. They strongly advised us to terminate the pregnancy to safeguard her health. Reluctantly, we chose to follow their counsel.

With the very reason that I chose to marry eliminated, I found myself at a profound crossroads. I couldn't help but question if I had rushed into this decision. Clearly, I had made a mistake by not waiting at least eight weeks to determine the viability of the pregnancy, and I failed to conduct adequate research. I was simply following my flawed, misguided heart.

Now, I was arrested by my flawed perception of a righteousness that I was in no way living up to. "I want to be a good Christian and I know God does not like divorce," I told myself. However, there was nothing Christian about the behavior that led me to my current situation. Furthermore, I married before the mayor, not God. I didn't see my own hypocrisy at the time. I realize now that I was reconciling my relationship to God's law by cherry-picking what I would obey and what I would not, rather than reconciling my relationship with God Himself and allowing Him to lead me out of my own foolishness.

As I grappled with my predicament, the football season officially began, and some intriguing developments unfolded. David Wilson announced his retirement due to re-aggravating a serious neck injury that had sidelined him the previous year. This left three RBs and a FB, effectively taking care of the roster.

I distinctly recall the special teams coach's expression after my initial preseason runs. It was a look of disappointment, not because they were bad plays, but because he knew my special teams reps would be limited. My potential as a runner was evident, and it was clear that I would be playing a significant role in the upcoming season.

Chapter 20: I Don't

As I'd mentioned previously, the biggest purchase of my rookie season was the investment of $15,000 to acquire my jersey number from Peyton Hillis. I have no regrets whatsoever about this decision. The previous year, I had taken number 44 to the Heisman race, and I wanted to continue building my legacy with it in the NFL. That number made me feel like myself. I really felt like myself behind that number. It was a big number and it had clean, sharp edges, like the corner of a heavy table, like my shoulders. You knew exactly what you were going to get from me when you saw the 44 on my chest. Finally, it was my older brother's number, and it was he who inspired me to pick up the sport.

My second biggest purchase was Marilyn's ring, and the price tag wasn't far behind the cost of the jersey. I do regret that decision. Marilyn showed no consideration for the fact that I had only just started making money and hadn't yet established a solid financial foundation. She simply chose what she wanted. Her mother was right by her side to co-sign her inconsiderate decisions. I really did ignore every possible warning sign, and there were many.

The season started out rough. We began with a loss away to the Detroit Lions followed by a loss at home to the Arizona Cardinals. Rashad Jennings was the starting RB at that point in the season. Peyton and I backed him up. Losses in the NFL are magnified tenfold. Every move made on the field from practice to game day is captured on film and analyzed by the coaching staff and your teammates. From there, the product you put on the field is analyzed by the media and then the country at large. Win or loss, everyone has something to say, an opinion, a suggestion, a comparison, a story to share. It is truly just as much of a psychological experience as it is physical. You need talent and toughness to play the game. But you need some tough skin and a level head to lose the game.

On the other hand, when you emerge victorious, everyone and their mother is eager to slap your bottom and shout hooray. Those

☆ After the Last Snap ☆

first few days of the week, everything is right in the world and the mistakes from the previous week fade into insignificance. It is an eight-month-long rollercoaster ride of unpredictable, emotional highs and lows.

The rookie season was well underway on the home front, reflecting our performance on the field. I was experiencing a series of losses. The first topic that occupied Marilyn's thoughts as a new wife, after our nine-month-long relationship, was why I had not designated her as the primary beneficiary in the event of my death. Initially, I was taken aback. I attempted to dismiss the conversation altogether. However, my shock turned to anger as she persisted in bringing up the issue, even going so far as to claim it as her right as my wife. It quickly escalated into an argument, marking our first significant disagreement since we came together. To my dismay, this topic resurfaced time and time again. She even involved her parents in the discussion. Cathy-Anne, in fact, sided with her daughter and pointed out to me that all of her friends' husbands had designated their wives as primary beneficiaries of their estates. I responded that all of her friends were old ladies over the age of 60 who more than likely, had been married for years, not a month. This argument grieved me to my core, and it came up again, and again, and again. I can't describe how upsetting it was to be in a relationship with someone who was so unabashedly obsessed with self and with money that they would fight me for the rights to my money in the case of my death while I was still very much alive. Not to mention, she hadn't participated in earning any of the money she was fighting for.

I had a feeling that this woman and I were not right for each other. She was self-centered but I was too busy and too insecure to consider leaving. I thought maybe she could change, and I was afraid of what others would think if I left so soon. I realize now that I cared too much about others' opinions. I convinced myself that I never quit anything, but that wasn't true. I dropped statistics the first week when I decided it wasn't right for me. I should have dropped Marilyn like I did statistics. But I was young and foolish and insecure. I stayed in it, and the longer I stayed, the more stressed I became. To cope, I turned to marijuana. It was the only thing we really bonded over. I was stuck in a twisted cycle.

☆ Andre Williams ☆

As the season dragged on, the stress took its toll. The losses on the field mirrored the growing distance at home. I immersed myself in practice and games, often staying late just to avoid going back to the apartment. The Giants were experiencing their own challenges, and the added burden of a tumultuous personal life only made things worse. I felt like I had no one to confide in, because it was I that had made the unilateral decision to marry. My teammates were busy with their own lives, and coaching staff only cared about what was happening on the field.

Chapter 21: Rookie

My rookie season stands as the highlight of my entire NFL career. In 2014, I emerged as the team's top rusher, amassing 721 rush yards with 7 rush TDs, and 121 receiving yards. That small stack of receiving yards was a source of pride to me, as catching the ball had never been my forte. There I was, with a c-note from Eli Manning. Most of the time, I was catching a simple wide route into the boundary and stealing yards sprinting up the sideline or securing the 5-yard "middle-of-field" late, check down. I owe much of this success to Eli. His superpower as a quarterback was "excellent touch." Eli could give me an accurate ball, with just enough sauce for my green hands to handle. He gave everyone a ball like that. His graceful precision was instrumental in my development as a receiver, and for that, I am truly grateful.

My first start came in game 6, during an away game against the Eagles at Lincoln Financial Stadium. In the absence of the entire RB room due to injury, I was the sole runner left standing. Apart from one bone-crushing run on power, I was ineffective, and our offense laid an egg, resulting in a disheartening 27-0 loss. Did we have some struggles at the offensive line position? Yes, but the reality was more complex than that. We had struggles with a lack of leadership that year. There was no definitive leader to rally us through adversity. While Eli led by example as a consummate professional, he was not the galvanizing leader. I think we did have a lot of high character, professional men that loved the game, but we were not a close-knit team.

It was clear that there was a power struggle unfolding in the coaching room between the young Ben McAdoo, our new offensive coordinator, and the seasoned head coach, Tom Coughlin. However, the significance of wins and losses held a different meaning for each of them. Regardless, the players were compensated regardless of the outcome, and as a draft pick, I felt secure. Little did I realize how greatly this power dynamic would

☆ Andre Williams ☆

impact my young career. But ultimately, my lack of understanding extended beyond the realm of the coaching room. I failed to comprehend just how much my personal life would come to influence my professional journey. This was an aspect that I had complete control over, but regrettably, chose not to exercise.

Odell Beckham returned from injury like a crack of thunder in Game 9 against the Indianapolis Colts, posting 156 yards receiving in his first game as a pro. This gave our offense some life, but it wasn't enough. We managed to lose the game 40 to 24. We went on a bender, losing 7 games in a row until week 14 against the Tennessee Titans.

It was an away game for us. It wasn't raining on game day, but the field was wet & soft from the previous night's rain. The grass was yielding under our movement in the wet clay dirt. The equipment staff had recommended packing long spikes, and it was evident that they would be necessary after we went out to warm up.

That day, we had our way with the Titans. They didn't have a chance at stopping our offense. We won the game 36-7. It was my first 100+ yard game. Odell and I went for a buck thirty a piece. I had a 60-yard TD after bobbling Eli's toss on a sweep to the left in the first half. After that, Coach Johnson left me in the game. I got lathered up and took my time to wash off on the Titans defense. We ate the clock and scored the victory.

We managed to pull two more consecutive wins out of the season against the Washington Redskins and St Louis Rams. I think it's funny that as I write this, Washington no longer holds their name, and the Rams no longer inhabit St Louis. It's been 6 years since my last game in the NFL and already, I am from a different era of football.

It's worth mentioning that I had my second 100-yard performance against the Rams in St. Louis. I was really starting to understand the flow of the game a bit better at this point. I could not dictate the flow of the run with a good set. At the pro level, the defense stuck to their fundamentals 9 times out of 10, but with patience, opportunities presented themselves that allowed for my abilities to flash and shine.

On a particular play early in the drive, I hit the crease just right on the inside zone and accelerated. It was clear that the safety responsible for run support did not anticipate what was about to happen, as he was completely unprepared for the collision. I kept going, and the run would have gone for 80 yards and a score if it hadn't been for Aaron Donald's incredible hustle. As I cut back inside towards the goalposts to avoid a defender, Aaron saw his opportunity to close the gap and make the tackle. I was thrilled to see him and Odell earn their Super Bowl rings in 2022. They deserved them more than anyone else from our draft class.

With a week 17 loss to the Eagles, my rookie season came to an end with a disappointing 6-10 record. Shortly afterward, Coach Coughlin was replaced by McAdoo, who stepped up as the new Head Coach sporting a bowl cut and an oversized suit at his first press conference as HC. It was a clear sign that things were about to change in a bad way. However, it was my personal life rather than my professional one that had me unsettled. Now, with no football to distract me, it was time to face the music at home.

Chapter 22: Real Eyes

I made some impactful decisions in the off-season of 2015, some of which greatly improved my quality of life, like when I decided to undergo PRK eye surgery to correct my nearsightedness. The PRK surgery did correct my nearsightedness and cut my dependence on glasses and contact lenses. The value I received for my $6,500 was some of the best money I have ever spent. If you're considering it, proceed. I highly recommend it. Be sure, however, to follow the recommendations from your doctor on the pain management directives. Regrettably, I turned down the painkillers and went straight home after my procedure, and as a result, I endured three excruciating days of pain once the numbing drops wore off. Spare yourself from unnecessary hardship and at least pick them up while you still have time.

There were other decisions I made that year that would shape the trajectory for the next decade of my life. I thought about the best way to explore my newfound freedom. Now I had a platform, I was in the biggest media market in the country, and I had money in my pocket. There were many opportunities to explore, and there was no longer any time to waste playing PlayStation.

In an effort to stay close to work and make my first sound investment, I made my first real estate investment in 2015: a townhouse in Secaucus—a prime location in my eyes, being just a seven-minute drive from the training facility in East Rutherford. Marilyn was vexed that I didn't buy in the neighborhood she preferred, the one with the more expensive condos across town where all the other players were living. At this point, I had learned to ignore her nagging mouth and cope with her negativity as best as I could. My method involved smoking and then diving into my work.

I started to dabble in aromatherapy. I delved into the art of soap making and dedicated my off-season to setting up a fragrance lab in my townhouse. Chemistry had always fascinated me, and I thoroughly enjoyed studying the effects of saponification on

☆ After the Last Snap ☆

different mixtures of essential oils and carrier oils used in my soaps.

I found fulfillment in my time in the lab that summer. As I delved into the world of scents and soaps, conducting research, I pondered the possibility of one day seeing my artisanal creations in stores. I had a marketing agent named Luke, who would visit my house to discuss ideas, take pictures and videos, and present opportunities. During one of our meetings, he asked if I would be interested in meeting his friend Eamon Walsh. I accepted the invitation and went to his office in a WeWork building in Manhattan.

Eamon came to me and said something to the effect of, "Hey man, you are a running back in the NFL. How would you like to create your own signature shoe?" He was deeply involved in the footwear business and on the brink of launching his own footwear brand, OneGround Footwear. Eamon told me he had access to an exclusive factory in Spain that was known for producing the Balenciaga Arenas, and his designer had just finished a stint with Nike.

This was not soap bars, and it certainly wasn't PlayStation. The concept intrigued me and sparked my interest right away. I saw an opportunity. This was an invitation to another sort of lab, but this time I would have the chance to produce a luxury product. I understood that it wouldn't be free, but after immersing myself in the creative process in the fragrance lab, I yearned to acquire the knowledge of crafting something high-end and wearable. I was down for a little pay-to-play.

For the following eight months, I plunged into the realm of shoemaking alongside Eamon. When I wasn't immersed in football training or matches, my focus shifted towards building a brand and honing in on what I thought the perfect shoe could be. I eventually named the brand, Runningman.

I drew inspiration for the Runningman from iconic brands such as Vans, PF Flyers, and Converse. But instead of cheap cloths and polymers, I used premium cowhide leather for the upper, luxurious lambskin for the interior, and a 100% rubber sole, resulting in an elevated, premium casual shoe. The addition of ostrich leather on

☆ Andre Williams ☆

the gusseted tongue added a distinctive touch. After finalizing the sample, I produced 200 pairs in black and 200 in white.

The Runningman quickly garnered attention in the fashion and apparel industry, opening doors that I never anticipated. My status as a New York Giant, combined with the allure of the Runningman, provided me with access to a myriad of trade and fashion shows, allowing me to network with influential players in the clothing industry, both large and small.

I was initially confused about how I ended up in these spaces and what my role should be. I was passionate about the creative process and proud of my work on Runningman, but I was a full-blown pro footballer. I had not yet grasped the difference between being a creator and a salesman, nor was I prepared to yield the time necessary to bridge the gap between the two.

That began to shift once I met Roy, but we'll revisit that later...

Chapter 23: Descent

The 2015 NBA All-Star Game was held in New York City at Madison Square Garden. The city was alive with things to do and places to be for All-Star Weekend. Of course, as a young promising NY Giant rookie, I had access to all of it. My local agent called ahead. The door was always open for us.

I'd never been to an NBA All-Star Weekend. Marilyn and I took an Uber into the city to see what it was all about. The way it worked was, my agent would keep me informed on what was happening near me. If something piqued my interest, he'd call ahead to secure my place on the guest list, with entry granted to Andre Williams +1.

We had a wonderful time enjoying the city together, day drinking, and connecting with new people. Our first stop was a house party in a modern townhouse in Stamford Village. We mingled there for a couple of hours before heading to Beauty & Essex for lunch. We then made our way to a hotel in Times Square, where we explored a handful of gifting suites. We collected a bunch of items that never made it home with us.

As the day turned into night, I contemplated our final destination and settled on 'Bounce Sporting Club' – It was a good pick. The vibes were on point, and the owner was grateful to have us in the building for the night.

After about an hour, Rob Gronkowski and Chandler Jones showed up. We'd studied the scouting reports, we knew each other and upon recognition, they graciously invited us to join their reserved table. At that point, the energy in the place reached an all-time high and we felt at ease. We sipped our drinks and took in an entertaining scene. We couldn't help but enjoy ourselves.

The night wore on and as it grew late, I was ready to satisfy my hunger craving with a slice of authentic NY pizza and head home for some rest. Marilyn had a different plan. She wanted to stick around for the after-hours scene, but I wasn't particularly interested. Before leaving, I expressed my gratitude to Rob and

Chandler, and we headed towards the street. I didn't need to search far for a taste of delicious NY pizza, and I was in line for a slice of sicilian with teacup pepperonis.

Marilyn kept trying to persuade me to prolong our night out and explore more. I was entirely content with my two heavy wedges of Sicilian pizza. I couldn't ask the night for anything else. I promptly arranged for an Uber to take us back to Secaucus, much to Marilyn's displeasure. Satiated, pleasantly buzzed, and feeling drowsy, I disregarded her protests until we arrived at our apartment.

Our luxury complex was situated on the quiet end of the town. There was one other player who stayed there. Management stayed out of our way for the most part, and it was easy to keep a low profile there, but we didn't go unnoticed around NJ or NY as a Giants draft pick. I did my best to stay out of trouble. There were rules we had to follow. 'No smoking inside' was one of them because it was an easy way to prevent avoidable disasters. I never wanted to hear a fire alarm, and we didn't know or trust our neighbors. Yet, here Marilyn was, getting ready to smoke a joint in the apartment. It was February, and it was cold outside, but these were the rules we lived by to keep myself out of trouble and keep a good thing going.

Clearly, Marilyn was trying to start a fight. I was left to wonder why she was willing to jeopardize our stability for her own spiteful desires. I am sure she felt secure in her privileged background. It was obvious that she had little regard for the impact her actions had on my livelihood.

She remained adamant about smoking inside, so I snatched the joint out of her hand, crushed it, and flushed it down the toilet, foolishly thinking I'd resolved the issue. She was speechless as I left her to have a shower. When I finished and was leaving the bathroom, the sound of running water in the kitchen drew my attention. I went to see what it was and found my winter jacket soaking in the kitchen sink. It didn't matter to me that it was an expensive piece by Gucci, but it did matter that it was my only jacket, and it was mid-February.

Now I was furious. I stormed into the closet, grabbed Marilyn's $3000 Hermès purse and Louboutin heels that I had bought for her.

☆ After the Last Snap ☆

I pulled the heels off the shoes and tossed everything out the window. Now Marilyn was fired up. She was shouting and cursing at me and looking for something else to destroy. She picked up my Mac computer and hurled it across the room. As I moved to retrieve it, the computer's broken screen sliced my hand open.

Marilyn's demeanor changed when she saw all the blood. I knew I needed stitches because the bleeding wouldn't stop. Marilyn was apologizing to me as I left the apartment, whimpering to take her with me. I declined. It was 2 A.M. as I drove myself to the Meadowlands hospital for stitches, pondering how I ended up married to such a crazy little girl.

Chapter 24: Her 23rd

In March, we headed to Miami to begin the off-season training period. Our plan was to stay there for six weeks. I secured a beautiful condo in Sunny Isles right on Collins Avenue. I was scheduled to train with Pete Bommarito five days a week and spend the rest of my time soaking up the sun with Marilyn, eagerly awaiting the day she would finally mature. Her birthday was approaching at the end of the month, and it couldn't come sooner, I thought. She continued to persistently argue with me about the same old things like a silly little girl asking her daddy for a pony or a birthday party. But Marilyn wasn't asking for either of those things. She wanted beneficiary status in case I wound up dead. This was the all-consuming topic that infected our daily lives up until her birthday.

Marilyn desired sushi and hookah for her birthday dinner. Once I returned from my training at Pete's for the day, I freshened up and we proceeded to Sushi Samba. Opting for outdoor seating, Marilyn wasted no time in launching her campaign to push her position on the beneficiary topic. We hadn't even ordered drinks.

I can't pinpoint any exceptional talents Marilyn possessed, except for her one uncanny ability to persistently pester the love of Christ out of me. The sheer extent of her nagging was truly astounding. No matter how hard I tried to steer the conversation towards something meaningful, Marilyn continued to dominate with her incredible ability.

As I reflect on it now, I am torn. Do I deserve to be scolded or commended for enduring it as long as I did? At the very least, I can proudly attest that I gave every bit of time and effort to our relationship that I had to give. It was a wasteful use of time, but I maintained my integrity and remained loyal to my principles and to Marilyn.

After dinner, we took an Uber to a hookah bar where her nagging persisted through drinks and smoke. Marilyn was sure she could convince me to guarantee that she would benefit financially

☆ After the Last Snap ☆

from my demise, dim-wittingly unaware that such a conversation disqualified her from ever obtaining such a benefit. I would never give her what she wanted. Eventually, I decided I couldn't continue. I told Marilyn that I was done celebrating her birthday. It was late, and I was ready to go home.

Similar to Sushi Samba, the hookah bar was an outdoor venue on a wide strip with various establishments on either side. I settled the bill, and as we started walking back to the car, Marilyn suddenly collapsed on the cobbled path. I was speechless and annoyed. I knelt down to check if she was breathing and when I nudged her, she came to and murmured that she needed to use the bathroom. Twenty minutes passed before she reappeared from the restroom.

When she reappeared, she acted as though nothing had occurred. I called for a car, and we stood in silence, patiently waiting for our ride. I couldn't help but wonder if she had an explanation for her sudden episode. It was completely out of character for her, and I had no knowledge of any existing medical conditions she was dealing with. We climbed into the car, and as we began our journey back home, I broke the silence and confronted her, "Marilyn, why did you collapse in the middle of the street? What was that all about?" I asked, hoping for an explanation.

"In college, I was diagnosed with anxiety attacks, a consequence of an emotionally abusive relationship," she responded.

Finally, she'd moved me to anger. Was she implying that I had been verbally abusing her? That I was the cause of her sudden collapse? "Do you think I'm verbally abusing you, Marilyn?" I asked her bluntly.

"That's not what I said," she snapped back. I was without words, overwhelmed with disgust. *This relationship is done for*, I thought to myself. I told myself that when it was time to return to New Jersey, I'd put an end to this sorry state of affairs.

When we got back to the condo, I sat her down and told her straight up that I was done with her bullshit and that I was ready to end our marriage. I told her if she spoke the word "beneficiary" just one more time, the next thing I would do was head to the airport for the next flight back to New Jersey, and I didn't care if she was on the plane with me.

She immediately said that she was sorry and that she did not mean what she said in the car and that she'd had too many drinks. But I had already resigned, and my exit was imminent. I was only here with her to complete my training. I knew I had to leave her as soon as we made it home. Marilyn wasn't going to change; she'd only get worse because Marilyn was not mentally stable, and I had no business putting up with it.

I successfully completed my training with Bommarito in Miami by keeping my distance from Marilyn as much as possible. After training with Pete in the morning, I would go for a run on the beach, lounge by the pool, or work on action items with Eamon over the phone for the Runningman. We made it back to the house in Secaucus in mid-May.

Chapter 25: Fine Print

This chapter is titled "Fine Print" because, until now, I failed to read the detailed terms and conditions that governed my relationships, my career, my faith, my principles. Regarding myself, I had moved through life being so moved by emotional attachments rooted in the flesh and ignorant, youthful idealism. Now, with my first year of marriage behind me and my second year in the NFL ahead, the mental strain I faced at home prompted me to pause and scrutinize the fine print. My marriage, my job, my Bible, my heart. Had I read the terms and conditions at all?

My principles informed me that marriage was the right foundation for my family, and my principles were true. If I was prepared to have a child with Marilyn, I should be married to her first. The issue was that we did not marry because we built a friendship based on trust and understanding which led me to love and choose Marilyn as my life partner. No, we only married because of a reason born from us having sex. If that wasn't the case, I am sure Marilyn and I would have gotten as far as friends. I probably would have lost interest in her like I did Hillary.

My principles informed me that signing a prenuptial agreement with Marilyn was wrong. I saw it as a failure to begin with a hedge against failure. In my heart, that equated to fear and that was the wrong attachment to commit to paper regarding my marriage. My principles were true. I would never sign a prenuptial agreement with my wife. There is no plan B, and I mean that with my entire heart, mind, and soul. And so, it wasn't so much good faith as it was blind trust and mere ignorance that urged me to move forward with Marilyn without knowing if her intentions for me were good.

It's clear now that my thinking was completely wrong because I hadn't read the fine print. I had both my parents in my life, and I knew there was a God. It wasn't that I didn't have proper guidance, I just chose not to heed their wisdom. Now, I was beginning to suffer the consequences, and the suffering and the consequences were only just beginning.

It wasn't too late to leave yet, but I had a flawed theology that froze me in fear and indecision, believing that God would frown upon me if I got divorced. I had not been actively engaging with my Bible or spending time in prayer, so I was unable to discern God's will for my life. I'd forgotten that my salvation was free, and I couldn't agree on what was right anymore. I was hesitant to be the one to initiate the dissolution, feeling that it would add another spiritual strike to my name. I felt compelled to honor the commitment I had made to this woman. She was my responsibility now… but it was not too late to leave.

I was a half-stepper, frozen in fear and indecision even though I knew deep down I needed to leave to save myself, my career, and my mental well-being from decay. I postponed my departure, pretending that Marilyn would miraculously improve and mature. I isolated myself instead of seeking help from others. I resorted to smoking another bowl, shifting my focus to the next opponent, the next workout, or the next business meeting.

Then I discovered Marilyn's hidden stash in her office desk drawer. I can't remember what I was searching for that day, but I was shocked when I opened the drawer and found three prescription bottles for various medications and a pack of cigarettes. Who in the hell was this person I was married to? Why was she on such a heavy dose of Adderall? How long had she been taking anxiety and antidepressant medication? I didn't even bother confronting her about it. I was truly unhappy with her, and it was all too much. I'd become tired of her.

It seemed like the discovery of cigarettes and pills was the straw that broke the camel's back. The selfishness, ingratitude, lies, and manipulation had become unbearable. I did not know this woman, and it was painfully clear: she loved the celebrity lifestyle I afforded her, but she didn't love me. The constant nitpicking and arguments over trivial matters exposed her and exhausted me. It was the house, or it was the money. I didn't want to hear it again. The lack of substance or logic anywhere in our conversations or our arguments was suffocating.

☆ After the Last Snap ☆

There was no sense of dreams or ambition in her words, only an unhealthy fixation on reality TV shows, where we could go next, and who we could meet up with. I was done with all of it, fed up with every self-serving statement.

I would break the news that I wanted to end the relationship during breakfast the next morning. I took her to the local diner and ordered my usual: banana pancakes with extra crispy hash browns, topped with cheese and a country-style sausage link. Although I wasn't hungry, I ate slowly and waited for the right moment.

When the moment arrived, Marilyn was prepared. She didn't seem surprised or break into tears. Instead, she had a response for me—she was pregnant.

"Fool me once, shame on you. Fool me twice, shame on me," that old song by Flowers for Dorian, epitomized my relationship with Marilyn Grey. She knew my flaws better than I did, and she understood my "fine print." I always wanted to be a young dad, and I really do care deeply about my kids. I didn't know how true this was until Barron was born into the world and suddenly my priorities had shifted.

Chapter 26: Baby On the Way

Looking back now, fully understanding the extent of Marilyn Grey's manipulative nature, I cannot be certain whether she was truly pregnant when she informed me of such at the diner that morning. However, she knew that I would hesitate if she mentioned a baby, and I did. My feelings about Marilyn didn't change, but now I was completely arrested. I wasn't prepared to abandon my pregnant wife and subject my child to unnecessary hardships. Marilyn did actually conceive my child sometime in May or June of 2015. Through a blood test, we discovered that it was a boy. This time, he endured the journey smoothly for the past eight weeks and beyond, without any complications.

Above all, I was eager to meet him. When Marilyn became pregnant, her demeanor changed. She was composed and easy to handle for a while. I confronted her about her use of medication for her undisclosed mental issues and urged her to do whatever it took to stop taking the pills while carrying our son. She reassured me that she knew better, didn't actually need the pills, and would take good care of herself.

In the grips of anticipation, indecision, & worry, the preseason arrived, and a new NFL season was upon us, ready to consume my time and my mind. Any decisions about home life would have to wait until the end of the season.

Two things vividly remain in my memory. Firstly, it was undeniable that the season did not go well. Coach McAdoo implemented an offense that was considerably simpler than before. Unfortunately, this meant that defenses easily predicted our plays. Additionally, Shane Vereen was added to our RB group as the scat back and received significant attention. Consequently, we moved away from a power running game that often found use for a hefty 230-pound running back. Naturally, I felt misplaced in McAdoo's offense. Throughout the year, my main tasks were spelling the

☆ After the Last Snap ☆

other RBs and ensuring the protection of Eli's blindside, or running predictable short down zone runs. Regrettably, the season did not end favorably for me.

Part of this was my fault. I failed to capitalize on the previous year's success in terms of receptions and receiving yards. It's not that I didn't want to; I simply found myself unprepared to transition from being a check-down route runner to the featured receiver, as our new offense sometimes demanded. I didn't dedicate enough focus to that aspect of my game in the offseason. Shane excelled at it, taking numerous targets for touchdowns in the red zone on the angle and angle out routes. In the NFL, the mentality is "if it works, do it again," and Shane did it again and again. He deserves all the credit for his accomplishments during his time in the league.

The second memory that stands out from 2015 is reconnecting with De'shonia, the only friend from college outside of football whom I managed to keep in touch with. A peculiar shift had occurred since I married Marilyn. The longer we stayed together, the less mental energy I had to spare for other people. We were losing games, and I felt like I was losing time on the field. At home, I felt like a loser as well.

I had reached a point of no return with Marilyn. In a way, she had achieved what she had been fighting for. I now realized this and felt my strength slipping away. In the game of football, there are constant ups and downs. I was familiar with the downs, having come from a school like Boston College. But this was different. I had never felt like a loser at BC. I was not a loser. However, I was undeniably losing a part of myself now. This was not how I was supposed to feel with my first child on the way. Marilyn was giving me something, so why did it feel like she was taking something from me? I needed to talk to someone, but I didn't know who that someone was.

My family had already warned me about Marilyn, so I knew running to them wasn't an option. I could already hear their "I told you so" reply. None of my close teammates were married, so I felt lost and misunderstood. However, the first game of the season was against the Cowboys in Dallas, where I had a friend, De'shonia.

The last time we had spoken was about a year ago when I was in Chicago with Marilyn before the draft. She called me in tears, seeking advice about her relationship with Derrick. Rumors about him had reached her ears since he had left for the University of Delaware. She even helped him complete his transfer paperwork, but she suspected there might be someone else.

Derrick and I were long-time roommates and teammates at BC. However, during my senior year, he made a terrible decision that almost cost him his place in school. Along with some other players, Derrick got involved with a freshman girl who turned out to be the daughter of a professor at the school.

Stories like these seemed to occur all the time. There was even a woman who used Craigslist to seek out a sexual encounter with a cohort of the football team. I had no interest in being a member of that cohort. I loathed to see the dorm room this sultry encounter was taking place in. The woman actually came to the school twice, once my freshman year and again my senior season. I heard that she even showed her hospitality to the recruits who were visiting for the day. Rumor had it that her husband was a die-hard BC football fan. Hyper-sex is fascinating to some, and it is not uncommon to find it in its various forms during a typical college experience, but it didn't sit well with me.

When the professor discovered what had happened to his daughter, he relentlessly pursued those involved. Derrick and others were implicated and expelled from the campus. Although Derrick initially lied to De'shonia about the reason for his expulsion, it was clear to me that she did not deserve to endure the hurtful relationship she was in, and I saw no reason for the lie to persist. As a friend, I felt ashamed for not being forthcoming with her earlier. I revealed the truth about Derrick to her on the phone that day in Chicago. It was like the phone call that night after the victory over Wallenpaupack. De'shonia listened to what I had to say, then she thanked me for being honest and ended the call. After that phone call, we didn't talk for a long time. I knew she was dealing with some deep regret. But her time was not wasted because even though Derrick was a dog, she proved herself loyal and loving. She was more than that. She was what a real woman looked like, a queen. Other than my own mother, I had never known a woman whom I respected more.

☆ After the Last Snap ☆

When the Cowboys appeared on the schedule in 2015, and I remembered that De'shonia was from Dallas, I was desperate to reconnect with her. My heart jumped in my chest when De'shonia responded with an emphatic "Yesss!!" It made me incredibly happy to hear from her. My mood and my mind were immediately elevated. In fact, as soon as it registered in my mind that I would be seeing her, my mind began to wander back to a place that it hadn't been since high school. An idea from a dark place crept up in my mind. *Should I get her a room at the hotel we'd be staying at?* It would be incredibly easy to do so. I wrestled against the thought the entire week leading up to the game.

During that period, Marilyn was roughly four months into her pregnancy, and as time went on, a deep sense of sadness settled within me. I had reached a point where I no longer desired to be in a relationship with Marilyn, yet it felt like it was too late to walk away. The most disheartening part, however, was that she only seemed interested in me for my achievements, completely disregarding the real me.

She showed no support for my ideas, belittled my passion for the Runningman, and refused to spend any time with me in the fragrance lab. To her, it was an eyesore and the ire of her disgust with the house she did not choose. Instead, she wasted her time engaging in mindless chatter about reality TV shows and constantly complained about my lack of attention towards her.

For months now, I recognized that Marilyn was not my equivalent or soulmate. We were not properly yoked. Nevertheless, that was no justification for compromising my principles and breaking my vows. I remembered the deep rotting feeling of regret that I felt when I betrayed Ayla back in high school. Now I was married with a child on the way. I refused to make the same mistake again. I wanted nothing to do with that heavy sin. No, I would not jeopardize my integrity or my marriage. I would give Marilyn, our family, and our unborn baby boy a chance. Perhaps he was the key to leading us towards genuine personal growth. It was crucial for me to discover the truth.

As we were accustomed to in our teenage years , I would meet De'shonia in Dallas as a friend, confide in her and seek reassurance that I was doing the right thing. I would not be booking a hotel room for De'shonia. Nor had I any plans to inform Marilyn about who would be attending the game with me.

Chapter 27: Giants Lose by One

I will admit that as I traveled to Dallas, the Cowboys were the least of my worries. I knew I wasn't starting, and there was still time to book the hotel room. I fantasized about her, not because I wanted to have sex with someone else, but because I craved intimacy with someone real. Intimacy... I wished that De'shonia could be the one who could in-to-me-see. There are few things worse than being legally bonded to someone that caused you to feel lonely inside. It is a kind of prison or slavery. I fantasized all the way to Dallas; but I left the fantasy on the plane. I knew De'shonia. I understood that she had principles that did not bend. Not once in our four years at BC did I see her bend, nor would I try to bend her. We made it to the hotel, and I walked forcefully past the check-in counter, hoping to beat the line at the elevator. Before I'd even dropped my bags off in the room, I was on the phone with De'shonia to notify her that I'd arrived.

She came to pick me up in a silver Mitsubishi Mirage. She stepped out of the car to hug me. As my eyes came to rest on her face and her figure, I was pierced with the reality that I'd ruined my life with Marilyn. I was staring at someone worthy of me. I hugged her and felt her body against mine. Everything about her was satisfying—her skin, her eyes, her smell, her smile... I remembered her pretty mouth and the power I knew it contained; the power to smite. I stepped away from her, walked to the passenger side of the car, and got inside. She could have taken me anywhere at that moment. I was already in a trance.

De'Shonia took me to an outdoor lounge nearby. We settled into a cabana with a cozy twin cushion seat. I took one last risk and inquired if she would like a drink, but she politely declined. It was clear that she hadn't changed since college—still the sweet southern belle. She carried herself with grace.

☆ Andre Williams ☆

Taking a breath to compose myself, we began to converse. She opened up about her decision to move back home after leaving Boston. She spoke of the loneliness she felt after parting ways with Derrick, and how cruel he and his family had been to her for ending the relationship. It stung her that he never had the decency to apologize for his deceit.

I offered her solace as best as I could. While I couldn't provide her with the answers she sought, I knew it wouldn't be long before someone came along who recognized her worth, helped mend her broken heart, and took care of her.

When it was finally my turn to express my feelings, I poured my heart out to her. I told her I felt like a failure because I found myself stuck with a spoiled girl who constantly challenged me and didn't support my ideas. And now, with a baby on the way, I couldn't bring myself to abandon her, even though deep down, I knew she was only after my money and my celebrity. I confessed my hope that our child might bring about some positive change in Marilyn and in our relationship, but in reality, I had little faith in that, especially now, sitting here with her. My heart was truly sad. I kept glancing at my watch, acutely aware that our night meetings were inching closer, and I would have to leave this place. We sat together for as long as we could, taking in every moment together before reluctantly making our way back to the hotel.

When we returned to the hotel, it was apparent that De'shonia shared the same sentiments as I did. We were both reluctant to let each other go. She asked if she could ride the elevator with me back up to my room. She could have asked me anything in that moment. I was already in a trance.

We ascended the elevator in silence, and as the doors opened on my floor, she made sure that no one was waiting to enter. There was no one in sight, and De'shonia drew me close, planting a gentle kiss on my lips with her pretty mouth. She whispered her goodbye and gently pushed me away. My mind exploded as I staggered backwards out of the elevator. It was a simple peck on the lips, a fatality. I was smitten.

I couldn't hear a thing for the remainder of the night. My soul had left from my body to linger within the confines of the elevator.

☆ After the Last Snap ☆

I nodded my way through meetings, downed two bottles of water, and melted into the bed.

The following day, we faced off against the Dallas Cowboys and suffered a narrow defeat by just one point, 27-26. After the game, I crossed paths with De'shonia once again at the designated meeting spot for players and their visitors. Thankfully she had brought along one of her male childhood friends to watch the game with us. It was easy to hide the elephant in the room and act as if nothing had transpired between us the previous night.

On my face, I wore a facade of frustration over our loss, yet deep down, my true disappointment arose from the realization that it was time to return home. I hugged De'shonia goodbye and told her it was good to see her, and I left in a dark cloud with the team.

I knew that we couldn't talk anymore once I left. She wasn't just a friend from our school days anymore, and she was more than a "what-if" road trip fantasy. I knew with certainty that there was something deep and wide beyond the door of our relationship. The proof was still there, lingering in the elevator, and it had to be left there to die. I was headed back home to my wife, who was four months pregnant with my son. I would stay true. I texted De'Shonia when we were on the ground in NJ:

"I have to give my relationship everything that I have, Dee. It will work out or it will fail. I really can't say what will be. But if it fails, it will fail because Marilyn and I are simply not for each other. I am okay with that. But it cannot be because I was double-minded, and I broke my promise to my wife. You and I are more than friends. We know that now. Let's not talk anymore."

Dee didn't fight me. She made it easy. She said, "Okay," with a red heart emoji next to it. It was the worst loss of the season.

Chapter 28: Roy the Maker

There is little else to say about the 2015 season. We ended with the exact same record as the previous year, 6-10. However, my impact on the few victories we did have was diminished. This was concerning for several reasons. I wasn't McAdoo's draft choice. I was part of the plan that just got pushed out the door. The new plan wasn't any better, but what mattered was that in McAdoo's plan, I didn't have a significant role. I had become expendable, and I would have to prove myself in the upcoming off-season. At that time, all of this was going beyond my comprehension. I was preoccupied with the challenges of life.

Emotionally, I was suffering because the woman I had chosen as my wife had revealed herself to be relentlessly ungrateful and unsupportive. However, she was also fertile, and in a few months, she would bring our first child into the world.

Physically, I suffered from a torn labrum that was causing shoulder subluxations. That was 100% affecting my on-field performance and hampering my ability as a runner. The Giants medical staff didn't have an answer apart from offering mediocre "maintenance" exercises. I was sure a second surgery on the same shoulder was not the answer.

Faced with this challenge, I sought to invent a solution. I dedicated myself to designing a padded shoulder harness capable of stabilizing my shoulder joint and guarding it with a high-grade combination of force-dispersing foam and polymers. This project, code-named Exxos Unlimited, had been a passionate pursuit of mine since my rookie season. I delved deeply into the design and prototyping processes, collaborating with a mechanical engineer to develop a concept that was theoretically feasible. Upon completing the design using CAD, I initiated the construction of early prototypes in partnership with a ballistics company based in Oregon. I was learning to grapple my challenges with creative

☆ After the Last Snap ☆

force. Even as early as the summer of 2015, I was learning to business my way through an obstacle. I can admit, I was a natural at the creative part, but I had no concept of the business side.

Although I didn't have any answers, I discovered solace in immersing myself in my work. Focusing on my physical well-being also brought me a sense of relief. Thus, when the season concluded in December, Eamon and I finalized the production of the Runningman shoe and produced the first 400 black and white pairs. I spent time in the lab, making soap, I eased my mind with marijuana smoke, and we booked another trip to Miami for off-season training. Barron would be born by the time we made it to Miami in the spring of 2016.

It was NYFW 2016, I was working with a teammate of mine by the name of Marcus Harris on a fashion show project. This project was called 'Giants on the Runway.' Marcus had a clothing line of his own he called 'Royality Rael.' Our intention was to showcase our clothing lines in a fashion show by combining our styles into different fits for a handful of our teammates. Marcus was in charge of the tops, and he was collaborating with another brand owner by the name of Mike Cherry to provide pants for the models. My input was footwear, with the Runningman shoe. I intended to model for the fashion show as well. It was the 'Giants on the Runway' show that allowed me to have the pleasure of meeting Roy the Maker.

Roy was the product developer for Mike and Marcus's brands. He reached out to me one day by text to introduce himself. He was wondering if I could possibly schedule to meet up with him for custom measurements of their collections. He was small and unassuming, but also he had a style about him that let me know he'd spent some time living in New York.

I led him into my living room, which had evolved into my fragrance lab and office. As he glanced around, I engaged in small talk about what I was up to in the lab. He stayed silent and clutched onto a small leather bag even as he proceeded to take my measurements. Although I offered him water, he declined and then surprised me with a question. Gazing at the Runningman shoe, he inquired, "Did you create this shoe?"

"Indeed," I confirmed.

"Why did you create it?" he prodded.

☆ Andre Williams ☆

"Because it was cool!" I shot back.

Roy then remarked, "They are cool, but how do you plan to sell it?"

"I haven't thought that far ahead, sir. I'm simply focused on creating something cool," was my response.

Our ensuing three-hour conversation delved into product manufacturing, football, and martial arts. Roy imparted invaluable knowledge and insights, positioning himself as a mentor who could elevate my product development to the next level. The information he freely shared was well beyond what I had paid to learn during the eight months of developing the Runningman. That night, sleep eluded me as I felt a surge of energy, signaling that I stood on the brink of a life-altering decision – one that would shape my destiny and set me on an enduring quest.

I pondered deeply on the significance of my encounter with Roy that day. My mind was racing. One particular statement he made lingered in my thoughts. Roy assured me that he had the ability to repair any injury or ailment in my body, and it would be a simple task for him. I shared with him my shoulder issue, and how the team doctors had informed me that there were limited options to address the problem, apart from maintaining it. Roy confidently declared,

"Anything below the chin, I can fix. If you break your brain, I can't fix that, but anything else is easy."

As I laid awake that night, my mind consumed by the conversation with Roy, I found myself captivated by his words. It was the off-season, after all. What did I have to lose? If Roy could repair my shoulder, now was the ideal moment to take a leap of faith. However, there was another lingering thought in my mind. The Runningman was undeniably impressive. Its classic style and impeccable craftsmanship set it apart. However, a shoe from a professional athlete, even a running back in the NFL, simply wasn't sufficient. The market was saturated with shoes. What was lacking? What was I yearning for? Then, a groundbreaking idea struck me like the unexpected prick of a needle. I couldn't wear fitted jeans without ripping my pants. There was a glaring absence of athletic fit denim on the market.

☆ After the Last Snap ☆

I texted Roy at 3 in the morning and told him what was on my heart. I asked him what I had to do to spend more time with him to repair my shoulder. I asked him for his thoughts on an athletic fit jean. Roy called me back in the morning and said, "If you are excited to work out, then I am more excited. I'll come pick you up tomorrow." Roy and I trained mornings at the Giants Quest Diagnostic training facility. I trained relentlessly with Roy for a span of 23 days, only taking breaks when he advised me to, recognizing when my body needed rest from the intense regimen he had planned for me. This form of exercise, rooted in martial arts, was entirely unique to anything I had ever experienced. There was nothing close to a kick or a punch as the term 'martial arts training' might bring to mind. Instead, the training revolved around military calisthenics, isometrics, and both simple and complex movement patterns sustained over time.

Roy had a profound way of explaining his approach to exercise, delving into the metaphysical realm. He said, "The Qi is of the body, and the body is of the mind. By mastering the mind, one gains control over both the body and the Qi." At the time, I didn't fully grasp the concept, but comprehension wasn't the goal. It all revolved around discipline, consistency, and triumphing over the discomforts imposed by the weight of one's own body.

I weighed 234 pounds when we began working out in February of 2016. When I left for Miami at the end of March, I had managed to get down to 217 pounds. If I hadn't already booked the trip, I would have preferred to stay in NJ with Roy straight through the training season because this exercise was the most effective form of training I'd ever done.

After training those 23 days with Roy, I never experienced another subluxation incident. In less than one month, my shoulder became stable through exercise and proper nutrition. Positions and exercises that were once off-limits became possible, such as sleeping with my hands behind my head and doing pull-ups. I was completely addicted to Roy's special training. As time went on, Roy became one of my closest friends and he entrusted me with a task—to name the unique martial arts training system that he had created by combining the best of all the martial arts forms he had mastered and omitting what he believed to be unnecessary. I called it Daeqido, meaning "Big Vitality Way". I went on to study Daeqido under Roy for a solid four years. Not only do I credit Roy with extending my football career, but he also restored my wrist after a botched surgery to repair torn ligaments had left me with almost no dexterity in my dominant hand. Without Roy and his Daeqido training, I might be an invalid today, due to the pain, weakness, and lack of flexibility I experienced in my wrist after the surgery.

In February of 2016, I made another important move with Roy. My signing bonus, received as a fourth-round pick in 2014, amounted to about a quarter of a million dollars before taxes. I decided to invest most of it in the stock market with the assistance of my financial advisor from Merrill Lynch. However, after making the investment, I couldn't shake off my uneasiness. I was actively looking for another investment strategy for my money. As previously mentioned, I shared my idea for creating athletic fit denim jeans with Roy. He pointed out that no one was doing it and encouraged me to be the first, but with a twist. He advised me to not just create any kind of jeans, but to make the best jeans possible using top-quality fabric in order to compete with the leading brands in the market. When I told Roy about my idea for athletic fit denim jeans, he said, "no one is doing it. You would be the first one. But don't just make anything, make the best. Use the best fabric so you can compete with the best brands in the market." What he said hit me in a place that was familiar and highly satisfying to my nature, "compete with the best." Hence, just two weeks after meeting Roy, I took the biggest financial risk of my life. I called my advisor, Travis, and instructed him to subtract $120,000 from my ETF portfolio. I used this money to place my first order for fabrics and officially begin the development of my denim line. And with Roy's help, so began my journey into the world of Japanese Selvedge denim.

On February 1st, I made the payment to Roy and sealed our deal with a handshake to kickstart the development of my denim line. I crafted a stylized version of my initials to create a compelling logo and christened the brand AW, an abbreviation for All Weather Selvedge. I had no desire to name the brand after myself, but I followed Adriano Goldschmeid's merchandising

☆ After the Last Snap ☆

principles, with his denim brand AG jeans. AW was simple and it was sharp, and there was already a precedent that it could work well in the market.

Chapter 29: BZW

On February 16, 2016, my first child, Barron Zavier Williams, was born. Marilyn did accomplish an incredible feat by gracefully giving birth to my perfect little boy. I am certain that Barron is God's special gift to me for persevering through the challenges of my relationship with her. I am truly grateful that he arrived in this world as nothing less than perfect. His existence is the single thing that allows me to not completely regret my relationship with Marilyn.

If you are reading this and feel that I am being too hard on her, I believe that's only because you haven't gotten to the good parts of this story yet. I can only say that unless you witnessed my daily life with Marilyn, you cannot fully understand the experience of unbound misery of a selfish and spoiled woman, the verbal abuse she dealt on the daily, and my own feelings of inadequacy that grew deeper the longer I stuck around. This was a woman that was consistently unhappy unless she was spending money or in the mix, and when she wasn't doing one of those things, I was the focus of her ire.

But on February 16th, I found myself deeply admiring her in a way that I couldn't deny. In just 17 minutes, she brought Barron into the world. When I laid eyes on him and saw the watermelon shape of his head, we locked eyes, and I knew that this was my child. What's more, I knew that this child was me! He was a version of myself that I had cast into the future. Something clicked in my mind that led me to a revelation: if Barron was me, then that meant that I was a version of my father, and that meant my last name was greater than my first name, because it was the last name Barron carried that would move on into the future after I was gone. What was I going to do today that was going to ensure that Barron was equipped in every way to carry on our legacy? What was I going to do today to build up the foundation underneath him so that whichever path he took would be a solid one?

☆ After the Last Snap ☆

A love for this little boy appeared in me that was hard to explain. I was a man, but Barron made me a father. He completed something in me that I didn't know was missing. He gave me the purpose of legacy building. I was in love the moment I held him.

Marilyn's first words to me after giving birth were, "Now you are mine, and you can't get rid of me." Her words made me cringe, but I was still basking in the joy of meeting my son for the first time, and I brushed it off. Her statement was a hint at our future and a threat. 2016 would unfold as one of the most challenging years of my life. Emboldened by the fact that she now had a child to hold over me, Marilyn's behavior grew much worse. Between February and September, our troubled relationship would deteriorate. Barron's arrival couldn't stop it.

I received a call from my sister Krystal that day, hours after Barron was born. Our conversation went like this:

"Congratulations Dre! Mom told me you just had your baby boy."

"Thanks, big sis."

"I want to come and see him. I'm going to take off work next Monday and Tuesday and spend the night at your house."

I hesitated. I was still in the hospital and would be there for at least a couple more days to ensure Barron's health. I was uncomfortable with her sudden declaration. My sister didn't have children of her own and had never stayed at my house before. I had no idea what the first week of Barron's life would entail. How could I commit to having my sister over so soon? I carefully crafted my response, saying something like,

"Krystal, I am still in the hospital. Hopefully, everything checks out with Barron in a couple of days, and we make it home without any issues. I don't know what next week will look like, so let's talk about it again this weekend?"

She agreed, and we hung up shortly afterward.

By the grace of God, everything checked out health-wise with Barron, and a couple of days later we left the hospital with him. We had arranged to do sleep training with a night nurse named Silvi, and she showed up later that night. Silvi discussed with us the importance of establishing a proper feeding schedule for Barron. Every three hours starting at 8am, 11am, 2pm, 5pm, 8pm, 11pm, and so on. This routine would make it easier for him to sleep through the night and set us up to eventually wean him off the night bottles as he grew. Silvi spent the first month of Barron's life in the nursery, sitting in the big rocker chair, watching over and feeding him throughout the night. This provided great comfort and convenience for us, and by the time training season in Miami began, Barron had a solid sleep schedule in place.

    I made it my priority to give Barron his bath every night. We had a little baby bath flower that fit into the sink. I would warm it up with the hot water and lay him down on it and wash his little caramel body with the baby soap. I don't think there is an experience in the world that matches having and caring for your fresh baby. It is truly special. I just knew I had to come home every night and give my baby boy his bath. I was in love.

Chapter 30: Family (Un)ties

Next week Tuesday rolled around, and I still hadn't heard from my sister over the weekend. It left me in this awkward limbo of not knowing if she still planned to visit. If she did, cool—if not, no skin off my back. But man, the house was packed as it was. Diab was coming over to see Barron. I had tapped him as Barron's godfather. He had some business to handle in NJ the following day and planned to crash on the couch in the basement living room—our only remaining available space.

Barron's grandmother, Cathy-Anne, had also arrived from Stamford. We got her set up with a blowup bed in the main floor living room, right next to the kitchen. Silvi, naturally, was there and spending the night, making frequent trips upstairs and downstairs to access breast milk stored in the refrigerator. The house was fully occupied.

The doorbell rang, and to my surprise, it was my pops. He came for an unexpected visit to see his grandson for the first time. Shortly after, Diab arrived with his girlfriend, Shelby, and his mother, Noelle. Then, I got a text from my sister saying she was on her way. Suddenly, the house swelled to eight people, including Marilyn and me.

I couldn't shake this pang of unease. Barron was just a week old, and I worried about exposing him to too many germs so early. Marilyn seemed even more troubled. She wasn't comfortable with the unexpected influx of visitors and was self-conscious about the post-delivery challenges new mothers face.

I reassured Marilyn, but also myself, that everything would be fine. I promised to make sure everyone left before Silvi arrived for the 8 PM night feeding. Pops threw Diab some money to grab pizzas for everyone. We had a blast hanging out, eating, and paying our respects to my beautiful baby boy. As the evening dragged on, Noelle and my dad prepared to leave. That was the perfect moment to inform my sister that the house was too crowded for her to stay overnight.

Looking back, I should have called her when she texted to say she was on her way. I could have explained the full house and let her decide if she still wanted to make the drive from Stamford, CT to my place in Secaucus, NJ. It's a haul—more than an hour. But I got distracted by the people already in the house and didn't make that call.

When I finally told her she couldn't stay, Krystal's reaction was far from pleasant. She looked at me as if I had slapped her. It was inconceivable to her that I would ask her to leave. I knew I'd hear about it later from my older brother and my mom. Krystal had a knack for broadcasting any grievances she had with me to the whole family.

Despite everything, I was happy everyone came to see Barron. He was a beautiful sight to behold. But I wished Krystal had respected the fact that I was a married man with a one-week-old baby and not just pop up whenever she pleased.

The next day, my older brother, Danique, called me. He asked why I kicked Krystal out in the middle of the night and even asked what I would have done if she got into an accident on the way home and died. I was offended. That was a dreadful question, and it didn't matter how much I tried to explain myself. Krystal had started a fire, and we had a heated exchange. Barely 30 minutes later, my mother called, asking the same question as if they'd rehearsed it together. She was even more upset, and again, we had another intense argument.

This was nothing new. A similar drama unfolded the previous year when I traveled through Connecticut to Rhode Island for an appearance at a casino. I stopped in Stamford to have lunch with Krystal and see how she was doing at her new job with Bridgewater Associates. She landed the job because she asked me to reach out to my financial advisor, Travis O'Brien, to see if he could help. I did, and soon enough, Krystal had a position at one of the largest asset management firms in the country.

During lunch, I asked her, "How do you like your new job, Krystal?" Her response stunned me. She said, "I don't like it. At this point in my career, I don't think I should be anyone's assistant."

☆ After the Last Snap ☆

I was floored. Krystal was 27, hadn't gone to school for finance, nor had she worked in the field before. Yet, she was displeased with her title. Entitlement at its finest.

We finished our meal, and I asked if we could split the bill 2/3rds, 1/3rd since Marilyn and I both ate. Krystal gave me a look like I had slapped her but grudgingly agreed.

The following day, Danique called me, questioning why I made Krystal pay for lunch. He argued that as the man at the table, it was my duty to cover the bill. He even offered to compensate me later if I refunded Krystal. But I held my ground. It didn't matter what I said, Krystal had already started a fire, and we had another heated exchange. Later, my mother called and cussed me out for making Krystal pay for her food.

I made Krystal pay because she was my older sister with a great job. She wasn't entitled to a free lunch just because I played in the NFL. I denied her request for a $25,000 loan to start a restaurant earlier that year for the same reason. She wasn't entitled to a loan just because I had the money. I'd never seen her cook a meal, take care of a baby, or run a business. I was married with a one-week-old baby and didn't need more entitlement in my life.

The aftermath left me grieved. I felt isolated in my marriage and alienated from my own family. My football career with the Giants was hanging by a thread. It felt like the air was getting harder to breathe.

Instead of focusing on the negative, I zeroed in on what I could control. I kept building my body and my clothing brand with Roy the Maker. At the end of the day, I'd come home and give Barron his bath. That was my therapy. Those few minutes were a refreshing grace—an investment in the innocence of a new life I was responsible for creating. Barron loved his baths with Dad, and I loved his joy. It refreshed my spirit.

Chapter 31: Zavier

I needed to let Barron find his footing in the world before traveling south for training, so we gave him some time to build his immunity before heading to Miami towards the end of March. This year, instead of hitting Bommaritos for another training season, I threw myself into Roy's Daeqido practice. Leaving New Jersey for Miami brought a twinge of sadness, but my wife encouraged me to go. I embraced it because Roy handed me a fitness challenge that looked impossible at first: 1000 pushups and 300 pull-ups daily for 5 days, then 1500 pushups and 400 pull-ups for another 5 days, followed by 2000 pushups and 500 pull-ups for 5 days, and capping it with 2500 pushups and 600 pull-ups per day for the final 5 days.

At first glance, it seemed impossible, but Roy believed I could conquer it. Watching him, a man in his fifties, pull off extraordinary feats made me trust his insight into the body and his assessment of my capabilities.

If I could finish this quest, I'd have done something no other player dared. It would give me an edge. But deep down, I knew I needed to spend the off-season working with a quarterback or investing in a personal jugs machine. That would've been the smart move—learning from my past mistakes. Instead, I let emotions dictate my choices, and I didn't take the initiative. My body thrived, but my mind was fraying. Once again, I was running from my weaknesses straight into more problems. This time, I fled to Miami.

When Marilyn and I were in Miami, my first set of samples arrived. I hadn't told her about my business with Roy. She thought he was just my trainer. When the samples came in, I broke the news to her. She was furious that I spent "our" money without talking to her first. No surprise there.

But I didn't care about her words or feelings; the moment I opened those boxes and saw the first jean sample, I knew I made the right call. The fabric came from the famous Kurabo selvedge mill in Japan, and Roy's own wash house handled the finishing. The quality was exceptional, and I saw the massive potential for my denim line. I knew I was right to invest in this. AW could become a household name.

My confidence in AW was so high that I devised a plan to keep Marilyn busy. I created a denim line just for her, hoping she'd be so distracted that she'd let me work on mine. I drained my savings and, with Roy's help, launched a sister brand for AW. In honor of Barron, we named her line Zavier, his middle name.

The strategy worked, for a time. When the Zavier samples arrived from overseas, she was blown away, just like I was. Those samples were phenomenal. I believe that if Marilyn would have actually launched the Zavier brand, she would be a multi-millionaire by now. Instead, Zavier became the straw that broke our marriage's back, leading to our divorce.

In Miami, my days were a blur of intense training sessions, long beach runs where water met sand, and eating good food by the pool. When I wasn't training or eating, I meticulously organized the brands, gearing up for a monumental launch. The climax of finalizing AW's production order was approaching, and I had to ensure it aligned perfectly with the preseason. Time was ticking; by the end of summer, camp would begin, and there'd be no room for personal ventures.

Chapter 32: Growing Pains

Marilyn had childhood friends from Stamford, the Celmers, who had moved to Florida. They lived in Windsor, an elite gated community in Vero Beach. Much like Marilyn's father, Mr. Celmer had struck gold in the finance world, particularly in Real Estate Investment Trusts. The Celmers had two daughters, Melanie and Marla, with Marla being the younger by a year. As part of our Miami trip, we spent a weekend at the Celmers' lavish Windsor estate.

Mr. Celmer loved skeet shooting. Mornings were spent on the course, blasting clays out of the sky. Afterward, the real indulgence began—feasting and drinking. I enjoyed our time there, but the palpable sense of superficiality gnawed at me. Everyone in Windsor seemed well-off, yet there was this constant need to flaunt their status. Marilyn slipped into the role effortlessly, showing off her professional athlete partner and flashing her emerald-cut diamond ring at every opportunity.

We'd done the Windsor rounds the previous year, but this time was different; we had baby Barron with us, barely two months old. He was growing fast, but the milk-drunk stupor from breastfeeding wore off even quicker. No matter how much he drank, Marilyn always seemed to have more, but Barron needed something heavier than just breast milk.

To make sure Marilyn had the energy to care for Barron while I trained, I took the night shifts. I cleaned him up when he woke up wet or stinky and endured his protests when we first took away his 2 am bottle. I stayed firm, rocking him back to sleep. But as he grew, he started waking up too early, messing with his feeding schedule. I suggested introducing baby cereal to his diet, mixing it with the breast milk. Marilyn was hesitant, worried he wasn't ready for solids. I tried to make her see that Barron wasn't an average

☆ After the Last Snap ☆

baby—he was the son of a pro athlete and needed more food. He was hungry, just like me. But she wouldn't budge.

The feeding debate persisted throughout our stay in Windsor, even spilling into dinner conversations with the Celmers. Normally, we'd eat at one of the community's restaurants, but on our last night, we dined at their home. I can't remember what was on the menu, whether it was homemade or catered, but Marilyn brought up Barron's feeding issues to Mrs. Celmer. She responded by sharing her own baby stories of Melanie and Marla — crushing chocolate chip cookies into milk, a trick from her mother. She assured Marilyn that it was perfectly normal, especially with Barron's lineage. I smirked. While it may have worked for her kids, I knew it wasn't right for Barron. He needed nutritious baby cereal, not cookies. I finished my meal, relieved Marilyn got a second opinion that seemed sensible.

After dinner, I helped Mrs. Celmer clear the table to show my appreciation for their hospitality. As I prepped the sink for dishwashing, Marla reappeared from her room, her boyfriend trailing behind. She had excused herself earlier, and now she shot Marilyn a sly wink and smile, hinting at some mischief. Spotting me at the sink, she spat out the first piece of garbage that came to her wilted mind, something about how I was a good slave for washing her dishes.

Everyone else must have been too shocked or embarrassed to respond, choosing to ignore her vile comment. To my dismay, the one person who laughed was my wife, Marilyn. That night, I told her I wouldn't go back to Windsor again. I didn't bother explaining why; Marilyn was having a good time and didn't seem to care.

That moment haunted the rest of my time in Miami that spring. I was baffled that Marilyn, who had given birth to our child, a child who shared my name and heritage, could still display such disrespect toward her husband, a man of color. Would she ever grow up? Was change even possible for her?

Chapter 33: Before the Storm

There were two tasks left on my off-season checklist before the start of the 2016 season: OTAs and preseason camp. We returned from Miami in early May, giving Barron time to readjust to the northern climate. The shift from the ocean breeze and crashing waves to the humidity and bugs of Secaucus also seemed to shift Marilyn's mood. While I was relieved to be home and ready to get back to work, she seemed less than thrilled.

One particular afternoon, we ordered Chinese food for lunch—chicken and broccoli, and vegetable lo mein. As we enjoyed our meal, Barron slept peacefully in his bassinet beside us. But my peace was short-lived, disrupted by Marilyn's relentless complaints. She started criticizing our home again, the fragrance lab in the living room, the kitchen backsplash, the sand-colored marble floors. Everything was hideous to her.

I kept my mouth full, chewing slowly, swallowing her ungrateful words until they spoiled my appetite. Finally, I couldn't take it anymore and confronted her. I demanded to know what she had done to earn a single dollar, what financial contribution she had made to buy the house she resented but comfortably lived in with our child. Her response? "It's our money, Andre, we are married!" She hurled a soy-sauced broccoli at my face.

Without hesitation, I overturned my plate of oily lo mein noodles over her head. As if rehearsed, she reached for her phone and said, "I'm going to call the police and tell them you are putting your hands on me." Instinct took over, and I snatched her phone away before she could dial.

Marilyn turned feral. Her fair skin flushed hot pink, her clear eyes burned red. She struck at me with slaps and kicks, snarling, "GIVE ME MY PHONE!" I held her back at arm's length, my gaze shifting to Barron. He remained unfazed, sleeping soundly in his bassinet despite the chaos.

What was I supposed to do? I couldn't let her call the police; there was no telling how they might handle the situation. Could I talk sense into her? I tried appealing to her for Barron's sake.

"Marilyn! Barron is trying to sleep! Please stop yelling!" I pleaded.

"GIVE ME MY ****ING PHONE, ANDRE!" she roared back.

When she started cursing, I knew reasoning was out of the question. She was completely consumed by anger. I moved to the ground floor, distancing Barron from the turmoil. Marilyn followed, lunging and slapping, careful not to draw blood, aiming only blunt blows. Her intention was clear: provoke me into hitting her so she could call the police with a fabricated story.

As we reached the ground level by the garage, I confronted her with an ultimatum. "Marilyn, if you don't stop yelling and calm down, I'm gonna smash this phone!" She only yelled louder,

"GIVE ME MY ****ING PHONE!"

In an impulsive moment, fueled by a mix of anger and hopelessness, I made good on my promise. I hurled her phone to the floor with all my might. The device shattered into fragments and unexpectedly erupted into flames.

It was as if the demon animating Marilyn had been hiding in that phone. I stomped out the fire and headed back into the house. Marilyn calmed down somewhat, tears streaming now. Knowing I had crossed a line, I went upstairs to the kitchen table, phone in hand. I called Marilyn's mother, Cathy-Anne, and told her, "Here, please talk to your crazy daughter." Then I found Marilyn downstairs and handed her the phone.

She retreated upstairs to talk with her mom. I stayed in the kitchen, watching Barron peacefully rocking in his bassinet. My mind was blank. After some time, Marilyn came down, packed bags in hand, ready to leave. She said she wouldn't be sleeping at the house tonight because I was violent and dangerous, and she felt unsafe. She was taking Barron with her.

I let her go. I didn't ask where she was going.

Chapter 34: Cold Summer

OTAs are like the preseason's shadow, a time to mesh the team together, introduce the offense to new members and draft picks, and build some cohesion through workouts and bonding. I vividly remember the first team meeting where the offensive coordinator shared photos of our offseason lives. When Barron's face popped up on the screen, the room echoed with an audible "aww."

At that moment, I felt a mix of pride and sadness. Pride in Barron, but shame over the strained relationship with his mother. I was imbalanced, with my siblings drifting away and me withdrawing from everyone else. I had been ignoring calls and texts from Barron's godfather, Diab, afraid of the questions I wasn't ready to answer. Eventually, he stopped reaching out. I was self-isolating, self-medicating, and stuck in the muck of my anxieties. I smoked a bowl. I made soap in the lab. I made sweat with Roy. I gave Barron a bath.

This year at Big Blue HQ felt different. It was my third year in the NFL, I was a proud father, and I was preparing to produce 2000 pairs of the finest jeans on the planet. But despite these milestones, I felt disconnected. I was in the midst of the most significant period of my young life, and yet I felt an overwhelming sense of dissatisfaction. Instead of thriving and expanding, I was mentally stagnating in the midst of my own white hot potential.

It seemed like my teammates were having the time of their lives, but I felt like a misfit. The world I had grown up in felt increasingly unrelatable, and I couldn't understand what I had done wrong. I wasn't wasting time in clubs or chasing women all night. I was handling my responsibilities as a man, husband, and father. So why did I feel used up and unfulfilled?

☆ After the Last Snap ☆

These were the questions that kept haunting me, and the quieter my mind became, the louder they shouted. I needed therapy but chose to escape instead. I convinced myself, "Less time on the ground, more time working." To maximize productivity, I bought a weed vape pen. It became an invaluable tool. Perhaps not the most advisable method, but the widespread cannabis use within the league made it seem normal.

When the AW production order arrived, I met Roy at our warehouse, where we organized all nine styles on the storage racks. Roy then walked me through the art of executing a flawless photoshoot. With the help of a skilled photographer and videographer, all I needed to do was recruit models, select an ideal location, and set a date. Roy was an incredible business advisor.

I hung up a handful of AW samples in my locker at the training facility. It wasn't long before teammates were sniffing around, curious about AW. Even Victor Cruz, Mr. Hugo Boss himself, showed interest. He wanted a pair of the Brad Antiques, but in my clouded mind, I thought it only fair to make him pay unless he participated in my photoshoot. He declined both.

Looking back, I missed a golden opportunity. I should have generously handed out AW jeans to any teammate who could fit them. These were the best money could buy, and once worn, their quality would've spoken for itself. By adopting a more charitable approach, the media content possibilities would have been endless.

In the end, I took the miserly path. Still, I managed to persuade a handful of teammates and assembled a group for my photoshoot. We gathered at the AVE, a luxurious apartment complex where many players resided during the season. Roy, a selfless genius, provided tremendous guidance in business and fitness. His mentorship was invaluable during this period. In these realms, I still navigated with confidence.

But despite all the progress and achievements, I couldn't shake the cold feeling of being unfulfilled. My internal battles raged on, leaving me questioning everything, especially myself.

Chapter 35: Fitness Quest One

I hadn't completed the fitness quest yet. I'd dip my toes in the water, knocking out a couple of hundred push-ups, then deceive myself into believing I'd finish the rest later. Of course, it never happened. When I calculated the numbers, it seemed impossible—35,000 push-ups and 9,000 pull-ups in just one month. I couldn't wrap my mind around it. But this was the fitness quest Roy had given me, and I had one last chance to complete it before the season began.

With OTAs over, there was one final break before the season. This break usually started in late June and extended through most of July, with our preseason reporting date at the end of July or early August. Marilyn typically spent the summer with her family at their beach house in Nantucket, and that's where we planned to spend our break. It would be Barron's first visit to the island, as he was only five months old.

On Nantucket, I honed my determination and calmed my mind to conquer the fitness challenge. There was no room for procrastination. As John Grey's son-in-law, I had full access to the fitness club where he was a member. Roy emphasized maintaining my leg strength and endurance alongside the fitness quest. This meant running and keeping up with my realwalks, best done along the shore where the water meets the sand—a perfect elemental challenge.

I established a daily routine. Every morning, I woke up early to attend to Barron's 8am bottle and spend some quality time with my son. Afterwards, I ordered breakfast from Stubby's, a local eatery known for its Jamaican cuisine. I often opted for their ackee and saltfish with fried dumplings breakfast platter. On days I didn't go to Stubby's, my family and I would head to the fitness club and

☆ After the Last Snap ☆

have breakfast by the pool. Once everyone was sorted, I headed to the gym.

The secret to completing 1000 push-ups in a day is to do them all in one go—not necessarily in a row, but in continuous sets until you reach 1000. Do them all in one sitting, don't save any for later because there will always be an excuse to do something else. It has to be all or nothing.

In the beginning, I divided the 1000 push-ups into sets of 20, followed by 10 pull-ups. Occasionally, I challenged myself with sets of 25. Some days, I focused solely on push-ups; on others, I prioritized pull-ups. Changing the routine kept my mind engaged and prevented my body from getting used to a fixed pattern—crucial because familiarity breeds boredom, and this quest was already challenging enough. Days 4 and 5 were always the toughest, with soreness and exhaustion making it excruciating to pull myself up on the bar. Yet, I kept reminding myself that the only way out was to finish.

Finally, I completed the first phase: 5000 push-ups and 1500 pull-ups in just five days. I felt immense pride. With the initial phase done, I realized that all it took was sheer determination. I knew I had the strength to conquer this quest.

It didn't become easier after that. I won't pretend it did. But as I persevered, my mind grew stronger. By the time I had completed over 10,000 push-ups, my determination to finish the quest intensified. I was achieving a remarkable feat; I couldn't imagine more than a thousand people on the planet had accomplished this. I desired the bragging rights, but the rewards went far beyond that. I took a two-day break between each leg of the quest.

The instructions were to keep working on my legs alongside the bar work. Twice a week, I ran two miles along the untamed shoreline behind the beach house. After every workout, I took a realwalk of 1000 yards on the shore. Roy called it the realwalk, and that's the name I prefer. Completing a straight 1000-yard realwalk made regular walking feel effortless and gave me the strength to run harder than anyone.

Monday marked the start of the next leg of the quest. Somewhere in this journey, something extraordinary and painful happened. I felt sharp, scorching sensations in my arms during a set of pull-ups. I looked at my arm and saw veins sprouting in places they had never been. My body was visibly changing before my eyes. I was eager to see the final outcome.

During the last leg of the quest, God sent me a friend to help motivate me. A young Kyokushin fighter named Ivan saw me in the gym one day and was impressed by my physique and workout intensity. After we introduced ourselves, he vowed to finish the fitness quest with me.

Ivan showed up and managed to complete a full day with me. His determination was remarkable. And guess what? In the end, I successfully completed the entire fitness quest:

- 1000 push-ups & 300 pull-ups, 5 days
- 1500 push-ups & 400 pull-ups, 5 days
- 2000 push-ups & 500 pull-ups, 5 days
- 2500 push-ups & 600 pull-ups, 5 days

It took a total of 28 days. By the end, my arms and chest were the largest they had ever been. My upper body was massive. No amount of weightlifting could generate the incredible pump completing this quest did. The pump lasted for about three days, then decreased considerably over the next week, but my arms remained rock solid. I was in the best shape of my life and eager to see what my efforts would produce on the field.

At that time, the situation between Marilyn and me was relatively stable. She was in a controlled environment; we had our little arguments, but I stayed in the gym and on the beach as much as I could, and her parents were nearby. Cathy-Anne was the glue holding our relationship together longer than it should have. John was an eccentric with high IQ, good with numbers but socially and emotionally awkward. Cathy-Anne was his opposite, intelligent but emotionally so, with a bright, extroverted personality. They rounded each other out well but had spoiled Marilyn with their obsession over things and experiences.

Marilyn's strong desire to emulate her mother was evident. She sought a wealthy partner to indulge in a carefree life of luxury and travel. It became clear that I wasn't the man she was seeking. I wasn't her father; I wasn't John Grey.

☆ After the Last Snap ☆

Leaving Nantucket, I returned home alone, while Marilyn stayed with Barron and her family. It made sense; I'd be busy with the team at camp, and she wouldn't have my support.

Back in Secaucus, NJ, I found a relative peace. There was no ungrateful nagger to come home to, but there was also no beautiful baby boy to bathe. I had bathed him every night since his birth, and I felt his absence deeply. That evening, I sat alone on the deck outside the kitchen, lighting marijuana in my bowl. As I pulled on my pipe, staring off into the horizon, I pondered how different my life would be if I had never met Marilyn. If I had a reset button, would I press it?

I would have peace if I did, but I wondered if not meeting her was worth the price of not meeting my son. I couldn't justify the cost now that he was here. I yearned for peace, and I yearned for my son. The only conceivable path to those things lay ahead in the future, not in the past, and there would be no instant "easy button" to press to get there.

Chapter 36: A Big Break

The sense of urgency at Big Blue HQ was palpable that year of 2016. Ben McAdoo was in his second year as head coach, and the pressure was on after a disappointing 6-10 showing. The stakes were high, but I remained unfazed. I'd completed the Roy's fitness quest, and I had an exciting, new confidence in my body. I was healthy again, and I felt invincible. When I cradled the football in my arm during preseason, it felt like only God Himself could pry it from my grasp. My entire body exuded strength and vitality. I was in peak physical condition.

The Giants had selected a running back named Paul Perkins from UCLA in the 5th round that year. They also signed Bobby Rainey from Baltimore and Orleans Darkwa in free agency. I had met Bobby at a Christian conference for NFL players, called PAO, the previous offseason. He struck me as a solid guy, and I was rooting for him to make the team, even though we now had five running backs on the roster. Not everyone would make it through preseason. It felt like a month-long game of Clue, wondering week after week who would be the odd man out in the running back room. Never did I imagine it would be me, the Heisman finalist draft pick. I was certain I was safe.

Records show we kicked off against Miami and lost 27-10, but I achieved the highest rushing yards of the game with 41, making a strong statement in preseason game 1. Yet, I hardly recall anything from that preseason—except for two very distinct moments.

By this point, I had developed an unhealthy relationship with marijuana. I wasn't addicted to getting high; my goal was to retreat mentally. I smoked all the time to escape, even at work. I found ways to get to that safe space in my mind where no one could reach me, not even me. Despite the self-discipline I'd honed over my body, I lacked control over my emotional well-being. I felt I had to hide from my thoughts to feel balanced and dodge uncomfortable questions. Whenever I had a moment to myself, between meetings or workouts or lunch, I'd take a couple of tokes from my weed vaporizer in the bathroom and keep floating above the issues. I always had eye drops, so unless you truly knew me, you could never tell how faded I was.

Truthfully, I wasn't the only one engaging in these behaviors, but I had become too comfortable. My smoking habit had become too frequent, and one day, I got too high.

It went like this:

We were headed to the field house after the morning install meeting to rehearse a couple of new plays. I took a bathroom break before hitting the field house. My eyes looked fine, but I was spacey. "Doesn't matter," I told myself. "I can handle a jog-through."

I was up first with Eli to run the bubble screen. "No problem," I thought. Eli started out in the gun with me on his left side. He rolled through his cadence and snapped the ball. I released on a deep wide route. On the 4th step, I got my head around and looked for the ball. But I was already late. The ball was already on me. My sedated body couldn't react in time to track it. My hands woofed through the air, and the ball hit my legs and dropped to the ground. There was an audible groan in the field room, then silence.

I picked up the ball and walked back to the huddle. Coach McAdoo called Rashad to replace me and run the play. We ran through it twice, and I was successful the second time, but the damage was done. Fifty percent is a failing grade.

Later that day, in the pre-practice meeting, Coach McAdoo made a crude joke about me. He said I couldn't catch an STD in a whorehouse. People laughed. It was a funny joke. It was a bad sign—a clue.

The last moment I remember from that preseason was the final matchup against the Patriots on September 1st. I was the last running back to touch the football that game. A reporter reminded me that historically, it was a bad sign to touch the ball last and asked if I was worried about making the team. I told him I wasn't, but deep down, I wasn't sure.

It was September 2nd, final cut day. Marilyn and Barron were back from Nantucket. I had left the hotel days ago when camp broke and was back at the house with them. I woke up next to Marilyn for the first time in a month. It was still early, and she wanted me to stay in bed, but my mind was already racing. I got up, freshened myself up in the bathroom, and then headed downstairs to the kitchen. I plopped Barron's milk in the warmer and sat in my office.

The mail and packages had accumulated over the past month during my absence at camp, creating an obnoxious pile of clutter. I took it upon myself to sort through everything to pass the time. Among the parcels, I found a package containing Zavier jeans samples. Unsure if Marilyn had seen this set, I set it aside to give it to her later. As I continued sorting through the mail, Marilyn emerged through the archway with Barron cradled in her arms. He lay on her chest with his eyes half-open, knowing it was time to eat. It was a few minutes past 8am. Barron was six months old.

We greeted each other again, and I extended the sample box toward Marilyn, saying, "Whenever you find the time, take a look at these samples. I'm not sure if you've seen this set yet."

She snapped, "Why would you have samples of Zavier that I haven't seen yet?" Her tone was testy.

I was confused. All the samples had been coming to the house. How was she supposed to see them when she'd been away for the last two months?

"You were in Nantucket for two months, Marilyn. All the Zavier samples have been coming to the house, and I've been receiving them for you here."

She shouted, "Why are you always treating me like a fucking child, Andre! This is my fucking company!"

I was astonished. What had I said to elicit such a negative response? It was barely 8am, and she was cursing and screaming at me. Most importantly, she had Barron in her arms, and he didn't need to see or hear any of it.

I told her quietly, "Marilyn, please watch your mouth and lower your voice in front of Barron."

She turned up even more. "I'm not a fucking child, Andre! Don't tell me what to do!" She shouted again, "Why do you have samples that I haven't seen yet!"

☆ After the Last Snap ☆

I was done engaging. I wouldn't argue in front of Barron. The sensible thing was to walk away. I rose and passed by her. As I descended the steps toward the front door, Marilyn suddenly kicked me in the back. My front foot slipped, but I caught myself by gripping the rail. I turned around, meeting her gaze. She stood at the top of the steps, peering down at me as if she was completely certain I would never reach at her and squeeze the life from her neck.

I had planned to sit on the front porch and let her cool down, but now it was time to leave. I retrieved my keys from the table in my office, put on my white Runningman sneakers, and stepped out the door.

"Where are you going?!" she shouted. I didn't respond. She rushed past me and perched on the hood of my car. She was barefoot and Barron was still in her arms.

It was a black 2016 Cadillac CTS. I settled into the driver's seat and started the car. Rolling down the window, I called out firmly, "Marilyn, get off the car and go back into the house with the baby. It's time for him to eat."

"You're not going anywhere, Andre!" she yelled back defiantly.

I revved the engine, but she stood her ground. I needed a different approach. "Marilyn, look at what you're doing. It's 8 in the morning, and you're sitting on top of the car with a baby in your arms. The entire neighborhood is watching you, and eventually, one of them will call the cops. I don't know who they will take to jail, but I promise it will be the last time you ever see me. Get off my car and take Barron back in the house."

This struck a nerve. She looked around, fell silent, slid off the car, and walked back towards the house. I drove away.

I drove around aimlessly, pondering what was happening in my life. I called Roy and recounted what had happened. We had a lengthy conversation, and he agreed to meet me at the mall later that day, advising me to try to relax until then.

Marilyn called me relentlessly until I blocked her. Then she used *69 to call from a blocked number. She sent me close to 100 text messages, accusing me of being at another woman's house and neglecting our child. I went to the Verizon store to change my

☆ Andre Williams ☆

number, but she broke into my email to find it. I blocked her again. There was nothing left to discuss.

I met Roy at the mall around noon, and we spent a few hours together. We enjoyed a meal, and he offered the support I needed. He pointed out the obvious truth—I had a real problem to confront now. He was right.

It was around 3pm when I remembered it was cut day and I was supposed to keep my phone on in case I got the dreaded call from Big Blue HQ. I hadn't passed my new number to the team, so I texted our player liaison. Thirty minutes later, the call came. A voice that knew my name but belonged to a face I had never seen said:

"Hello, is this Andre Williams?"

"Yes, it is."

"Okay, I'm sorry to tell you this, but I'm calling from player personnel with the New York Giants. We are gonna let you go. I'm gonna need you to gather your iPad and your playbook and report to Jerry Reese's office as soon as possible. Is that understood?"

"Yessir."

"Alright. We'll be seeing you shortly." Click.

Just like that, my time with the Giants had ended. I drove back to the house to grab my iPad. Thankfully, Marilyn had left with Barron. I grabbed my items and headed to Big Blue HQ for my exit meeting with Jerry Reese.

I sat in his office, looking him in the eyes, waiting for what he had to say. He told me some vague nonsense about not being on enough special teams. I tuned out most of what he said after that because except for field goal and field goal block, I had played on every single special team since my rookie season. It became clear to me why the Giants had leadership issues. Jerry had no value to offer in his final evaluation.

It became clear to me why the Giants had been plagued with profound leadership issues. There was no reason for pretense left between us. This was the last opportunity for Jerry to be completely honest with me about his evaluation of me as a player in the hopes that I could use what he said to continue to grow, and he had nothing of value to send me off with. It seemed that either they had no genuine interest in developing players or they simply lacked that

☆ After the Last Snap ☆

ability. After watching the Giants commit the Saquon Barkley debacle, I have no hope in 2024 that things have changed since then. If history repeats itself again, then Saquon will go on to earn a ring with another team before he's done playing.

I don't know what I did for the rest of the day, but I returned home after dark. Marilyn was there with a dumb look on her face, uncertain about what I would do or say. We exchanged words, but I had been through enough. I told her I wouldn't field any questions tonight. I was exhausted. All I wanted was to shower and get some rest. Luckily, I had a king-size bed to sleep comfortably without touching her.

I woke the next morning to my first day in limbo. Uncertainty lingered, but one thing was sure: I'd have breakfast at home. However, before I could finish my meal, my phone rang. It was Erik, my agent. His voice buzzed with excitement—San Diego Chargers had claimed me off waivers. The representative would contact me soon to arrange my flight. I was headed to San Diego today. I thanked Erik, hung up, and felt my wounded heart healing in the warm rays of the California sun.

I broke the news to Marilyn. She was all smiles about San Diego, excited. She didn't understand she wasn't coming.

I explained, "I could have been going down the street to DC or Philly, Marilyn. It wouldn't matter. You have a problem, and you need to talk to someone. You think you can put your hands on me in front of my son, and I'll act like it didn't happen? You're staying here with the baby and getting help. There's no California for you and me."

She was shocked, then laughed. "Look at me and look at you, Andre. You think anyone will believe I put my hands on you? What are you gonna tell them? I kicked you? You didn't even fall. You think you can leave me here with your baby?"

She was unrepentant and unwell. I had to leave. If I didn't, the only outcome would be injury, death, or jail, and Barron would be the real victim in every scenario.

As I grappled with the situation, my phone rang. It was the Chargers, setting up my plane fare. I was on a plane to San Diego later that afternoon.

Chapter 37:
Move of God, Act of Man

As I boarded the plane bound for California, a revelation dawned upon me. It became clear that my departure from the Giants was more than just a series of unfortunate events—it was the handiwork of God. Was there a quicker or more efficient escape than what had unfolded in the last 24 hours? I doubted it. I was being propelled as far away from Marilyn as quickly as I could, and none of it was by choice. If not for these events, would I have left? God, it appeared, knew the truth and intervened on my behalf. This realization emboldened me further in my resolve to leave Marilyn in the past.

This was the hand of God at work in my life, shaping events in a way I could not achieve on my own—urging me to leave. My life with Marilyn had become unmanageable and perilous, with no clear route of escape. Yet, amid the turmoil, I saw God's plan unfolding. It was evident that God was revealing His grace and mercy to me. While I was grateful for His favor, I now realize that I took His favor for granted because I did not seek His will for my future. I said thank you and kept going in my own direction, a grave mistake.

San Diego, California, is truly a stunning city. Words cannot adequately capture the immense sense of relief that washed over me that evening as I arrived there alone. With great anticipation, I made my way to Bolt HQ, where the head coach and my new teammates awaited me. It was an exhilarating time, for the veteran duo of Philip Rivers and Antonio Gates were gracefully passing through the twilight of their remarkable careers. Meanwhile, our starting RBs, Melvin Gordon and Danny Woodhead, were poised to make a significant impact on the field. Melvin, in particular, was about to embark on an exciting second year.

☆ After the Last Snap ☆

The Chargers were navigating a captivating phase, as the ownership earnestly sought to bring about transformative changes and elevate the team's image. It was a quest driven by the undeniable desire to secure a long-awaited championship, an accolade that had thus far eluded them.

They had a GM with a keen eye for talent, evident throughout the organization, including the locker room and coaching staff. However, there was something about the laid-back West Coast vibe and the team management protocol that led to an overall lackluster output. Furthermore, our head coach, Mike McCoy, was a soft man who did not play to win. Instead, he played not to lose, which, coupled with the team's utter lack of conditioning, yielded disastrous results.

I vividly recall my first day suiting up for practice with the Chargers. The locker room, although a bit dingier and more unkempt than in New York, became my own, complete with my #44. It was everything I could ask for, and at that moment, I felt content. In my first offensive meeting, it quickly became apparent that mastering the offense would be a formidable challenge. The playbook was extensive, and the pass protection far more intricate than what I was accustomed to. Nevertheless, I was resolute in my determination to take it one step at a time and thrive.

It was evident that Melvin Gordon wasn't pleased to see me. Our college journeys closely paralleled each other. He was the 2000-yard rusher of 2014, winning the Doak Walker that year and becoming a Heisman finalist, just like me. I could sense that he viewed my presence on the team as a threat, and his attitude confirmed it. Although his rookie season didn't go well, he didn't have much reason to worry. As a first-round pick, the organization wouldn't easily give up on him. In fact, they made significant efforts to build the offense around him that season. And it paid off handsomely for Melvin and the Chargers, as he had a remarkable year.

When I arrived, I didn't interact with Marilyn a whole lot. I was still consumed by the aftermath of the recent events, especially hurt by what she had said the day I left. Being away provided some respite, but it also meant being away from Barron, which made me miss him terribly.

Chapter 38: W.I.N.O.

My relationship with Marilyn unraveled rapidly after I departed for California. It took very little to unravel it. As soon as I arrived on the West Coast, I wasted no time reaching out to Cathy-Anne. I felt compelled to inform her of the incident where Marilyn, while holding our six-month-old child, attempted to kick me down the stairs. I explained to Cathy-Anne that Marilyn showed no remorse and even ridiculed me before my departure. I made it clear that I would not settle for anything less than Marilyn seeking the assistance of a qualified professional.

Cathy-Anne questioned me as if she doubted that the events I described had truly happened. It seemed that she was too proud to admit that her daughter was capable of such behavior. Finally, Cathy-Anne presented me with an ultimatum. She assured me she would speak to Marilyn and do everything in her power to get her the necessary help, but she wondered if that would be sufficient to reconcile us. She made it clear that if I was set on leaving her, she would be obligated to do whatever it took to safeguard her daughter's best interests.

In my mind, the situation seemed simple. Marilyn had crossed a line for the second time with a physical altercation in front of our son, which I had already forgiven her for once. Despite my own faults, this time would be the last. It was a dangerous situation, and there would be no more chances, regardless of her mother's opinion.

I had hoped that having a child with Marilyn would improve our relationship, but it had become obvious that she believed it gave her the right to mistreat me. Her true character disgusted me. I had no intention of introducing her as my wife in San Diego. Despite being the mother of my child and legally married, she was simply a W.I.N.O.—wife in name only. It was crystal clear that she needed help, and if she didn't get it, it would only make it easier to keep her at a distance.

☆ After the Last Snap ☆

Marilyn immediately began bombarding me with endless inquiries as soon as the first week started. "Have you fully settled down? Where exactly are you living? And when can you bring me and Barron over to stay with you?" she interrogated me.

I was only half surprised by her lack of genuine interest in getting help. I was already well-acquainted with her manipulative methods. She would commence by incessantly pestering me, and if that failed, she would attempt to manipulate me by making me feel guilty or eliciting my compassion. But not this time.

My response was, "Have you spoken to your mother about enrolling in therapy, Marilyn?"

Marilyn immediately jumped to gaslighting. She made comments about how much Barron missed bath time with his dad, apologized for the argument, and emphasized that she would never do anything to hurt her family because they were what she cared about the most.

I felt deeply disappointed in myself and ashamed. How could I have allowed myself to become a victim of such a cheesy impostor? After she left my question unanswered, I decided to leave her without a response. The next day, her text was harsh, and she seemed angry. She sent me an ultimatum of her own.

"If you won't fly me and Barron out to California, then you might as well divorce me. I won't stay here alone in this house while you are out in California doing whatever you want."

Her words were an alarm. The timer on our relationship had run out. It was time to wake up and go our separate ways. There would not be another snooze option for us.

I wasted no time on thought. I responded, "Let's do it, Marilyn. Let's get divorced." It had become the only viable option. I had given Marilyn every part of myself. Perhaps she did not possess my heart, but she certainly captured my soul, and unfortunately, she had carelessly mistreated it. Nonetheless, my conscience compelled me to honor my commitment to my marriage until its conclusion. And now, it had reached its inevitable end. With her own words, she had finally granted me liberation. Although my relationship with God left much to be desired, I still possessed a rudimentary understanding of scripture. The words of 1 Corinthians rang out loudly in my mind: "To the rest I say this (I, not the Lord): If any brother has a wife who is not a believer and she is willing to live with him, he must not divorce her... However, if the unbeliever decides to leave, let it be so. The brother or sister is not bound in such circumstances; God has called us to live in peace."

1 Corinthians 7:12–15

My journey towards peace would commence in San Diego, albeit at a considerable cost. When two entities fuse into one and are subsequently torn apart, both entities suffer damage, and neither piece maintains its original form. It is an inevitable consequence.

Interestingly, natural law operates in peculiar ways. If I were to leap off a building and implore God to rescue me during the descent, if it aligns with His will, through His boundless mercy, my life would be spared. However, does that signify that I would evade the consequences of my initial leap? Absolutely not. The price must still be paid, and the toll could manifest as paralysis, disfigurement, or fractured bones.

That's precisely where I found myself: perched on the edge. Marilyn challenged me to leap from the towering building, and without a moment's hesitation, I took the plunge. Little did I know, I was about to fall a great distance, and break more than a few bones along the way. I was disfigured for a time, paralyzed for a season. But God would have mercy on me, and today I do not look like what I've been through.

Chapter 39: The Skull & The Wolf

It September 11th, the day of the season opener against the Chiefs. I was on a twisted high now, all too excited for the new season I was entering in my life, not realizing the heat of hell rising around me.

The ambiance at Arrowhead Stadium, home of the Chiefs, evoked strong memories of BC's away games against Florida State. The architectural design of the stadium, coupled with its Native American symbolism, transported me to a place that felt strangely familiar. As I gazed upon the lush natural grass and the expanse of the big blue sky above, I was captivated by the electric energy emanating from the massive crowd. The atmosphere was perfect for football.

Acknowledging that I had only been a part of the team for a mere eight days, I knew that my chances of gracing the field that day were slim to none. I didn't mind that though. I was looking forward to watching a great game unfold and understanding what my new team was capable of.

Traveling to Kansas City with the team was great fun. Once we were up in the air, Philip Rivers organized a game where everyone had the chance to enter their name and per diem money into a big pot. Later, he would draw a name from a bag and the lucky winner would take home the entire pot. These men knew how to relax and have a good time with each other for sure, but I had questions.

Before we embarked on our journey, the customary travel meal was an all-you-can-eat BBQ wings feast. Once we boarded the plane, we had our pick of snacks for the flight. My personal favorites were the M&M's, Häagen-Dazs ice cream bars, and crackers with cheese. It was safe to say that the Chargers didn't prioritize the team's nutrition as well as they could have. Our group was talented but poorly conditioned.

☆ Andre Williams ☆

I couldn't help but wonder how much this would affect us during the game. I also wondered about the proficiency of our offense in executing the pass protection so early in the season. It was complicated enough that I hadn't understood its nuances by the time we hit the field that Sunday. The good thing was that the offensive line consisted mostly of seasoned players and their experience helped to mitigate the complex adjustments we had to make from team to team. This was crucial because our playbook was deep. It was a far cry from the simplistic offense we ran in New York. I was excited to sit back and watch us perform while suppressing the small albeit silly hope bubbling inside that perhaps, I'd see the field today.

That day, I discovered that the Chargers' offense truly was electrifying. The huge playbook showed its strength right away and it seemed as if we had more tricks in our bag than the Chief's defense could manage. We surged to a 21-0 lead by the 2nd quarter, and if it weren't for some late defensive mistakes, we would have achieved a shutout by halftime. However, despite the opposition managing to score, we entered the locker room with an impressive 21-7 lead. Our performance was outstanding.

I made my contribution to the team by sharing my excitement and ensuring that everyone was properly hydrated and had a few snacks during our break. The coaches made their adjustments and shared their remarks, and we returned to the field as halftime came to an end.

I was confident that we would continue to perform at our best, defeat the Chiefs, and leave with a victory. However, to my surprise, the opposite occurred. It felt as though we had left our energy in the locker room, as our offense came out lacking the necessary push. We struggled to sustain successful drives, while the defense could no longer contain Alex Smith and the Chiefs, leading to back to back scores for them. Throughout the entire second half, we only managed to score 2 field goals. The game ended with a disappointing loss, with a final score of 27-33.

I felt a great sense of disappointment.

We retreated back to San Diego in defeat, I returned to my single apartment to contemplate where to begin the looming season of divorce. I decided it would be best to keep the lines of communication open with Marilyn as we worked through it. I did not want

☆ After the Last Snap ☆

to drag out the process and it didn't seem all that complicated to me.

Considering the circumstances, our marriage had only lasted two short years, and we didn't possess much in terms of shared assets apart from the house. Personally, I was content with that. My plan was straightforward: sell the house, divide the proceeds fairly, and establish a sensible parenting schedule for Barron. Admittedly, scheduling would require careful consideration due to my football career, but I was confident we could work through it gradually. Naively, I anticipated that this process would be relatively easy. However, reality had a different plan in store for me.

At this stage, Marilyn and I mainly communicated through text. I shared my thoughts with her, much like I did in this book, hoping for reciprocal feedback. Her response set my soul on fire.

She said to me, "Are you kidding? Parenting time with Barron will definitely not be equal, Andre. Do you even know what size diaper Barron is wearing right now?"

The grief was instant and nauseating. I was overcome with fear and anger because I realized that it didn't matter how far away I got from Marilyn. She was still close enough to torment me because she had Barron, and he would be her ransom in the divorce. Outside the sun was still shining, but for me, there was a sudden darkness setting in over San Diego. The new season high was gone. I was spiraling downward.

In the NFL, there is a rule stating that players obtained through the waiver wire must remain on the active roster for a minimum of two weeks before being released. The team's general manager was keen on having a comparable alternative for Melvin Gordon, and that's why I was picked up. Despite having a more successful rookie season than Melvin did, he showcased remarkable improvement in the first 2 weeks of the season. Consequently, I was demoted to the practice squad in week three of the 2016 season in order to make room for a replacement on the defense due to an injury.

I would be dishonest if I pretended that I wasn't utterly crushed by this news. At that moment, I was in the prime physical condition of my life, and now the opportunity to truly showcase it would only present itself during practice sessions. Head Coach McCoy did his

☆ Andre Williams ☆

utmost to console me. He emphasized that I was constantly just one injury away from being thrust into a position where I would have to perform, and he advised me to wisely utilize my time to familiarize myself with the offense and hone my skills. His words held truth, but that didn't make the transition any less difficult. What stung the most was the staggering 80% decrease in my salary. My projected earnings of $500,000 suddenly plummeted to $100,000 before taxes. The impact this would have on me was staggering but I couldn't see this at first.

The bubbling spring of expectation I felt on gameday had gone completely flat. There was no longer any chance I'd be seeing the field. I was deflated. My days at Bolt HQ became monotonous. My value to the team was defined by how many reps I could give on the look team and nothing more.

Under normal circumstances, this setback wouldn't have hit me so hard. I have been in the position of the underdog before. It was nothing new. But now, I yearned for my son. It had been three long weeks since our last encounter. My relationship with Marilyn was strained, particularly after our conversation about parenting time. Our relationship had already become foreign. Adding to the hardship was that Barron was still too young to speak. It wasn't as if I go around Marilyn to speak to him. I was in pain.

In my moment of vulnerability, I committed a grave error. Regrettably, I failed to seek guidance from anyone regarding my divorce prior to selecting an attorney. Instead, I resorted to a simple Google search and came across an individual with satisfactory reviews who would handle my case and initiate the paperwork at a relatively low cost. With my finances severely strained, the thought of the retainer fee devouring nearly a third of my salary terrified me. Although I did what was necessary, I made this decision without wise counsel.

Ultimately, I enlisted the services of Tanya Freeman, an African-American attorney from a firm located in Parsippany, NJ. Initially, I believed that perhaps a woman of color would possess the necessary empathetic insight to understand my emotional turmoil and effectively advocate on my behalf. Unfortunately, reality proved my assumption incorrect.

☆ After the Last Snap ☆

Tanya somehow convinced me to keep quiet about the fact that Marilyn had tried to kick me down the steps, even though that incident was the main reason for our separation. She suggested filing for irreconcilable differences instead of extreme emotional damages, claiming it would make me seem like less of an angry bully and give me a better chance in court against Marilyn's aggressive attorneys.

I was deeply confused by this, but I decided to trust Tanya's advice. On September 22, 2016, I served Marilyn with the divorce papers, and she did the same to me. She had the backing of an expensive law firm, Skoloff & Wolfe, and I couldn't help but feel intimidated. The Grays were not playing around.

At the time, I underestimated the impact of the divorce proceedings, thinking it would be straightforward due to our short-lived marriage, regardless of how Marilyn behaved. Furthermore, I was too distracted by my immediate career challenges to fully comprehend the gravity of the situation.

Chapter 40: Beaujolais

Wake up, drive to practice, hot tub, shower, eat, sit through a host of meetings that didn't involve me. Prepare for practice. Get used up. Eat. Sit through the meetings again. Lift. Go home. Sink deeper into divorce litigation. That was my day.

Amidst it all, the highlight was running the ball on the look team for the defense. It felt like an honor, especially facing such a formidable defense. Melvin Ingram at his prime, Joey Bosa's rookie season, and the likes of Casey Hayward and Darryl Stuckey in the secondary—we were stacked. The competition was sharp, and I did my best to show them up.

That was when I experienced my daeqido super strength. It wasn't about lifting heavy weights—in fact, I had grown tired of weightlifting by then. I focused on meeting the minimum requirements. But I discovered a different kind of strength: controlling my body. In specific situations, I could become an unstoppable force or an immovable object.

Team run for the defense went like this: If I finished the play running full speed and the defense hadn't managed to wrap me up or break my stride, it was a clear loss for them. The coaches would howl, spit, and slam their hats.

"Get that ball out!" DC coach Pagano barked.

Losing the ball while running is the running back's gravest sin. That would break my energy, end my streak. I was trotting back to the huddle for the next play when Ingram came up from behind to tomahawk the ball. He failed, but his hand was now wedged firmly against my chest under the ball. Brandon Mebane jumped in, grabbing me around the waist, trying to hold me up while Ingram did his best to rip the football loose. Now I was having fun.

I lowered my center of gravity and torqued my body violently to the left. Melvin lost his balance and grip, and Mebane was thrown to the ground. I made it back to the huddle with the ball.

☆ After the Last Snap ☆

Clements, the look team QB, patted me on the butt. Joe Barksdale let out a loud whoop as they watched me shake off the abuse.

I possessed great physical strength, but outside the football field, it held no significance whatsoever. The true battle that consumed me was of the spirit and of the soul. I should have turned to my Bible for guidance, instead I was entering battle without a weapon. How could I possibly wage war in the spirit without the wisdom of the Creator and master of the soul and spirit? I did not pray and ask God why I was living in anguish every day. I chose to numb my pain instead, with smoke and alcohol. I was setting myself up for a beating.

I made a habit of visiting the CVS down the street from my apartment after practice. Hard liquor never settled comfortably on my palate, but I did enjoy a decent bottle of red wine. This particular CVS had an interesting selection for a local pharmacy. There was a French wine there with a beautiful name: Beaujolais. I gave it a try. My apartment complex was set at the base of some hills and camping trails. I was on the fourth floor, with a balcony overlooking the foliage and palm trees. At night, if the sky was clear and the moon was out, it would illuminate the landscape and create a beautiful scene. Most nights, I sat on the balcony and had a drink.

PartyNextDoor had just released their third album. I had it on repeat as I uncorked a bottle of Beaujolais, lit my bowl, and let the music, the drink, and the smoke enshroud me, hiding my mind from the day's problems. Exhaling the stress, I surrendered to the night's ambiance. I knew this wasn't the solution, but I was at a loss for answers. I felt utterly alone. I longed to confide in someone, but all I could do was pour another glass.

"Yeah, I met you in Texas, and I left you in Texas..."

Lyrics to "Nobody" by PartyNextDoor met my ear. He was trying to remind me of someone I hadn't talked to for over a year. De'shonia... I found her number in my phone. I called it and put the phone up to my ear.

"This call cannot be completed as dialed..."

Her number had changed. I hung up the phone. I took another drink of Beaujolais.

☆ Andre Williams ☆

Wake up, drive to practice, hot tub, shower, eat, sit through a host of meetings that don't involve me. Prepare for practice. Get used up. Eat. Sit through the meetings again. Lift. Go home. Sink deeper into divorce litigation. That was the day.

But today would have a different ending because De'shonia had left an email in my inbox. It read,

> **Hey Dre! I'm just checking on you. My dad told me that you got cut from the Giants. I hope everything is okay. Call me.**
>
> **~De'shonia**

There was God again. I couldn't reach her the night before because I had the wrong number. The very next day, she emails me with her new number. Was the setup not divine? Could it be any more obvious that we were destined to speak again?

I dialed the number she provided in the email, and this time, she answered. I poured my heart out to her over the phone, reliving the entire year since our moment in the elevator in Dallas. She was prepared for it all, attentively listening to every word. And then, she spoke those magical words that I longed to hear: "I've got your back." The feeling of having my friend back was everything I needed at that moment. She was better than the moonlight and the Beaujolais.

We talked for over an hour that night and every night after that one. She told me what she'd been up to since we lost touch. She held a management position with Puma and had been spending time alone, doing the best she could to heal from her past.

We could have saved each other from the darkness we were facing now if I had taken the initiative and done the right thing back then. It was clear that she had always been my match. I knew it the day I saw her on upper campus and looked into her pretty mouth. Yet, I let her endure the trauma all those years. I was ashamed. Surely, I didn't deserve to have her share the weight of my burdens now.

But here we were again, figuratively staring each other down. We couldn't get the time back, but there was still a chance to find out what we missed. There was still a chance to help each other heal.

Chapter 41: Edge of Mind

When my mom called me after Marilyn and I had exchanged divorce papers, I knew it wasn't going to be good news. She told me that Marilyn had reached out to her, spilling the news about our impending divorce. According to my mother, Marilyn insisted that divorcing her would be a colossal mistake on my part. Her threats were palpable—she said she would leave me broke and alone and that she planned to marry another man who would take care of her and our child.

The darkness within me grew as the divorce process unfolded. I was grappling with the reality of having a child with someone I felt I no longer knew. This stranger was now not only pitting herself against me but also causing conflict with my mother. It was clear that there would be no amicable resolution here, no handshake and parting ways. Marilyn was gearing up for war, using every resource at her disposal—her parents' money and our son, Barron.

The constant question in my mind was, "When will I see Barron again?" Once the papers were signed, Marilyn stopped sending pictures. Our relationship, already dysfunctional, was now shattered beyond repair. She claimed I didn't even know Barron's diaper size and made it clear that equal custody was out of the question. My heart had grown cold towards her. I could barely find the will to speak to her. But it had been a month since I last held Barron, and the ache to see him grew stronger every day.

The Chargers' bye week in November seemed like the perfect opportunity to get some quality time with Barron. I thought I could take him to Georgia to meet my mom, who had yet to meet her grandson because she hated flying. It seemed like a good idea to offer Marilyn a break from looking after Barron on her own. But when I brought it up, Marilyn vehemently opposed the idea. She insisted that Barron stay in New Jersey and proposed that I rent a hotel nearby. She would allow me to pick up Barron for only a few hours at a time, ensuring he slept in his own bed every night.

I knew her intention was to provoke me, and it worked. She had no right to dictate how and where I could spend time with my son, yet that's exactly what she was trying to do. But I also knew I couldn't forcibly take him without serious consequences. The next day, I sought counsel from my attorney, who recommended filing a motion and litigating it in court. Despite my emotions and naivety about the legal process, I agreed. Our petty conflict had escalated into a full-blown war.

I submitted a motion to the court the following week. I made a heartfelt plea, recounting my unwavering presence in Barron's life since his birth. Despite losing my job and having to relocate across the country, my only request was to spend quality time with my son. I wanted Barron to meet his grandmother in Georgia. I shared how I had always given Barron his baths at night and fed him his morning bottle. I expressed my immense joy in continuing these routines during my week off in November.

Reading Marilyn's opposition to my motion felt like a punch to the gut. It was a dark web of lies. She intended to use my football career against me, claiming I had moved to California without any intention of seeing Barron. She said I had been an absentee father, aggressive towards her, and that she feared for her safety when I was around. Marilyn insisted it would be dangerous for me to have Barron overnight, claiming I had never cared for him alone. She asserted that I needed constant supervision while Barron was with me and even suggested involving independent child psychologists to conduct separate custody evaluations, trying to undermine my position in every way possible.

I couldn't believe what I was reading. Marilyn's response left me speechless. I instantly regretted not filing for divorce on the grounds of severe emotional distress. Her behavior was beyond extreme, and under the guidance of my attorney, I had let her off the hook. Now she was free to continue her abusive ways, unmitigated. Our court hearing was scheduled for November 21st, the first Monday of the bye week. Even if my motion prevailed, arranging for Barron to visit his grandmother on such short notice seemed nearly impossible. Marilyn had already emerged victorious.

Wake up, drive to practice, eat, sit through a host of meetings that didn't involve me. Prepare for practice. Get used up. Suddenly, it was a grind to make it through the day.

My emotional state was lousy. I was in sunny San Diego, living the dream of playing pro football, but some days, the pain made me wish I wasn't there. The only relief I found was temporary—on the balcony at night, with a green bottle, weed smoke, 808 beats blaring, or De'shonia's voice in my ear. But the pain never left. Every morning, I woke up stewing in anger and missing my son. I stayed by myself, avoided making friends, and kept my negativity to myself. Besides, I didn't have money to burn on hanging out.

My expenses were already out of hand on my reduced salary. Between the mortgage on the townhouse in New Jersey, rent in San Diego, and general living expenses, the situation felt overwhelming. To make matters worse, Marilyn still had access to our shared credit card, which I couldn't lawfully close. She continued to shop without restraint. September's credit statement revealed a staggering $20,000 balance, with $4,000 spent on a single trip to Aritzia. My attorney told me there was nothing I could do before the court date.

The practice squad check and my savings would cover for now, but I was doubtful of my financial viability. The $30,000 retainer I paid my attorneys to take the case worried me the most. How many times would I have to refill the retainer before the divorce was over? I spent sleepless nights drifting in the dark, wondering if I would become another NFL statistic. Anger, worry, and sadness were nudging me towards the edge of my mind.

De'shonia and I had been talking regularly for over a week, and she could tell I wasn't doing well. She offered to fly to California to check on me, and I agreed. Seeing her would be incredible, something to look forward to amid the chaos.

In early October, we started making preparations for her visit. I bought her a plane ticket for October 22nd. We had an away game against the Falcons that week, and I wouldn't be traveling with the team. It was the perfect opportunity to scoop her up from the airport and make the most of our time together.

☆ Andre Williams ☆

The day after purchasing the plane tickets, De'shonia called with surprising news. She had transferred her job with Puma to Carlsbad, California, just a 40-minute drive from San Diego. She wasn't just visiting California; she was relocating here. She planned to give her apartment and car to her sister and leave Texas for good. She asked if this move was right, willing to bet it all to come and see me.

I was astonished by De'shonia's dedication. She knew about the drama with Marilyn, that I already had a child, and that my football career was uncertain. Still, she wanted to face it all with me. There was a tiny piece of my broken heart that wanted to doubt her intentions, but I was so emotionally handicapped that I didn't dare question her. I needed to see my friend.

Besides, I knew this woman. From our teenage years until now, she had always shown nothing but virtue. I couldn't let my brokenness drive her away. I thought back to college, to the moment I saw her carrying Derrick's bedpan filled with urine to the bathroom after his knee surgery. I remembered our time together in Texas, smitten by her pretty mouth in the elevator, and how painful it was to leave her behind. I wanted her to come to California. I wanted her to stay. I told her yes with my whole heart, or what was left of it at the time. I took a couple steps back from the edge of my mind and waited for her to arrive.

Chapter 42: A Love Letter

I was in the city hanging out around the San Diego Airport. It was a Saturday afternoon and I was waiting for your flight to come in. You were due to land any minute now. I looked up and I saw a pink plane queuing up the runway. I knew it was your plane, I could feel it. A few moments later I got a text on my phone. It was you. It read,

"I'm here." There were butterflies in my stomach when I parked my car outside the airport in the arrivals lane and waited for you to come through the doors. I don't remember the waiting, i just remember laying eyes on you and thinking to myself,

"Damn.." and nothing else, my mind was blank. My heart was beating hard when I stepped out of the car to greet you. Your embrace felt like peace. I put your suitcase in the trunk and I drove us to Café Bené for bubble tea. You asked me to order for you. I got us both the hot taro flavor.

I can't recall what we talked about. I just remember how happy I was to be there with you. Your beauty was a liqueur, and your presence intoxicated me. My God, did He take his time with you. My eyes couldn't get enough of your smooth, soft, chocolate self. Inside and out, there was no flaw in you.

This was not like our meeting in Texas at all. All inhibition was gone now. You were here for me and I was here for you and we both knew that this was forever and there was no going back. We bet everything on that. I needed you to rescue me from my dark and desperate circumstances, to raise me from the dead. In return, you only needed to be seen. There was no fair exchange in our meeting, but it was your longstanding virtue that made your royalty so obvious to me.

I see you Noble Dreamstar, and with honor, I am on assignment until death to care for your needs, to protect your heart, to cherish your body, and to heal your soul. To say I love you, is more than a feeling, it is a promise.

It didn't matter how broken we were on the inside because our healing began the moment our eyes met there in San Diego. You saw me, and I saw you and I knew everything would be okay after that. My chin raised up. My back straightened. My posture improved. I was more of myself again as we sat there smiling at each other.

We finished our bubble tea over an hour ago but we were still there, lost in each other. It was time to head back to my apartment so you could put your bags down, clean yourself up, and make yourself at home. We climbed back into the car and as I drove off with you, my mind ran wild with wet ideas.

This gorgeous chocolate woman was about to take her clothes off and shower in my room. This gorgeous chocolate woman was going to sleep next to me in my bed tonight. This gorgeous chocolate woman... I wonder if she knows what's on my mind. The ride back seemed like forever.

I opened the door to the apartment and let you in. I followed behind you as you toured around our space. You stopped in the bedroom and put your bags down. You turned around and looked me in the eyes and you asked me a question that didn't need an answer,

"I don't know if you're still married... should we wait until later or are you ready for me now?"

We'd been waiting for each other all these years. We had hurt ourselves waiting. The wait was over and it was time to stop hurting ourselves. My marriage was certainly over. I was ready for you, so I took your hands and I answered you with a gentle kiss.

You kissed me back and started to undress. I saw your body and there was no stopping it now. We were crossing the threshold. First my shirt was off, and then my pants were gone too. You were on your knees, staring back at me from the edge of the bed. You received me for the first time, and my body knew your body. Your perfection was almost too much to bear. I already loved you, and now I was helplessly in love. I wished in vain that you and I had never known anyone else, but it didn't matter now. I was standing on top of the world.

☆ After the Last Snap ☆

Chapter 43: Enter Hades

It's true—this wasn't the ideal situation to begin a relationship. But Dee and I were like two peas in a pod, soaking up the San Diego sun and making the most out of our circumstances. I got her a long-term rental car, and she worked her job at Puma in Coronado. We weren't alone anymore. I focused more on work and worried less about missing Barron. My confidence was coming back.

All of this was important because I would need every ounce of strength to handle what was coming during the bye-week. Unfortunately, the stage was already set, and I was sailing into the storm on a raft with no paddle.

When the bye-week finally came, I left De'shonia in California to work, and I flew back to New Jersey for my court date against Marilyn—the skull, and the wolf.

Upon my arrival on Sunday, the first thing I did was check on the house. Marilyn wasn't home; it seemed she had gone back to Stamford with her family. To my surprise, my key no longer worked in the front door. She'd changed the locks. The garage opener was in my Cadillac CTS, which I had already arranged to be transported to California. I had lost access to the house and hadn't planned for that.

I had a neighbor named Vanessa who lived two doors down. She was married to a tall Polish man named Martin, and they had two young kids together. While we didn't know each other well, Vanessa had often tried to engage with me in the cul-de-sac and become friends. Unfortunately, she always seemed to catch me in the middle of a spat with Marilyn. I never gave Vanessa the time, but now, seeing her minivan in the driveway, my spirit urged me to knock on her door. I followed my instinct.

☆ After the Last Snap ☆

Vanessa was surprised to see me when she opened the door. "Andre, where have you been!" she exclaimed.

"I just returned from California. I'm a Charger now," I replied. Concern filled her eyes as she welcomed me inside. I poured out the sequence of events that led me to her home, and the more I spoke, the larger her eyes grew. By the time I finished, she was picking her jaw up off the floor, her complexion flushed with surprise and disappointment.

I apologized to her for being distant since moving into the neighborhood and now seeking her help. She shook her head and reassured me, saying that her house was my house and that I could spend time with Barron and even stay the night if necessary, as they had a spare room.

I was truly grateful and told her I would take her up on her offer. I didn't want to deal with the expense of a whole week in a hotel. We exchanged numbers, and I promised to update her after my court appearance the next day.

The following morning, I took a car to the courtroom. Marilyn arrived late, flanked by her two attorneys. She looked ghostly pale and noticeably nervous, but her lawyers appeared collected and composed. I knew their names from the paperwork we had been exchanging—Beth, a frail and pallid elderly woman, and Jordan, a young man with an olive complexion and slicked-back black hair. These were my true opponents—the skull and the wolf.

Tanya, my attorney, arrived and started discussing the day's proceedings with me. It seemed there would be minimal interaction between Marilyn and me in the presence of the judge. Instead, the attorneys would convene privately to resolve matters and then meet with the judge behind closed doors. Marilyn and I had no choice but to wait patiently. Given that this situation was entirely unfamiliar to me, I placed my faith in Tanya to fight on my behalf.

I waited anxiously as the hours dragged by. Finally, Tanya emerged with an update: Marilyn would no longer rely on the credit card, but spousal support would be determined by the judge. This left me feeling uncertain and uneasy.

To add to my frustration, I found myself locked out of my own house, with no immediate solution. According to the court, Marilyn was considered the primary parent, and the house was her primary residence. Until the entire case was resolved, the status quo would persist. Tanya seemed optimistic, but I felt a sense of confusion creeping in. These weren't the issues we had set out to address in court.

After another long wait, Tanya returned, her demeanor less cheerful. She relayed that Marilyn remained steadfast on the parenting arrangement. It was either supervised parenting time or no access to Barron at all. Having been absent for over two months, Marilyn held all the cards. It was a punch to the gut, an unjust cruelty often imposed on fathers in a divorce.

With no other options and the moments of my bye-week ticking away, I grudgingly conceded to supervised parenting. I wasn't going to leave for San Diego without laying my eyes on Barron. Tanya nodded and disappeared once more. When she returned, it was time to face the judge.

Standing before the judge felt like awaiting a sentence for a crime I didn't commit. The judge issued the final order: indefinite supervised parenting for my interactions with Barron, the supervisor to be mutually agreed upon and hired at my expense. We were required to hire independent child psychologists to evaluate our relationships with Barron in order to establish a parenting agreement. Additionally, I was ordered to pay $5000 a month in spousal support until the divorce was finalized.

It felt like a bomb had exploded. I was shell-shocked, at a loss for words or actions. Tanya advised me against challenging the ruling, gesturing to a number hastily scribbled on her notepad: "$72,000," suggesting the case could be settled at that price. Glancing at my phone, I realized it was already past 4 PM. I was supposed to have picked up Barron from daycare an hour ago. It was too late to arrange supervised visitation for today. However, Marilyn agreed to meet me at the daycare so I could feed Barron lunch before she took him home.

Tanya offered me a ride to the daycare so I wouldn't have to wait for an Uber. Surprisingly, we arrived before Marilyn. When I entered the daycare, I found Barron sitting alone on the floor, crying inconsolably with no one attending to him. I immediately scooped him up, and as soon as he saw me, his cries stopped. He recognized his dad, resting his head on my suit jacket. Holding him close, we swayed back and forth—a painful moment seared into my memory.

Marilyn arrived shortly after with Barron's food—a store-bought orange mixture of vegetables and fruit. I heated it and spoon-fed him right there in the daycare. He was delighted, babbling and bouncing as he stacked blocks and patted my lap. After he finished eating, Marilyn took him away. I sat there, thoughtless and broken. After some time, I ordered a car and headed back to Vanessa's house. That night, over dinner and red wine, I discussed the court ruling with Vanessa and Martin.

Marilyn insisted that Rochelle, a babysitter we knew from my time with the Giants, supervise our visits. She shot down the idea of Vanessa, our neighbor with two kids, supervising me at her home. To add insult to injury, I would have to pay for my six hours with my son. I realized my mistake in court—submitting to Marilyn's abuse to placate my emotional state over Barron. There would be no mutual agreement; I would play by Marilyn's rules or leave empty-handed.

The next day, I picked up Barron from Marilyn according to her text message instructions. She told me to wait in my car until Rochelle arrived. When Rochelle pulled up, we rang the doorbell. Marilyn handed Barron to me, and when I asked about his diaper bag, she replied, "That's your responsibility," shutting the door in my face. Marilyn had completely shed her disguise. I had fathered a child with the devil, and now she was ready to sacrifice our child on an altar of spite. Barron was asleep on my chest as if nothing was amiss. I swallowed the intense anger that sprang up in my heart and walked away.

We made our way to Vanessa's house. She was happy to see us reunited but went pale when she learned Barron was given to me without his diaper bag. Furious, she left immediately to get some supplies. I knew Barron's eating schedule hadn't changed, and he would be okay until 2 PM. I retreated to the basement with Barron, where it was quiet and shaded. There was a big comfy couch, and I laid down while Barron slept on my chest. Rochelle mostly let me be as I reconnected with my son that week. She didn't seem happy to be in the middle of all this, but she sat around and collected her money anyway.

Chapter 44: Secret Baby

Returning to San Diego at the end of the week was bittersweet. Marilyn, the Skull, and the Wolf had gotten the best of me. I saw my son, but it came at a heavy cost, and now I was on the verge of discovering something else about the Greys that would further diminish me.

Before leaving New Jersey, I made sure to clear my mailbox. It required a key to unlock, and fortunately, I had the only copy. The mailbox was stuffed to the brim, so I decided to take everything back with me on the plane. I had no desire to sift through the mail during my short stay in NJ; my priority was spending quality time with Barron.

Dee was still at work when I made it back to our apartment. There wasn't much to do until she returned, so I took the opportunity to shower and relax. Eventually, I got around to opening the mail. Among the letters, one stood out from Cigna, my insurance provider. Without delay, I opened it, thinking it might be for Barron. However, to my surprise, it was a notification of coverage for completed services—for Marilyn.

The document listed medical expenses for procedures Marilyn had undergone at Brigham Women's Hospital in Boston that August. She had been under the care of several medical professionals, including a gynecologist, an anesthesiologist, and a surgeon. As I read through the details, the truth became painfully clear. Marilyn had undergone an abortion, concealing her pregnancy from me and seeking her parents' assistance to fly her to Boston for the procedure while I was away at camp. She had made the decision without involving me, denying me the opportunity to know about our unborn child.

I tried to find some solace in the fact that we only had one child together. In the midst of a bitter and costly divorce, the last thing

☆ After the Last Snap ☆

we needed was additional complications from more children. But when I thought about how beautiful and perfect my Barron was and the possibility that there could have been a second child like him, my heart began to ache. The audacity of the Greys, deciding which of my children were allowed to live or die without my knowledge or consent, set me on fire. This was too much. I called Dee to share the news.

At this point, I believed my divorce was inevitable because Marilyn was incredibly spoiled by her rich upbringing, her mind wasted by stimulants and antidepressants. I knew that despite her limited capacity, she believed she was superior to me and would never submit to my direction for our lives and our family.

But as I sat there, digesting this new betrayal, I realized that the only one at fault in the relationship was me. Allowing her to remain by my side despite every blaring alarm signal she sent my way was an egregious error on my part. Although she was incapable of a healthy relationship with someone like me, I did not hate her for being who she was. I was still thankful to her for Barron, the beautiful boy she carried and birthed. However, when I discovered that she was willing to use Barron as a pawn for her own manipulative purposes and secretly abort our children, I did begin to hate her.

I despised Marilyn for interfering in my relationship with Barron and mistreating him out of spite. I also loathed John and Cathy-Anne Grey for enlisting the Skull and the Wolf to wage a deceitful legal battle against me, fueled by their lies and audacity.

With every offense committed, every dollar spent, and every curse I relentlessly hurled their way, my spirit became infested with hatred for Marilyn and the Greys, its roots growing deeper and deeper until it manifested itself in dark and bitter fruit. I found myself engulfed in a relentless battle, consumed by a state of mind that was far from my true self. Indifferent to the financial and emotional consequences, I cursed the Greys and their lawyers, while stubbornly fighting for unadulterated time with my son.

Chapter 45: Attrition

Melvin Gordon suffered a knee injury and wasn't able to recover in time for the regular-season finale against the Chiefs. The Chargers activated their insurance policy and called me up to the active roster in the Week 17 matchup, just in case Melvin wasn't ready to go on Sunday.

I didn't understand why the team was so desperate for him to play. We didn't have a real shot at making the playoffs. I believe Melvin knew he was injured, but he didn't want to give me the opportunity to outshine him. Consequently, he only practiced at half-speed with the first-team offense the entire week. I ended up taking all the reps with the second team. I didn't receive a single handoff or pass in practice that week. It might have just been my negative perspective at the time, but it was disheartening to realize that even with Melvin nursing a compromised knee, the coaches had little confidence in me and didn't rest their star running back. We were not properly prepared for the game.

Nevertheless, I was ecstatic to receive an actual game check. I desperately needed it as we approached the final week of the season. By that point, spousal support had kicked in, and my expenses had become overwhelming. Without that last game check, I would have entered the off-season completely empty-handed.

Friday arrived, marking our last day of preparation on the field. After practice, Melvin made the decision that he would not play on Sunday. I would be going up against the Chiefs. If Melvin truly intended to ruin my preparation by taking the reps that week because he feared witnessing my success on Sunday, he achieved his objective.

Game day arrived, and everything about it—the atmosphere, the weather, the field conditions—was exceptional for a season finale. Yet one unforgettable mistake overshadowed everything: the dropped ball on a check-down pass from Rivers. I checked the

☆ After the Last Snap ☆

protection and realized I was clear. I went through the motions as I executed my check-down route five yards beyond the ball. I figured the ball would be out to one of his favorite targets by the time I turned around. But to my astonishment, Philip actually delivered the pass to me. It was the first time Philip had ever thrown me a pass all year. I don't offer excuses for dropping the ball, poor preparation almost always lead to poor execution.

Other than the dropped pass, I had a decent performance running the ball. I accumulated 87 yards on 18 carries. I moved the chains well enough but unfortunately couldn't find the end zone. Our entire offense fell short, and it was our team's kicker who stole the show, emerging as the top scorer of the day. Despite our best efforts, we only managed to secure two touchdowns through the air with passes to Hunter Henry and Antonio Gates. The Chiefs ultimately triumphed over the Chargers in the season finale with a final score of 37-27.

The season had come to an end, signaling the time for me to return home—back to the war zone. Dee and I packed our belongings and headed east together for the first time. With my townhome off-limits for the time being, we needed to find a new place to live. We sought refuge in Pennsylvania in the meantime. Fortunately, my father resided there, and although he was just as upset as I was about how the divorce was unfolding, he was relieved to see me arrive at his home with De'shonia by my side. He had met her briefly while I was still in school and admitted to me that he wished I'd pursued her years ago. "If only, if only," I thought. Our daily excursions into New Jersey paid off when we finally stumbled upon an apartment with a reasonable price that was only six minutes away from my house. I wanted to be as close as possible to make the most of my time with Barron. To furnish our new home, we turned to CORT for temporary furniture. The apartment was secured and furnished. Finally, I was ready to reunite with my son.

Emotionally, these were some of the most challenging times of my life. At noon, I would pick Barron up and bring him home, and the fun would begin. We ate home-cooked meals, we napped, and we took rides around the apartment complex in his push car. Time always flew by, and suddenly it would be 5:40 in the evening, and

I'd be hustling to get him in his car seat and back to his mother. This routine continued from Monday to Friday, and by 6:05 on Friday evenings, Marilyn would be in the car with Barron, en route to Stamford, Connecticut. Occasionally, I'd pause for a moment, gazing at my empty house and wondering how I ended up in such a lowly place, before making my way back to my apartment to curl up next to Dee and lick my wounds. This pattern persisted throughout the entire off-season.

There would be no trip to Miami for training this year. I had no money left for it. Every dollar and all of my time were committed to the war. I never planned for things to be this way, but now I couldn't see any other option.

Instead of heading to Miami, I had to make trips to visit the psychologists for our custody evaluation, as mandated by the court. She chose Dr. Regis, and I chose Dr. Sebrin. I spent countless hours talking to each of them about the same subjects. It was an immense waste of both time and money. Indeed, that was the purpose, and there was no way around it.

The lowlight of this off-season happened during one exceptional evening with Barron at the apartment. He decided to resist his nap in favor of spending more time playing with his dad. Unless you have personally experienced the arrival of a baby boy in this world, it is difficult to convey the sheer joy of spending a few hours with your own one-year-old. It's incredible to watch them discover and explore the world. On this particular day, Barron was delighted to discover his newfound ability to turn handles, open doors, and greet the person on the other side. He continued doing this until exhaustion finally overcame him, and he couldn't resist his nap any longer. Eventually, he climbed onto the bed and fell asleep on my chest, as he often did. It was well past 5 PM by the time he finally drifted off.

I didn't intend to wake him. I texted his mother, letting her know that Barron had just fallen asleep, and I wanted to let him finish his nap before bringing him back. Her response was a flat refusal. Whatever. I was so tired of her nonsense and abuse. I stopped responding to my phone and soaked up our last moments together for the day.

☆ After the Last Snap ☆

Time flowed swiftly and as the clock struck ten past six in the evening, there began an intense banging on my apartment door, unsettling the tranquility of the moment. De'shonia emerged from the living room, her eyes widening with bewilderment, mirroring my own feelings. The relentless banging persisted, urging me to abandon the comfort of the bed and my son's head against my chest to investigate the source. Marilyn was there when I peeked through the spy hole. The dark fury that sprang up in my chest when I saw her face caused me to break out in a sweat as I resisted the urge to fling open the door and shake her until she went quiet. How did she manage to bypass the security desk in the lobby? Who had divulged the location of my room to her? Didn't she realize that people depart from this Earth every day due to a lack of basic respect?

I called her on my phone, and she picked up immediately, demanding, "OPEN THIS DOOR AND GIVE ME MY BABY!"

This woman was utterly deranged. There was no other explanation. I wanted so badly to open the door and help her lose her balls and find some sense. However, I knew that physicality would solve nothing and complicate everything. In reality, even though she didn't know what she was asking for, she had been provoking me for years towards that end. Instead, I firmly instructed her to stop banging on my door and to leave, as the exchange was to take place at the house in accordance with the court order. I made it crystal clear that if I opened the door and saw her there, she was going to have a big problem because I had already instructed security to alert law enforcement.

Barron was still fast asleep, while his mother carried on with her despicable behavior. But now it was time to bring him back. De'shonia was furious. She couldn't comprehend Marilyn's boldness. Normally, she wouldn't have come to the exchange, but this time she insisted on joining me. I didn't argue. Until now, Marilyn had no clue that De'shonia was living with me. Today, she would find out.

Marilyn was not there when we opened the door. I'm certain she was spooked when I mentioned law enforcement. She knew she was out of line, whether I was late to the exchange or not. We made our way to the car to secure Barron and exited the garage. It was then that we spotted her—Marilyn, in her black Audi SUV, waiting for us at the end of the road. She tailgated us the entire drive, and when I stopped the car in front of my house, she sprinted to the passenger side window and began banging on it, shouting, "GIVE ME MY BABY!" like a lunatic.

That's when De'shonia stepped out of the car, her anger boiling over. "STOP BANGING ON MY CAR WINDOW!" she barked. "THERE'S A BABY IN THERE, YOU CRAZY PIECE OF SHIT!" De'shonia was in her face now. "BACK THE FUCK UP AND GET IN THE HOUSE BEFORE I BEAT YOUR SKINNY LITTLE ASS." Marilyn was cowering now as De'shonia continued, "I HEARD ABOUT YOU, YOU DUSTY BITCH, SUCKING DICK ALL OVER BOSTON. GO SIT DOWN SOMEWHERE!"

I stepped out of the car, ready to calm the situation. I empathized with her anger but recognized that this was not the suitable occasion nor setting for such an outburst. As Barron observed from inside the car, I marveled at his ability to remain composed, never shedding a tear during these challenging moments in his life.

From the expression on Marilyn's face, it was evident that she was completely taken aback. Dee had successfully killed her malignant energy, leaving her in a state of quietude. Slowly, I circled the car, extending my hand to grasp Dee's. With a gentle yet firm tone, I urged her to return to the car. She complied.

Finally, Marilyn's voice squeaked, "Andre, are you going to let her talk to me like that? I'm your wife!" I shot her a glare. How had I gotten this far gone with such a crazy woman? I couldn't comprehend it. I opened the car door and took Barron out of the backseat. I kissed him goodbye and handed him back to his mother. Then we drove off.

The winter months flew by, and March arrived. I received a letter from the Chargers in the mail; it was a futures contract. They were giving me the chance to compete for a spot on the team for the 2017 season. We were heading back to Cali, and now I had mixed feelings. I couldn't believe how cold I'd grown in less than a year. I was fighting just to stay afloat financially and salvage my career, and I didn't want to go. I didn't want to leave my son again.

☆ After the Last Snap ☆

I desperately longed for the divorce to come to an end, so I could finally move on with my life. However, it seemed like there was no end in sight for the court delays, expenses, and petty conflicts. As long as money continued to drain from my account, there would be no resolution. My adversaries took every opportunity to frustrate and delay the proceedings. I was trapped, foolishly pursuing every fleeting moment with my son instead of devising a plan to salvage what remained.

By this time, I had already terminated my attorney's services. There was absolutely no way I would spend another $30,000 on someone who had put me in such a precarious situation. Unfortunately, I didn't have the funds to hire a new lawyer, but when I confided in Roy about my financial struggles, he wired me $30,000 within the hour.

This time, Patty Barbarito came into the picture, highly recommended by a contact within the Giants organization. Patty got on the phone with the wolf during our very first meeting and literally started cussing him out. In just one month, she not only crafted a parenting schedule that accommodated my coast-to-coast travel but also convinced the opposition that I no longer needed supervision during my parenting time.

Finally, my struggle yielded a stroke of progress. But all was not well. It's not easy to find joy when you've lost most of your rights to your child and property and you're forced to burn piles and piles of money with no end in sight. And despite holding one of the most prestigious jobs in the country, I was struggling to hold things together financially. Rejoicing over small victories was hard.

I only spent half of the OTA training period with the Chargers that summer because every two weeks I flew back to New Jersey to spend time with Barron. (Dee stayed in Cali to save money.) I had a conversation with Coach Lynn and explained what I believed needed to do. He nodded and said, "OK, you do what you think is best for your family."

Some might consider this a foolish decision. And maybe it was, but for me, it was important that Barron knew who his father was. I didn't care about anything else at that time.

☆ Andre Williams ☆

The summer break before camp was approaching, and our apartment lease was expiring. I couldn't afford to extend the lease, pay the mortgage, and rent in Cali for the year while also managing the spousal support and litigation fees. I felt like something was about to give. Every day, I called, texted, and pleaded with Marilyn in every way possible to leave my house and return to Stamford. Finally, in the summer of 2017, she agreed and handed over the keys. In exchange, I allowed her to go to Nantucket with her family for the summer, as was her custom, and she took Barron with her.

It was a small relief to return to the house I'd left behind almost a year ago. For a time, we were unburdened from the constant back and forth with a tyrant abuser. Vanessa and Martin welcomed us back into the neighborhood with open arms. On our first night back home, Dee and I sat down with them and enjoyed drinks.

Chapter 46: One Last Dance

Roy gave me a new daeqido quest to complete that summer, and it couldn't have come at a better time. This time, I embarked on a quest for endurance. Roy shared a story about how South Korea, despite not being exceptional soccer players, almost won the World Cup because of their unbeatable stamina. Inspired by this, my fitness quest was to progressively increase my running distance. I would run 5 miles for 5 days, then 7 miles for 5 days, 10 miles for 5 days, 12 miles for 5 days, and finally 15 miles for 5 days.

I had never run more than a mile before, but after completing 35,000 push-ups and 9,000 pull-ups in less than 30 days, I knew I had the mental fortitude to conquer this challenge. Some days, De'shonia ran with me, even up to the 7-mile leg, but after that distance, I was on my own. I started on the treadmill, listening to music and suffering through the sweat, but day after day, running in place and staring at the clock grew boring. I found that running outside made the journey more bearable.

I adopted the approach of taking 2 days off between each 5-day period, sometimes 3 if my body needed it. My running routes varied—from town streets to the local high school track and through the park. The pounds melted away as I clocked the miles. After completing the first 10-mile set, I was amazed to find that I had shed 8 pounds, bringing my weight down to 207 pounds, the lightest I'd been since joining the league. I wasn't concerned. I was confident I'd regain the weight once the running phase was over.

One time, during the 12-mile legs of my fitness journey in the sweltering August heat, I made the error of starting my run at noon, with temperatures hitting 100 degrees. I refused to let the temperature stop me. I strategically placed a large water jug at the starting line of the local high school track to fuel me every half mile. As I approached mile 9, I decided to switch to a cross-country route, passing through the nature reserve, which I knew to be a mile and a half. I figured that by the time I circled back to the track, my challenge would be complete.

I failed to consider the lack of water after each half mile. The scorching 100-degree heat hit me hard halfway through the park. I could feel my internal temperature rising, and as I made my way back, my insides started to scream in pain. I knew I couldn't stop, or I might not make it back. I was fighting painful cramps in my legs when I spotted my water jug in the distance. I reached the 12.04-mile mark on my distance tracker when I finally reached the water jug.

Reaching the 15-mile mark, just a week before my upcoming journey to California for camp, I must confess that I didn't fully complete the last leg of the run. However, running 15 miles even once, was a significant achievement for me. I didn't want to push my legs to their limit, knowing the extensive running I had in store for camp. Given more time, I believe I could have completed the full distance.

It was time to pack up and head to Cali for the season. I'd logged 185 miles that month, and I was about 215 pounds by the time we boarded the plane, my lightest playing weight yet.

I don't remember very much from my preseason camp except how much I disliked my position coach. The Chargers cleared house, and the staff was completely new. My running back coach was a guy by the name of Alfredo Roberts. Not only was he insulting and disrespectful, but he was also uninspiring and unapproachable as a coach. He was a tight end by trade and didn't know very much about the nuances of the running back position, so he got by, spending each meeting sucking on Melvin's toes. I know I got off on a bad foot with the coaching staff because of my frequent travel during OTAs, but apart from that, our personalities clashed badly. I did my best, but I think our dislike for each other was obvious.

That year, I lost my roster spot to Austin Ekeler. He would become the Chargers' new Danny Woodhead. I found myself on the practice squad, serving as a backup for Melvin once more. It was disappointing to lose to a rookie, but I was already mentally exhausted and had accepted it. I didn't fight it—I had bigger problems to deal with.

Wake up, drive to practice, hot tub, shower, eat, sit through a host of meetings that didn't involve me. Prepare for practice. Get used up. Eat. Sit through meetings again. Lift. Go home to Dreamstar. Sink deeper into divorce litigation. This was my reality.

That season, I discovered a new power granted to me from my off-season daeqido training: world-class stamina. It came in handy because many times we were a man down somewhere in practice and needed an extra body. I used my deep stamina well to show off, and I took as many reps as they would let me. I didn't get tired. I spent a lot of time catching balls on the jugs during my free time, before and after practice, and even during lunch. I also spent much of my free time on the treadmill working on my mile time. I got it down under 6 minutes with a personal best of 5 minutes and 53 seconds.

To my surprise, my luck turned around midway through the season, and the Chargers added me to the active roster. I was seeing the field again in limited instances, giving Melvin a spell and protecting Philip on pass downs. By December, I was running the 4-minute offense.

Marilyn and I reached an agreement for her to accompany Barron on a trip to Cali for a week during the season, with the condition that I covered the travel expenses and their accommodations. Despite this, I was still not allowed to spend overnights with him. Barron was just a year old when he visited Cali to spend time with me, and his athletic genes were already starting to show. I remember him shouting "FAST!" as he ran circles around the living room in the apartment. It was his favorite pastime.

My rookie teammate, Rayshawn Jenkins, also had a son named Ace who was the same age as Barron. De'shonia was close friends with Jenkins' girlfriend, and they arranged a playdate for the kids. Jenkins and I watched our children discover themselves and bond with each other while our partners prepared dinner. Rayshawn had a great big pit-bull, and Barron fearlessly sat on its back. I was struck with emotion in that moment as I watched him, understanding how few and far between these moments with my child would be from here on out.

I realized the necessity of having another baby boy. It was agonizing to have to fight for a moment of normalcy with Barron. It was torment to return him to his mom, knowing it would be a long time, and another court scuffle, before I saw him again. I knew we were moving towards a scenario where I wasn't going to be the dominant force in his life the way that I wanted to be. We were already there. The Greys made sure of that. This was not how I envisioned raising my son. After a year of divorce court and no end in sight, I was run down. I needed new joy in my life, and I needed to heal.

De'shonia and I started praying for a boy as we did that thing that a man and a woman do to bring kids into the world. Before long, something happened. It was November when De'shonia found out that she was pregnant with our first child. We prayed and hoped, harder. Nine weeks later, Dee took a blood test to check the sex of the baby. She woke me up at 2 in the morning with the results. It was a boy.

It only took me a couple of hours to decide on his name. I wanted to name him after an angel because he was a gift from God—a clear answer to my heartfelt prayers. I needed his name to serve as a reminder of this truth. I knew that angel names often end in 'el, so that's where I began my search. Our baby boy was due in July of 2018, and when I discovered that Ka'el was the name of the angel overseeing the stars of the Cancer constellation, I knew I had found the perfect name for him. He would be called Ka'el Malik Williams, meaning "Mighty Warrior-King-Faithful Defender." Our hearts were filled with an overwhelming sense of joy.

On December 10, 2017, I played my final game in the NFL. We faced the Redskins at home and completely dominated the field. With a comfortable lead of two scores in the final minutes of the 4th quarter, I was skillfully executing a 4-minute offense to run out the clock. However, as I took a handoff to the left side of the field on an inside zone play, I gained a few yards before a gang tackle ended the play. As I attempted to pick myself up off the ground from a kneeling position, one of the D-linemen came in late and belly-flopped on my back, exerting all of his weight on my right wrist. I heard a pop, and immediately knew something was terribly wrong. Looking down, I could see that my wrist was hanging grotesquely, and I was unable to move it. The pain was excruciating, far beyond what I knew to be normal. I didn't know it at the time, but that moment marked the end of my professional football career. Cradling my injured wrist, I left the football behind, and jogged off to the sideline for the very last time.

The sideline doctor initially believed the injury was a broken bone, but after a closer examination, it turned out that the ligaments in my wrist were torn, which is actually worse than a break. I was given two options for stabilization surgery: they would re-attach the ligaments and insert pins or a plate to immobilize the wrist as it healed. I was advised that the plate would be the superior choice as it would provide better wrist stabilization, and I would be able to manage any loss of mobility once the plate was removed.

I should have taken a moment here to think. I should have gotten a second opinion. Instead, I blindly followed the advice from the team doctor and chose the more invasive plate surgery. I know today that this was the wrong option.

The first surgical procedure took place on December 19, 2017. I was scheduled for a follow-up procedure three weeks later, to have the immobilizing plate removed. I went through a very painful three weeks with that plate in my wrist, but once it was removed, the real pain began. I was not expecting my wrist to be so incredibly useless after the surgery was complete, but it was. My wrist was almost completely immobile, and my hand strength was completely sapped. I was devastated at the outcome because the thought of confidently holding a football again seemed distant and uncertain. I knew in this state, it would take quite a while to recover.

The harsh reality of my current circumstances began to dawn on me with devastating clarity. I was grappling with a never-ending divorce battle and fighting to spend time with my son. I was struggling under extreme financial pressure and recuperating from a severe injury to my dominant hand. It was all too much, and I knew in my heart that my football journey was coming to an end.

It was sad to come to this conclusion, but I also knew that the injury was a message from God. He was nudging me into a place where the next step did not require me to make a choice. I now had a crystal-clear indication of the path I needed to follow because, at this point, I knew the only thing fueling the divorce were my resources. But with my compromised wrist, and no prospect of when I would be available to play again, my source of income would quickly dry up. It was time to embrace the end of football and bring closure to the divorce.

Chapter 47: Mere Formalities

Enter 2018. De'shonia and I have moved back east for good this time. We are one year and three months into the divorce and still neck-deep in an unprovoked war with the Greys. New Jersey is the battleground, and the Skull and the Wolf's litigative attacks on me have inflicted terrible financial and psychological damage. Great piles of greenbacks are burning all the time. My wrist is destroyed.

Despite these hardships, we manage to find some temporary solace. For one, we are finally back in the townhouse, and I am no longer paying double rent. There are new issues to conquer here—the carpets are riddled with Marilyn's Pomeranian piss, and the tub in the master bath is leaking into the ceiling of the kitchenette below. But these issues are fixable, and our friends are glad we are back in town. Most importantly, there is a little chocolate boy growing in Dee's tummy.

I am so excited to meet him. I cannot fully express the deep gratitude I have to De'shonia for blessing me with another baby boy. I love on her as best I can. She doesn't have to be here with me in the mess, but she is by my side, watching everything burn down around us, holding my hand, massaging my heart.

At this point, I'm numb to the torture I'm going through with Barron. The in-person psych reviews have begun now that I'm home from work. The child psychologists come to the house and watch us when we are with Barron, peering over my shoulder and asking questions. Greenbacks are burning so that they can take notes on what Barron eats, what time he takes his nap, who gives him his bath, the condition of the house, my relationship with Dee, Barron's attachment to her, etc., etc.

I hit a wall, financially speaking, in the spring. A monthly spend of fifteen to twenty thousand dollars can't continue anymore.

☆ Andre Williams ☆

There's nothing left. Now we are living paycheck to paycheck on workers' compensation dollars. With the injury and no contract, there is no prospect of me playing football next season. To be honest, I don't have the mental drive to push myself back into playing condition. I am tired of destroying myself on the field for the sole purpose of exploitation. I have informed Pat and her team that I can no longer afford their retainer fees. With a balance of over $50,000 on my account, there has been a noticeable change in their attitude. While they haven't withdrawn entirely, they have started to pull back, leaving my emails and phone calls unanswered at times. They prioritize more lucrative clients.

I am no longer able to pay Marilyn's spousal support. Surprisingly, stopping the payments hasn't resulted in any negative consequences; in fact, it appears to be the best decision I've made so far. Now, Skull and Wolf are discussing a resolution, and we have a date set for arbitration to discuss the terms of our divorce settlement.

Ka'el's arrival into the world is drawing nearer with each passing day. De'shonia is in the last trimester. He's kicking like a horse in the womb. He will be a special athlete. I can sense it. We have made arrangements for his delivery at Englewood Hospital in Englewood. The reviews are positive.

Dee's not on my insurance yet, but she will be. There's no doubt in my mind about it. De'shonia is a good woman, and I am not letting her go. I know this is true because I've experienced a bad woman. The hospital recognizes my status and has graciously offered to deliver the baby free of charge. We agree to work out the insurance issues afterward.

The time has come for Pat Barbarito and her associates to walk away from me. They won't represent a client who can't afford their fees. Oh well. Maybe they should have worked harder at fixing my bogus spousal support before we made it to this point. I can't even afford to pay my taxes this year. Interestingly enough, the $70,000 I have already paid in spousal support is the precise amount the IRS claims I owe. There is no remedy for this.

Nobody is getting paid—not the lawyers, or the Greys, or the government—but they will all make out just fine. The same can't be said for me. Pat's junior associate emails me privately to tell me he's sorry about everything and that I can count on him if I still have questions or need help. At the time, I believed he was being kind, but I would learn later that he is a snake.

The arbitration date rolls around now. I meet Marilyn and her lawyers in a NJ office of a court-appointed former judge. He is the neutral arbitrator. I'm pro se now. I feel cool standing alone against Marilyn, her hired help, and the court system. The arbitration is the final opportunity for Marilyn, Skull, and Wolf to carve away at my flesh.

The issue of custody is the first matter to settle because if custody is decided, then the financial issue mostly settles itself. I don't have much leverage to fight it anymore. The future is so uncertain now that I can't see how we will survive. I am injured and jobless.

Marilyn wants to be the primary parent, of course, meaning Barron would spend most of his time with her and go to school where she is. I already allowed her to move back to Stamford with Barron. It's his primary residence now. I tell her I'll agree to it if parenting time is split 50/50 until he starts school. We agree that during the school year, we will split the school vacations in half, including his summer break. Done.

The financial issue is all that is left. Skull and Wolf suggest that my 401k could be divided by half, and the months of overlooked spousal support could be deducted from my share, along with Marilyn's equity in the home.

In my perspective, Marilyn had no claim to any equity in the house. She never contributed a single dollar towards its purchase or upkeep, and she left it in a deplorable state. Moreover, there were numerous items missing from the house when she departed, but the lawyers won't vacate the issue of equity. I fight them down to a fixed amount: half of the 401k, along with $20,000 for the equity. However, Marilyn would bear sole responsibility for the penalties and taxes on the retirement account. Agreement reached.

Finally, we came to the topic of child support. At the time, I was unemployed, and they'd already taken everything they could find. They couldn't expect much more from me. Eventually, we reached a final agreement.

☆ Andre Williams ☆

That was all. From here, what was left were mere formalities. The entire two-year divorce had been settled in two hours of conversation. It could have been settled the same way years ago, and in doing so, we would have avoided all of the evil that we perpetrated against each other. Instead, by their behavior, my perception of the Greys was so terribly marred that I could only ever identify them as enemies. It was a shame. I don't understand why these incredibly wealthy people were so obsessed with burning all of my money. Was it all for the sake of spite? When everything was said and done, I'd still have the responsibility of being Barron's father. A dollar would never replace that, but it takes money to raise a child. After we came to an agreement, a court date was set in October for us to finalize our divorce. I didn't know it, but I was in for one last surprise.

July had arrived, and Ka'el's due date was now days away. Dee was ready to pop, and I found myself in a familiar and strange place. I was the veteran parent, and Dee was the rookie mom-to-be. For nine months I'd been coaching her to deliver the perfect touchdown—the birth of our beautiful baby boy. I knew they were both well-prepared. Dee had been eating like an athlete and exercising like a martial artist.

On July 12th, Dee began experiencing heavy contractions. I put our hospital bags in the car, and we made our way to Englewood Hospital. As fate would have it, it seemed like every mother in New Jersey had also chosen that day to give birth.

We were finally admitted to a birthing room after a long wait.

The nurse came in to see how far along Dee was dilated, only 3cm. Ka'el wasn't coming today. Because the delivery unit was so full, they actually sent us home. We'd have to come back tomorrow. Dee endured the night curled up on the giant Lovesac we kept in the kitchenette, groaning from the intensifying pains of labor.

By 8 AM the following morning, her contractions had become stronger and more frequent, signaling that Ka'el's time had come. We hurried back to the hospital, and on the afternoon of Friday, July 13th, 2018, Ka'el Malik Williams came into the world, weighing a healthy 7 pounds, 8 ounces. De'shonia showed incredible strength, delivering him vaginally without any

☆ After the Last Snap ☆

complications. Fresh out of the womb, Ka'el bore an identical resemblance to his brother, even down to his caramel skin. I was so, so proud of Dee and of the baby she made for us. Ka'el could never replace Barron, but he was my God-given comforter, to ease the pain of longing I felt for my firstborn. When he arrived, I gained new strength. Despite everything that was going wrong in my life, I was one step closer to wholeness. I had my family. I had love.

On the eve of finalizing the divorce, which was scheduled for October 11th, I found myself facing an unexpected twist. In my mailbox, I discovered a class action lawsuit sent by Patty Barbarito and her deceitful associates. Their intention was to sue me for the remaining unpaid balance on my account with their firm. To make matters worse, they planned to levy the funds from my 401k, once it was accessible through a court-ordered QDRO (qualified domestic relations order) at the conclusion of the divorce proceedings.

By now, I had become adept at navigating through the paperwork and filing it with the court without the need for legal representation. I delved into the lawsuit they had initiated against me and quickly identified a major error and a potential loophole. I found that there is a specific time frame within which I have the right to file a complaint to the BAR association in case there is a dispute regarding the amount of money they claim I owe. Pat was not permitted to file a lawsuit before this designated time period has elapsed.

Their lawsuit was improper, and the snakes wouldn't be getting their way. I crafted a response against their ill-conceived legal action, clearly highlighting the flaws in their case. Regardless of whether my assessment was deemed justified or not, I was resolute in my decision to gracefully step away from the courtroom tomorrow, without allowing this divorce to reach its finality. At least, that was the way I felt as I wrote my response. Pat Barbarito wasn't walking away with my hard-earned money.

Pat's Right Hand and the snaky Junior Associate arrived at the courtroom the following day. As we took our seats on the benches, I found myself sitting alone on one side while Marilyn joined Skull and Wolf. Right Hand walked in, brimming with excitement, and exclaimed to everyone, "Let's make some money today!" They

☆ Andre Williams ☆

joined Skull and Wolf, attempting to establish friendly relations and gather information. However, it was clear that Skull and Wolf were unamused. They were here to complete their mission, not to fraternize with rivals. I couldn't help but smirk. Right Hand seemed unaware of the progress I'd made in our lawsuit. The court system was slow like that.

Eventually, we were allowed into the courtroom and sworn in before the judge. The judge made his remarks, acknowledging that Pat Barbarito and their associates were encroaching on the divorce with their lawsuit. He also affirmed that he received my response to their suit and recognized that I was correct in my assessment; their lawsuit was illegitimate. The judge counseled us to step outside and reach an agreement or return another day for a divorce settlement.

In hindsight, I realize that I was overly confident in that situation, too smug with the fact that I had correctly assessed the illegitimacy of Pat's lawsuit. But I should have used the moment to gain leverage in the divorce, because now that I was struggling, the Greys were eager to make their exit. Now was the time to hold them hostage, like they had done to me when I was making money. If I had held out at that moment, I know I could have convinced them to pay off my debts to facilitate their exit.

I should have just walked out the door that day, but in my heart, I was just as eager as the Greys to move on and be with my family. I wanted to be a free man. However, for those who may be going through something similar, it is at the very end, when everything you have is burning and signed away and everyone is running to the door, that you have the most leverage. Divorce is a soap opera, a big fake drama. It's not real. The only thing real is what you agree to. Stay resilient and play smart to secure a favorable outcome.

In my overconfidence, I strode down the hallway, followed closely by Right Hand and Junior Ass. As we reached the end of the corridor, I turned around and locked eyes with Right Hand.

"So, gentlemen, what's the plan here? Make a deal that makes sense, or we all leave empty-handed. It doesn't matter to me."

Junior tried to interject, but I cut him off sharply. "I wasn't talking to you, and I have no interest in hearing what you have to

☆ After the Last Snap ☆

say. You talk nice, but you are a snake." He fell silent. I shifted my gaze back to Right Hand and waited for his response.

His initial proposal was to tap into the 401k and only claim the $65,000 they alleged I owed, instead of the entire account. I scoffed as I became a mime. I crumpled his proposal, tossed it into the air, and sent it sailing out of the park with a powerful swing of my bat.

"That idea is rubbish. What else do you have?" For the span of about 8 or 10 minutes, we went back and forth with lopsided proposals followed by stiff rejection. I started to raise my voice. They were wasting my time, and Right Hand was starting to get frustrated. Finally, Junior Associate took him aside for a brief conversation. Right Hand returned with a smile on his face. "What if we withdraw $25,000 from the 401k and establish a lien on your property for the remaining account balance?" I quickly did some mental calculations.

"I could work with that," I replied. We shook hands to seal the deal. Right Hand went over to Skull and Wolf to discuss our agreement and start working on the proposal.

After some time, he returned with scribbles on a piece of paper. I agreed to surrender $25,000 from the 401k after the QDRO and accepted a lien on my house. Marilyn was in charge of issuing the check to Barbarito and sending me my share. Right Hand was truly clueless. If Marilyn was responsible for issuing him the check but didn't have to sign the agreement, then both of us would be legally off the hook if they didn't receive their money. I signed the agreement, and we resumed our meeting with the judge.

Ten minutes later, it was done. Marilyn and I were officially divorced. I shook hands with Wolf. He was a smooth criminal, and I'd learned a lot from the way he played the game. He had my respect, but I did not like Skull. She was just an old, dusty puss. I walked off without a word to her or the snakes from Barbarito's office. We all exited the courtroom. Marilyn and I had parked in the same lot, and as we reached our cars, she turned to me, attempting to embrace me goodbye as if the last two years of turmoil were now irrelevant. I stepped back from her and extended my hand. We shook hands and parted ways.

Chapter 48: Aftermath

Finally, after 25 long months I emerged as a man set free, but the price I paid for my freedom was colossal.

My thriving NFL career had come to an end, my dominant right arm rendered useless, and my financial stability obliterated. I'd been beaten bloody, yet despite all of this, I had hope that the future would be bright. It was time to get back to business.

The first thing I had to do was access my 401k funds. When 2019 arrived, I was completely broke. Workers' compensation had run dry, and I was still months away from my severance pay. I needed access to my share of the 401k just to stay afloat. My 401k was worth just under $190,000 at that time. I walked away with $79,000 after splitting it with Marilyn.

I didn't make a big deal about dividing the money with her. She notified me when the courts released the money to her, and I kindly asked her to send me my portion. I made no mention of her obligation to send Pat Barbarito $25,000 from my portion first and she didn't ask about it. She was more concerned with the fact that it was her responsibility to pay the penalty taxes for withdrawing the money early. But we had an agreement, and she sent me my money.

I firmly believe that my first mistake after the divorce was attempting to salvage the house. In hindsight, I should have sold it, accepted the loss, and moved forward. However, I was utterly exhausted. Once I finally managed to finalize the divorce and breathe a sigh of relief, the mere thought of relocating, let alone dealing with a house full of belongings on a bum wrist and limited cash, overwhelmed me.

Instead, I decided to use half of my funds to make a one-year down payment on the mortgage. Although I was aware of an impending severance pay from the NFL, the financial feasibility of maintaining the house without a reliable income source was completely foolish. Despite this, I was resolute in my decision to keep up with the payments.

I never intended to give Pat Barbarito any money and it was never my responsibility to do so, according to the way her own team wrote the contract. She could collect from the lien when I decided to sell. I wasn't ready to make another move – I just wanted to enjoy my kids, in my own space, in peace. I took my money and bought time.

For the span of a breath, we experienced relative peace. Things were okay, but about a week after the settlement, Marilyn texted me to inform me that "Barron has a new man in his life. His name is Cramer, and he will be in Barron's life from now on." I responded with something like, "that's great. I hope he beats your ass." I'm not proud of my response. It was wrong and petty to wish bad things on the mother of my child, but karma was about to have its way, regardless. Cramer turned out to be that very type.

At each exchange thereafter, it was Cramer in the driver seat of her black Audi SUV when Marilyn pulled up to my house in Secaucus, to pick Barron up. That winter, I focused on rehabilitating my wrist and spending quality time with my boys. Barron, who was now three years old, had been talking and understanding for quite some time. He had grown used to the back and forth between New Jersey and Connecticut, to see his dad. However, there seemed to be some confusion brewing within him because at times he would refer to Cramer as his dad. Was Marilyn introducing Cramer to Barron as his father? I couldn't believe it. I knew Marilyn was capable of the most cruel behavior, but I never thought this guy would be foolish enough to play along. My wrist would have to hold up because I had never slapped a man left-handed. I wasn't concerned though, as I had more than enough strength to confront him.

Marilyn rang the doorbell to pick up Barron for the exchange but this time, when I opened the door, I left Barron in the interior of the house with Dee and Ka'el. As expected, Cramer was waiting in the car outside. I murmured that I needed to speak to Cramer for a moment and brushed past her. She followed close behind me. As I approached Cramer, he stepped out of the car to greet me, wearing a smile. This man was strange. I don't believe he sensed how ready

I was to throw my elbow if he answered my question the wrong way.

I approached, drawing close enough to inflict injury. "Cramer," I asked, "do you think you are Barron's father?"

He chuckled and promptly replied, "No, I do not."

"Right. You understand, but this dummy you're with doesn't understand shit," I barked. Once again, he chuckled softly and offered me his hand for a shake. Marilyn was silent. This man was clearly a creep, but he wasn't bold enough to assert himself where he did not belong. I kept my elbow holstered.

I found out later that Cramer was 40 years old. He had a son named Jacob who was around Barron's age. They became friends and Barron often talked about him. I can't vouch for the accuracy of what Barron said about Cramer and Jacob, he was only 3, but sometimes the things he said were concerning.

I don't know how Dee found her, but we ended up meeting Jacob's mother, Jenny. She told us Cramer's story. As it turns out, he was not only a creep, but also an abusive, manipulative womanizer who lived off of his parents' wealth. He reminded me of someone that I knew. We kept a vigilant watch over Cramer and Marilyn, while forging a close bond with Jenny. Together, we supported each other in ensuring the safety of our children.

There were some truly frightening times. We were privy to strange occurrences in Stamford, but Marilyn chose to remain silent about them. I didn't press because it wasn't my business but eventually, I did involve child protective services when it became apparent that there was a clear element of danger that could bring harm to Barron. After about a year, Cramer lost interest and slithered away once he realized that his ill-intentioned desires would not come fast and easy.

Last we heard about the man, he had a girlfriend that left his side early one morning to go and jump in front of a train. He was under investigation for a possible role in her suicide. Marilyn even testified in court against Cramer on Jenny's behalf, to help her gain custody of her son Jacob, confirming that he was indeed an abusive man.

Chapter 49: Liberty Fairs

De'shonia and I found a local church in Rahway that we started attending regularly. We had a mutual friend there from Boston College, an old teammate of mine named Colin Larmond. We started looking for a church because I had it in my mind that it was time to marry De'shonia. I was deeply in love with her. She had stood beside me in my worst times, and she bore me a perfect, handsome little boy. Together, they'd helped me heal through my trauma. I knew she was the one for me and with everything settled, there was no reason to wait any longer. But this time, we would do it the proper way, before the eyes of God and not the town mayor. Colin made the introduction to the pastor of the church, Lawrence Powell, and when the opportunity came, I let Pastor Lawrence know of my intention to marry De'shonia. He agreed to conduct the ceremony if we could successfully complete his marriage counseling course. We were very happy to take part in it together. After the months-long course, Pastor Lawrence held our marriage ceremony in the office of his church. Barron and Ka'el were in attendance, along with Colin, his girlfriend Amanda, and their daughter Addelia along with two elders from the church, Elder Izlar and his wife, Audrietta.

A full year had passed since my wrist surgery, and I could not properly hold a football in my right hand. The Chargers actually called me back in February of 2019, wondering if I was ready to make a comeback. I told them the truth. I wasn't ready. At this point in my life, I was out of the loop as far as football was concerned. I hadn't done any serious training since the injury. My wrist caused me real, daily pain and I just couldn't see how I could manage that pain in a pro football setting. Of course, I kept up with the physical therapy, but it wasn't helping at all. After some time, the workers' compensation moderator assigned to my case decided I'd had enough therapy, and I was "cleared" by a team doctor for full activity. It was a lie. There was no way that I could compete fully or partially with the condition my wrist was in, but they were done paying for my injury. There wasn't much that could be done without legal action on my part, and I wasn't prepared to pursue that angle yet.

I still had many things to settle since leaving the drama of divorce behind me. I was heavily invested in the parenting schedule I'd worked out with Marilyn. Our 50/50 parenting time would end as soon as Barron started school and that time was fast approaching. I needed to live that out, I needed to reclaim my health, and I was ready to play a new game. It was time to rebuild my denim company, All Weather Selvedge.

During the divorce, Marilyn and her attorneys were desperately seeking a way to profit from AW. However, I hadn't established a company or made any sales prior to the outbreak of the divorce. All my jeans were sitting in a warehouse in Edison, NJ but the only people that knew that were me and Roy, and we'd completely destroyed her brand, Zavier. She never trademarked or incorporated anything, and so there was nothing for her to take. I was still very wary of Marilyn, but it was time to form a company and begin to build some kind of legitimacy behind my brand. Just to be safe, I urged Diab and Nawal to form a company that I could use to conduct business for a time.

My original plan for AW was to secure distribution deals with major retailers and conduct business-to-business sales. Suddenly, all the time I had spent at tradeshows years ago came flooding back to me. I realized that I needed to get into a tradeshow to secure product orders.

Roy had worked diligently on my behalf, building my brand presence while I was lost in the bitter sauce of marital breakup. He generously gifted several pairs of jeans to influential individuals and made valuable connections in New York City in the process. One of those connections was Jovan, a talented photographer who happened to meet a well-connected woman named Sharifa Murdock while covering an event in the city.

As fate would have it, Sharifa was a partner at Liberty Fairs tradeshow, alongside Sam Ben Avraham. During that time, before the unfortunate onset of the COVID-19 pandemic, Liberty Fairs held a prestigious position as one of the country's leading trade shows for high-quality clothing and apparel. Jovan reached out to Sharifa, sharing details about our new selvedge denim company owned by a prominent sports figure, and she eagerly expressed interest. Before long, we had a meeting scheduled with the impressive Sharifa Murdock.

When it was time for the meeting, I neatly packed a suitcase with a sample of each style of jeans I carried, picked up Jovan in the city, and made our way to Sharifa's office. I didn't know what to expect but we sat down in the office and waited to be seen.

Finally, the time came for our meeting to commence. With my suitcase in hand, I strode into her office. I was nervous but I was excited too because I knew I had a suitcase full of gold. Meeting my gaze, she asked me simply, "Andre, what is your story? Tell me about your brand."

It was the most obvious question I could expect but I was caught off guard. It was the first time anyone had ever asked me anything denim-related in years. I did my best to recount the entire story, starting with Luke, my marketing agent, who introduced me to Eamon and convinced me to create the Runningman shoe.

I shared with her the story of how the Runningman guided me to trade shows, despite my initial lack of understanding about them. I recounted my meeting with Roy the Maker and how he asserted his influence by introducing me to the realm of Japanese selvedge denim. Following this, she inquired, "What led you to choose selvedge denim?"

"I love to compete, Sharifa," I explained. "When it comes to high-end fabric, Italy and Japan are the top sources. Specifically for denim, Japan comes out on top because they still use the original shuttle looms that Levi Strauss used to create his iconic blue jeans back in 1873, and they have preserved the art of creating denim wear as it was intended, a durable workwear fabric.

Secondly, under the right conditions, selvedge denim molds to the body for a truly unique fit and gains character along the way. These are the same fabrics that the leading producers in the market offer, and those are the competitors I aim to challenge. Perhaps not on price, but in the quality of my product."

☆ Andre Williams ☆

I went on to draw from my athletic background to make a mark in the fashion industry by creating my own unique fit of jeans. Before designing my own, I struggled to find the perfect pair. Now, I have the opportunity to redefine what an athletic fit truly means.

Sharifa seemed impressed, and as she carefully examined each pair of jeans, I could see her genuine admiration for my work. She checked each pair in silence and afterward, she offered me a booth at Liberty Fairs and promised I could attend free of charge since it was my first time. She even presented me with the option of showcasing at either the New York show, the Las Vegas show, or both. New York was a no-brainer. There was no doubt in my mind about showing there. I'd never been to Vegas before. The Liberty Fair trade show was the perfect reason to go. I expressed my intent to participate in both shows.

Sharifa was pleased but she informed me that the clock was ticking, as the show was just a month away. Most of the vendors already had their preparations nearly complete, being long-time members. As a newcomer, I had a lot of work ahead of me. However, after the meeting, I was filled with an incredible sense of excitement at this sudden new direction for my life.

July was an incredibly busy month, with Sharifa's team constantly in contact with me about the show. There was a long checklist of items that needed to be completed before the show. I had to ensure that all my digital assets were forwarded so that I could be properly represented on the tradeshow floor, the web, and in all the marketing materials that would be distributed.

I had a small booth assigned to me, and it was my responsibility to set it up in a visually appealing way for the buyers and attendees at the show. To prepare, I immersed myself in a crash course in visual design and sought the expertise of Roy, whose guidance was invaluable. With his help, I created product order sheets for the buyers, ensuring everything was in order for the event.

My booth required three sets of jeans and shoes in each style, a pack of S-hooks, a calculator, PO sheets, signage, business cards, and a healthy dose of creativity for its design. Before I knew it, it was time to pack up and head to New York for the show. The event took place at Piers 94 from July 22nd to the 24th, where I was among great denim brands such as Japan Blue Jeans, Jack & Jones,

☆ After the Last Snap ☆

PRPS, Neuw Denim, Naked & Famous, Railcar Fine Goods, Levi's, and many others.

It was truly fascinating to stroll through the room and observe the offerings of each brand, only to realize that my product was just as good, or even better, for one reason or another. My jeans were unquestionably authentic. It was an incredible experience.

I noticed Sharifa as she made her rounds. A look of concern was evident on her face as she expressed worry about the lower volume of buyers this year compared to usual. Because the experience was completely new to me and I didn't know what to expect, I was unconcerned.

On the final day of the trade show, the buyer from Bloomingdale's paid a visit to my booth to personally inspect my product. Her name was Anya. Although our subsequent email exchanges did not lead to anything concrete, the encounter left an impression on me. While I did manage to secure a small purchase order for 15 pieces from a store in NY over the course of three days, the buyer retracted the order and it ultimately fell through. Nevertheless, as Sharifa wisely noted, setbacks like these are often part of the journey for a first timer. The key is simply to persist. Despite this, the overall experience was invaluable, yielding numerous insights and a wealth of valuable content. Now, armed with newfound knowledge, I prepared to take the next step and head to Vegas.

Vegas was an even bigger spectacle than New York. The logistics of transporting my equipment there were more complex and costly, but I knew I was going to have a lot of fun and I was excited to explore the city with De'shonia.

It turns out my loctician had a timeshare in the area and was willing to let us stay there for free, which saved us a lot of money. De'shonia's mom, Arnette, was quite familiar with Vegas. She had remarried there the previous year and decided to spend the weekend with us to spend time with her grandson. It was a blessing. De'shonia and I would have the chance to explore the city together.

The trade show took place from August 12th to the 14th. This time around, I felt no nerves and was thrilled to be in the city for such a prestigious event with other well-known brands. I was confident that I would be a hit in Vegas and secure a major product order. However, it appeared that something deeper was affecting the retail world at the time. Sharifa had the same worried expression on her face. The buyer volume was unusually low.

Nevertheless, we had an awesome few days in Vegas. During the day, I dedicated my time to the trade show, but by six o'clock, I would eagerly escape to explore the city alongside Dee, leisurely sipping on the bottomless drinks from the Fat Tuesday vendors around the city. It was a vacation that we desperately needed.

Sadly, when it came to business matters, the outcome mirrored what I experienced in New York. There were no substantial orders for our products. In fact, there were no orders at all. Despite generating significant interest and attracting a handful of potential buyers, none of them made a purchase. Apart from a good time, I left Vegas empty-handed.

I did meet one interesting buyer though. Her name was Katie. She represented a denim boutique in Canada called Dutil. They had stores in Vancouver, Toronto, and Calgary. We stayed in touch after the show and after a few months, the relationship bore fruit and I signed a consignment deal with them. They took $15,000 worth of All Weather Selvedge denim jeans in two styles, George and Brad Ripe. The product was due to hit the shelves in all three locations in the spring of 2020.

Chapter 50: Roughnecking

There was a problem creeping into view around the final quarter of the year. While it had always been looming, as the months passed and the reserve cash dwindled, it became clear that maintaining the house was no longer feasible. Without a full-time salary, I couldn't keep up with the payments, yet I couldn't secure a full-time salary while dedicating myself to kick-starting my business. Despite the thrill of landing the Dutil account, it didn't bring the financial relief I needed.

The consignment order, though exciting, didn't provide immediate payment. In fact, the $15,000 product order would cost me money before generating any profit due to packing and shipping expenses to Canada. The items wouldn't even hit the shelves until the spring of 2020, so any profit would be delayed. It was clear that decisive action was necessary.

I found myself facing a dilemma: either I had to sell the house, or I had to find additional funds and buy some time. In the end, I chose to tackle both challenges head-on. Before the house was even ready to be put on the market, two major issues needed to be addressed.

Firstly, Marilyn had forgotten to turn off the water during the winter, resulting in burst pipes that caused flooding in the basement walls, leading to water seeping through the carpet during the summer. Although I promptly turned off the pipes for repair, the damage had already been done. Mold had taken hold in the basement, creating an unpleasant smell and visible growth when I lifted the carpet. It was clear that the entire basement required a thorough cleaning and renovation.

As if that wasn't enough, I also uncovered a second issue: the jacuzzi in the master bath was leaking water, causing a troublesome bubble to form in the ceiling of the kitchenette directly below. Not only did the tub need to be replaced, but the ceiling also required immediate repair.

My severance pay from the NFL came in right on time to help me complete the repairs and remodeling. The most pressing issue was the mold growing in the basement, so I took care of that first. Fortunately, I had a skilled friend named Ronnie, who owned a deli in town. Ronnie was very good with his hands, and he offered to take on the repairs and renovations by himself. Ronnie removed the mold and redid the floors with a handsome blue-gray tile. Once the basement was complete, we moved upstairs. I did a full remodeling of the master bath, enlarging the shower and completely removing the leaky tub. Fed up with the stains left by Marilyn's Pomeranian, I even went as far as pulling up all the carpet and replacing it with the interlocking tile material that looks like wood. After all was said and done, I was down to my last 30k, which was quickly depleting. I was running out of time, but an opportunity came my way at the last possible moment.

I spent a lot of time with Ka'el and Barron at the pool and the parks in Secaucus that summer. During one of my visits, I had the pleasure of meeting an older gentleman named John. He was always with his grandkids, William and his younger sister Shelby. It was during one of our conversations that John first mentioned the XFL, an intriguing spring football league owned by Vince McMahon and the WWE. Although the league had initially failed after just one season in 2000, it was now making a comeback for the 2020 season. Initially, I brushed off the idea, as I was unable to crawl around on the floor with my kids without experiencing nauseating pain in my wrist. How on earth was I supposed to confidently hold a football again?

But then, I saw old teammates of mine attending the tryouts. There was some press about potential 100k contracts for former NFL players. I was intrigued. It was a far cry from NFL money, but 100k for three months of work would certainly alleviate some of our financial burdens. When I learned that the last tryout of the year would be taking place at Montclair University, which was just a short 20-minute drive from my house, I knew what God was telling me to do. It was time to go back and play some football.

☆ After the Last Snap ☆

AW was developing at its own pace, but it was not the answer to our current financial needs. I knew that there was still a significant amount of time before I even came close to selling an item at a Dutil location. There were more trade shows to attend to pick up more accounts, but I was financially exhausted. I didn't have the means to continue attending those trade shows. Desperately needing the work, I reached out to Roy and explained my circumstances and presented my plan. If anyone was capable of fixing my wrist, it was him.

We arranged to meet at the Retro Fitness in town. It was never very busy (nothing in Secaucus ever was), and fortunately, my young friend Saummy worked at the admission table, so we were able to get in for free. Saummy was intrigued by what Roy was about to demonstrate to me.

In just two short months, Roy guided us through a seven-step advanced upper body program crafted to enhance the strength of the back and upper body, while simultaneously realigning the bones and joints in my shoulders, arms, and wrists. My instructions were to complete each step in order, stacking one on top of the other each day until I failed to complete a step, and by the time I was able to complete all seven steps, my wrist should be properly re-aligned and strong.

The initial step, named "long-handed pushups for 20," required us to place our hands shoulder's width apart while extending them past our heads. This alternative pushup technique creates an obtuse angle at the shoulders and vigorously engages the core and tricep muscles. It was tough but simple and after a few attempts, I triumphantly conquered the challenge on the very same day it was presented.

Step 2 consisted of performing handstands off the wall for a duration of two minutes. The idea behind "off the wall" is to execute the supported handstand position while facing away from the wall. Mustering the courage to flip up onto the wall with a damaged wrist was the first challenge, but enduring the pain in my wrist while holding the handstand for two minutes was the worst. It was incredibly painful. I failed many, many times on this step. It took me well over a week to overcome.

Step 3 was the inverse of step 2, it was the wall-supported handstand facing the wall for another two minutes. Handstands in this position turned out to be comparatively easier. While I still experienced deep throbbing pain in my wrist, it lacked the sharp intensity of the previous stage. Nevertheless, it took about a week to overcome this stage.

Step 4 was the midbody pushup for 20 repetitions. This challenging step required bringing the hands below the chest, towards the belly button. This stage was much less painful than the handstand, so I was grateful. It still proved to be quite difficult because it shifts your point of leverage from the shoulders to the core and lower back, and it becomes necessary to balance more of the body's weight in arms. After a few days, I beat this challenge and I was happy to make it this far.

Moving on to step 5, I had to execute planted pushups for 25 repetitions. The term "planted" indicated that my feet were off the floor, firmly planted on the wall. This position shifted the weight distribution from the floor and the hands to across the entire body since the leverage point for the feet was now vertical instead of horizontal. Consequently, my core was truly put to the test. I spent a lot of time mastering this step.

Step 6 involved finger push-ups for 15 repetitions, which surprisingly became the easiest of the seven steps as I progressed through the program. I managed to conquer this stage on the same day it was introduced. Step 7, the final challenge, consisted of backhand push-ups for 20 reps. It was an excruciating experience, and the pain was more intense than any of the previous steps. I don't recall how long it took to complete step 7, but ultimately, I managed to complete all seven steps in one session. My new objective was to continue performing the exercises until my wrist pain subsided considerably.

The road to recovery was not swift and Roy became concerned about my progress. He was not seeing the results that he expected from the training I completed. I was still in too much pain and although the exercise had squeezed much of the inflammation from my wrist, it wasn't enough. He advised me to get a second opinion of the state of my wrist. There was a sports medicine center that I knew about in Norwood, NJ called PH Institute. Many of the

☆ After the Last Snap ☆

Giants players were familiar with the spot because you could get great medical treatment outside of the normal team offering. I went to them to get a fresh look at my wrist. After some testing and x-ray, Dr. Phillips revealed to me that the bones in my right wrist had been misaligned during the surgery and were now fused at an anatomically incorrect angle. The limited range of motion and the persistent pain were a direct result of this underlying issue. It was not merely a matter of scar tissue and muscle atrophy, but to address those issues, the PH Institute offered an additional service that I gladly took advantage of. It was a minor surgery, much like a kind of liposuction for scar tissue. I put my wrist through two rounds of it before the XFL tryout.

Although regaining complete range of motion might not be immediately attainable, my primary concern was to regain the same strength in my hand necessary for football as in previous seasons. I continued to rep my seven-step AUB routine. The health of my wrist was already far beyond its starting point in terms of strength and flexibility, but I was not without pain. Prior to my training, I would never have imagined being capable of performing a handstand.

To complement my physical training, I partnered with the former Rutgers RB, Savon Huggins, for skills training. At the time of this writing, he is in his 4th year as the RB coach for Boston College. They have a special talent in Savon. His foot drills are next level, and he became a great friend of mine.

The moment of truth arrived with the tryout at Montclair University. The event consisted of the same combine events typically suited for athletes of my caliber. Among the notable attendees was Hakeem Nicks, the New York Giants' first-round pick in 2009. It seemed that, for various reasons, we were all eager to give the game another shot, enticed by the prospect of a brief three-month spring season, and the opportunity for a 100k contract. No matter which way we looked at it, the deal was sweet.

Overall, the tryout was an outstanding success from my perspective. The XFL organized a draft in October, and to my delight, I received a midday call from the Houston Roughnecks informing me that I had been drafted. De'shonia was excited to hear the news. We were returning to her home state, and she would

☆ Andre Williams ☆

have the opportunity to see her family. We prepared for the journey to Texas. Shortly after the draft, representatives from the Roughnecks broke the news to us about the enticing 100k contracts, that it had been nothing more than a ploy. It was disheartening to discover that Vince McMahon's deceptive image on TV was indeed reflective of his business practices.

However, at this point, I didn't mind giving the league a shot anyway. I really needed the money. Collecting $50,000 by mid-spring wasn't life-changing but we didn't need life-changing. We needed to survive and even though I was weary about the condition of my wrist, I was excited to give football another shot. I packed up a small assortment of jeans to ship out ahead of me. I figured I could fashion another photoshoot in my downtime and maybe even sell a few pairs to my new teammates.

I spoke extensively with the RB coach before we flew out to Houston for minicamp. He was a fantastic guy by the name of Wes Suan from Hawaii. He let me know how excited he was to have a player of my caliber joining the team and he would look to me to play a big leadership role on the team. He gave me a bit of background on the head coach, June Jones, a longtime head coach for the Hawaii Rainbow Warriors football team. Many of the coaches he assembled for the Roughnecks had played with him in Hawaii, including Wes Suan. June Jones wasn't just a man of faith, he was a genuinely good man, and his coaches had a lot of love and respect for him. Moreover, he had a solid offensive strategy.

The team utilized a 4 or even 5 wide formation exclusively throughout the game, compelling the defense to forgo their base defense and instead adopt a nickel coverage to avoid being overpowered by slot receivers. Regardless of the play called, the routes for the receivers shifted based on the defense's coverage, and the running back seldom encountered a stacked box to contend with. With the correct players and cohesive understanding among all team members, our strategy was designed to systematically exploit and overwhelm the defense throughout the entire game by creating advantageous matchups.

It became evident that Coach Wes anticipated me to be the starting player once the season commenced, as I was the most well-known RB on the team. I became more and more enthusiastic about

☆ After the Last Snap ☆

returning to football and was determined to seize the opportunity. Joining a talented team in a new city and immersing myself in an environment like the professional football world I was used to was invigorating.

Even still, this time around things were different. Money was a definite concern. Our accommodation for the season was provided by the team in a hotel, and Dee and Ka'el would be there with me. Renting in Houston for the season was out of the question. We had to make the best of the hotel. More importantly, my wrist was still a major issue. I could hold the football, but it wasn't comfortable and it ached at times, sometimes all day. This season was going to be a real challenge.

The minicamp presented a golden chance for the coaching staff to fine-tune the roster, carry out initial assessments, and begin to install the offense and defense. As the camp concluded, they promptly made some preliminary cuts and granted us some time off for the holiday. Determined to make the most of the occasion, we opted to celebrate the holiday in the vibrant state of Texas. Conveniently enough, Dee's father resided in San Antonio, a comfortable driving distance from Houston. Choosing to stay in Texas not only brought us closer to family but also allowed us to save some hard-earned money so that is exactly what we did.

It was customary for Barron to spend part of his holiday in Aspen, Colorado, with his mom and grandparents. This year, the split was the New Year for her and Christmas for me. We left Ka'el with his granddad and cousins in San Antonio, and Dee and I met Marilyn at the Dallas Airport. It was a three-hour drive from San Antonio.

The kids had a great time together. We took them to ITS Pizza, spent time together at the park, and ate good home-cooked meals. I always felt it was important to allow Barron to be still, just be a kid, and to take a break from the constant movement and travel he experiences on the other side with his mom and grandparents. I cherished our time together before the season, knowing it would be a while before I saw him again. More than anything, I just wanted him to know me. When our time was up, Dee and I drove him back to Dallas airport.

☆ Andre Williams ☆

Preseason started in January of 2020. It was time to put the pads on and show the Roughnecks what I really was. We were staying in the heart of the city, at the Marriott Hotel a short walk away from the Galleria Mall. A bus drove the team to the University of Houston every day where we held practice, meetings, and games. The city and the school was a beautiful place to call our home and they loved their new team.

The preseason played out as expected. Maybe I was a little rough around the edges skill-wise but that would work itself out over time. I won my matchups on my athleticism. That part hadn't changed one bit. All my power and strength was still there. My wrist held up surprisingly well. It was always on my mind, but it didn't give me much of an issue in the beginning. All in all, it was an exciting and promising time.

The first exhibition match took place at home against the Dallas Renegades. The play started with an inside zone run to the left, and the blocking was nearly flawless, and I accelerated through the gap for a 50-yard gain. As the game progressed, other running backs had the chance to showcase their skills. By the end of the preseason, I emerged as the clear starter for the Roughnecks, alongside three other talented RBs - James Butler, D'Angelo Henderson, and Marquez Williams. Our quarterback was PJ Walker, a standout from Temple University.

Our season opener on February 8th against the Los Angeles Wildcats was a home game that sold out the stadium, reflecting the enthusiastic support for professional spring football. Despite Vince McMahon's questionable reputation, the XFL had found a winning formula.

We were fortunate to have a fantastic group of coaches, and we were playing real football out there. We started strong against the Wildcats, and everything was going smoothly until PJ threw me the ball early in the second quarter. I was running the wide route on a check down into the right boundary, caught the ball, and turned up the field with the football secured in my right hand. The corner came down to make the tackle, and despite lining him up and lowering my shoulder, he managed to dive under it and take out my legs. I was airborne and landed hard, but I still managed to secure the first down.

☆ After the Last Snap ☆

Under normal circumstances, this hit would have been just a regular part of the game. However, this hit was different because his helmet made direct contact with my right wrist. It was the first time my wrist had taken such an impact since the surgery, and the pain I felt was otherworldly. I jogged off the field, doing my best to conceal the pain, but my wrist was completely incapacitated. It had no strength. I tried to work it back to life, but to no avail. I couldn't understand what was wrong, and the weakness persisted throughout the game.

My coaches were astonished. The offensive coordinator pulled me to the side and inquired if I could at least gather myself to handle pass protection, but deep down, I knew I would only put PJ at risk. I told him I could not. Now they were rotating in RB 2 & 3, but when James Butler scored on a run later in the quarter before the half, they left me alone for the rest of the game. I probably should have done more to protect my wrist before a full game of football, but it was water under the bridge now. I'd lost my seat.

PJ concluded the game with 4 passing touchdowns, while James secured the only rushing touchdown. Our victory came with a score of 37-17. After the game, the medical team conducted some tests, and later in the week, I had x-rays taken. It was determined that there was actually no damage to my wrist, and the pain was attributed to the disruption of scar tissue and nerve shock. We decided that an anti-inflammatory injection in the wrist would be sufficient in alleviating the pain and preventing any swelling. I agreed, received my shot, and promptly returned to work.

I received my first game check a couple of days after the game and was shocked to find out that the state of California was garnishing my wages for unpaid taxes from the 2017 NFL season. I owed them over $9000, and they were taking a significant cut. There'd been nothing left to pay taxes with after that year because of the horrendous $5,000 per month in spousal support. Expenses for supervised parenting time with Barron, flights back and forth to Cali, mortgage and rent, as well as the cost of relentless litigation, left me with nothing at the end of the year. I was furious and I was powerless. My check should have been $5,000 before taxes, but I was not even taking home $3,000. The divorce was officially over, but its aftermath was just beginning to unfold.

☆ Andre Williams ☆

As the season went on, the Roughnecks became unstoppable. PJ was a phenomenon, and our offense was formidable. However, 44 had lost the golden sheen he started the season with, at least in the eyes of the staff. James Butler had become the solid starter at RB, while I held down 2nd place. I continued to work diligently to sharpen my skills and dedicated myself to practicing daeqido to strengthen my wrist, but emotionally, I was bruised. I was glad to have my wife and son there with me in Houston. They gave me a reason to smile.

Chapter 51: Contagion

Bob Marley once famously said, "Every man thinks his burden is the heaviest." I had some heavy burdens of my own and they were getting heavier all the time. But it seemed the world was about to inherit a different kind of weight. This load was viral, and as it crept its way across the ocean towards the United States, President Trump was busy poking fingers at the Chinese, laughing off the threat. We all joined in the laughter, but in the end, the joke was on us.

In the week leading up to our game against the Seattle Sea Dragons, there were whispers and rumors that their starting center had caught something they were calling coronavirus. We shrugged it off. All the information we had suggested that with a 98% survival rate, it was nothing serious. It became a running joke that we were all going to catch the "rona." Seattle flew into Houston that Saturday, virus and all, and we played in another sold-out TDECU Stadium. James and I had developed a great one-two punch. I led the league that week in yards after contact, James had a nose for the end zone, and PJ was playing lights out at QB. No defense could contain our offensive barrage. We took the win.

That was Game 5. We were only halfway through our schedule, but that would be the final game of the season. March 11th, 2020, became the day everything started to shut down. The NBA suspended their league, marking the first domino to fall and signaling the official onset of the coronavirus pandemic in the US. The World Health Organization declared the virus a global pandemic that same afternoon. As large gatherings were banned for safety, our season abruptly ended.

Ironically, most of us were already sick. Ka'el was the first to show symptoms, unusually lethargic and with no appetite, but he bounced back the next day. By Sunday, I had uncontrollable sneezing fits. By Tuesday, I had a runny nose, and by Wednesday, I felt extreme drowsiness, and my nostrils were completely blocked. We got the official word that day—our season was over. I went home and slept through most of the day, and by Thursday, I was feeling better. But the situation across the country was dire. We had to report to the training facility one last time for our exit physicals. On the bus ride there, I noticed one of the defensive backs was noticeably ill, sitting alone, groaning, sneezing, and blowing his nose into a rag. He and several other players got tested for the coronavirus. Amazingly, their tests came back negative. My theory is that they probably had the virus, but the organization decided it was easier to clear everyone and send us home quickly, avoiding any costly responsibilities or liabilities. The league had shut down, and the money had stopped flowing.

Dee fell ill last, and her symptoms were the most severe. She had all my symptoms but also developed lung congestion, making it hard for her to breathe. The novelty of the pandemic combined with the horror show playing out on every news station made Dee's illness a bit frightening, but I had no doubt she would be fine. I wasn't buying into the CNN death toll ticker. This was just a chest cold, not the Ebola virus. But we did our part and quarantined in the hotel for 10 days before heading home. During this time, Houston resembled a ghost town. The larger venues like the Galleria Mall were temporarily closed, but smaller establishments like restaurants tried to remain open and serve the community.

We relied on Grubhub deliveries and trips to the local Jamba Juice for sustenance. Oddly enough, the gig economy didn't stop running. You could still get food delivered and catch a Lyft.

Dee made a full recovery by day 5, and I was grateful to God. I knew we were too young and healthy to be significantly harmed by the virus, but the constant barrage of grim news was nerve-wracking. The death toll counters on each major news station climbed by the hundreds each day. People masked their fear behind literal masks.

Honestly, it didn't make much sense. I remembered watching the movie 'Outbreak' and realizing that a simple paper mask offered little protection against an airborne virus. It seemed futile, especially considering that being in any building for an extended period meant breathing recycled air from outdated ventilation systems—sharing air, mask or no mask. If this was our national response, we were lucky it was only coronavirus.

Returning home meant facing some very big issues. My expenses were overwhelming, and I was drowning in them. The sudden loss of income and previous wage garnishment had prevented me from saving enough to cover even part of the year's expenses. We had just enough for the basics: food and gas. With the world shut down, there seemed to be no prospects for finding alternative income to cover my mortgage and car expenses. The thought was clear—my football days were truly behind me. The whole world was shutting down.

Then there was the matter of Dutil in Canada. My jeans had just hit the shelves at the denim boutique in March, but now the stores were closed. There was no revenue coming in from that in the near term. As hard as I had fought to keep the house and make a way, it was time to sell it. I remembered agreeing to a $65,000 lien on the property to move forward with my divorce. Selling would eliminate some debts, but I wouldn't make much, if anything, from the sale. The situation was grim.

I couldn't believe what was happening. How could I have achieved so much through sports and education, only to find myself on the brink of homelessness? I knew I'd made mistakes, but had destiny truly led me to a dead end? I refused to believe it. I constantly questioned myself:

Was there a path I could have taken to avoid this destructive conflict? I married the wrong person the first time for the wrong reasons, and we handled our relationship badly in the end. I let my anger overpower my common sense. Could I have swallowed my pride and used every bit of charm and wit I had to avoid a spiteful outcome? I was clever enough to do it.

Perhaps the right path was to leave Marilyn and my son behind. What if I had gone to California and never picked up another call from her? What if I had given my all to football to make a fresh start without her? Where would I be now? What would have become of Barron?

No one can say. But I do know that I respected the sanctity of my marriage and never raised a hand to Marilyn. A two-year marriage could have been settled in two months of meaningful litigation. Instead, because I dared to leave a toxic relationship, I was flayed, slice by slice, both financially and emotionally, until I bled out. The Greys had no reason to defame me as a father in court or squander my money. No one acted justly, and we can't predict the outcome of our collective decisions. How will all this impact Barron? Only time will tell. But I do know that you reap what you sow.

Now, what was the path forward through the current darkness? I didn't have all the answers, but I had faith. I wasn't the best Christian at the time, but I believed God created me to prosper and do more for His kingdom. I wasn't living up to God's standard for my life, but that didn't shake my belief that He would take care of us somehow. Despite my shortcomings, I had a good heart, a wonderful wife, and two perfect little boys—blessings of immeasurable worth. Deep down, I knew I had more to give, more to do.

Chapter 52: Valley of the Shadow

It was time to leave Houston, but where could we go? There was no point in heading back to New Jersey now. Losing the house was inevitable. We wouldn't be staying there much longer, and sticking around only meant trouble, especially since I had already decided not to pay my car loan for the month. The clock was ticking before the bank put me on the repossession list, and I didn't want to be around when they came knocking. We were on the run in the coronavirus twilight zone.

The pandemic was a double-edged sword. On one hand, the world shutting down meant that the economy had come to a screeching halt. People weren't making money, small businesses were suffering, and everything seemed to be falling apart. But on the other hand, the economic upheaval led to a complete standstill in financial obligations. Bills, payments, and loans were all postponed as everyone tried to cope. Governments stepped in with stimulus packages and printed money at an unprecedented rate.

So, even though I was facing financial hardship like never before, I found myself in a strange state of limbo. Thanks to government support, I was able to keep my head above water—barely.

When we got back from Houston, I immediately reached out to my father. Despite his separation from my mother, he had been maintaining their house in Schnecksville, PA. Whether driven by fate or necessity, it was time to go back to Pennsylvania.

My dad had concerns about the virus, worried about getting sick. I reassured him that we had all recently recovered and had the antibodies, so he wouldn't be at risk from us. With that settled, we packed our car with the essentials and set off on the hour and twenty-minute drive across state lines to our new home.

☆ Andre Williams ☆

Four years had passed since my parents split up. When my brother Danique had his first son, my mom left for Georgia to help raise him and she never came back. So, my dad had the ranch house on the hill all to himself.

We moved into the "grandparents' suite" in the basement—me, De'shonia, and our one-year-old son Ka'el. It was a far cry from our spacious townhouse in Secaucus, but we were grateful for the security and the support of family. This was our only option, and we were thankful for it.

Honestly, I saw this coming. I knew I didn't have a long-term solution for keeping the house, and I'd already spent too much money during the divorce. The house had become a sinking ship from the day I got injured 3 years ago.

I had finally come to terms with the fact that my football career was over. I accepted it. Football had been slipping away throughout the entire divorce because all I could think about was Barron. I let it slip through my fingers. Above all, I wanted my son to know his father. I achieved that mission, but now I had to figure out my next move.

Short term, our main priority was to get some cash. Even though we were living in my father's house, he wasn't going to pay our bills, and I didn't know how long we'd be allowed to stay. I took the initiative to apply for unemployment benefits. It took some time to navigate the application process, but eventually, we started receiving bi-weekly checks. This assistance ensured we had enough food on the table. Transitioning from a half-million-dollar salary to relying on government aid in just two years was a tough pill to swallow, but it was our reality. There was no room for pride or sorrow.

Fortunately, I had another potential source of income, although it would take time. I could secure a Line of Duty payment from the NFL for the injuries I sustained during my time in the league. It was a form of disability payment, and now that I was definitely done playing, I was eligible to apply. I had tried pursuing this on my own before joining the XFL, but I failed to meet the necessary criteria, even though my wrist was clearly damaged. This time, I sought professional help and hired a law firm called Pro Athlete Consulting (PAC). They offered to file my claim with no upfront cost, in exchange for a percentage of the payment they'd secure for me.

I signed an agreement with PAC, and the work began. Due to the COVID-19 pandemic, doctor visits were impossible to schedule, so it would be many months before I could get evaluated. We had to find a way to survive until then. De'shonia stepped up to support our family during this difficult time. She started working as a patient care technician at St. Luke's Hospital in Bethlehem, PA, fulfilling her dream of working in healthcare. With a pandemic raging, it was probably the worst time to start a healthcare career, but we weren't afraid of COVID-19.

I carefully considered the value of returning to the Lehigh Valley and how it could provide opportunities for moving forward. With a network of people who had followed my journey through high school and the pros, and real friends nearby, I realized I had the potential to leverage my talents, experiences, and assets to create a new path for myself.

I had a unique and highly effective exercise regimen I had never taught to others, and a legitimate denim brand with access to high-end product manufacturing typically reserved for major players in the industry. But these assets were largely undeveloped, and I had yet to establish a formal company. I had options, but it would take work to turn my potential into power again.

Chapter 53: In the Meantime

I thank God every day that He allowed me to find my wife when I did, and that she blessed me with another baby boy. Some might think it was improper for me to dive into family life during such an ugly tussle with Marilyn, but I have no problem with that opinion. I know it was God's mercy that my real wife appeared when she did. It wasn't just mercy on me, but on Marilyn too. I was already in a dark place, and had I been alone, there's a chance one of us wouldn't have survived. That's the honest truth. You can only push a man so far before he cracks, and I know how close I came to that point. So again, I thank God for sending me my wife at the proper time to prevent me from succumbing to despair or worse. Instead of being consumed by bitter despair, I found a balance between the bitter and the sweet. The sweetness was something to focus on, helping me retain my sanity and keep putting one foot in front of the other.

When we relocated to live with my father, Marilyn and I had to figure out a new exchange arrangement for Barron. After some consideration, we decided to meet at a Dunkin' in Morristown, NJ—a halfway point between us. However, on the first occasion that I was supposed to have Barron, Marilyn wasn't available. Luckily, her mother, Cathy Anne, offered to drop him off at my father's house as she happened to be passing through the area on her way to a retreat with Mr. Grey. Less work for me, so I didn't mind.

It seemed Mr. and Mrs. Grey were eager to see the impact of their actions and the repercussions of the divorce on Barron's living situation. They showed up at my father's house, descending the garage steps into the basement. I met them halfway down the hallway leading to our grandparent suite. I stopped them halfway, because if they advanced just ten more yards, they'd be peering

☆ After the Last Snap ☆

into my bedroom—a boundary I wasn't willing to let them cross. Nonetheless, I greeted them with a smile, shook John's hand, and thanked them for the visit. They smiled back, assured me it was no trouble, and left soon after.

At this phase, my main issue wasn't my fall from NFL grace or the loss of financial stability, but the emotional damage I'd endured over the last two years. The scars ran deep. I had been consumed by hatred throughout the spiteful twenty-five months of divorce, and it had profoundly affected my mental state. I became disengaged from the outside world, inactive on social media, and I didn't connect with friends. All I craved was quality time with my wife and kids in peace. While this mindset was appropriate amid the turmoil, it stunted my business growth, especially with the pandemic complicating things. I felt lost and unsure of where to begin.

Denim was on my mind, but how could I move forward? The losses were piling up, and sitting in that basement, I was too dejected to see a way forward with my company. The only two things that brought fulfillment were time with family and working on my body. Diab was definitely family, and he was one of the few willing to work out with me. We started working out together often.

I noticed a huge difference between New Jersey and Pennsylvania. Here, most people didn't seem concerned about the virus. You could walk into places like Target without a mask, and no one would bother you. Socially, the virus was an unseen specter haunting the town, but nobody could catch it in the act. The drama on TV didn't match our reality. According to the news, military ships were docked on each coast to handle the increasing number of sick and dying people in major cities. The death toll was in the tens of thousands. There was talk of a vaccine in progress, but it was deemed "years away," which I found hard to comprehend. Watching 'Outbreak' as a kid, I knew that airborne viruses rendered masks and social distancing useless. At this point, we'd all catch the virus, beat it, or croak. What was really going on?

Regardless, I was consumed by my own issues. I needed to start generating income, but seeking employment wasn't feasible. Even if I found a job, what about the future? At 13, I realized that a traditional 9-5 job would never bring me fulfillment. If football was really over, then it was time to build my own business. I'd already invested $250,000. There was no turning back. I thought about this during my workouts; breathing, sweating, and contemplating my next move. Often, I'd be working out in a pair of jeans. During one of these workouts, clad in my favorite moto jeans, an idea began to sprout. Why should Diab be the only one to benefit from my exercise routine? I was confident I could train others. But I needed a location—a gym. Access to a gym required a certification. Even if I got certified, gyms were "closed" due to virus laws. What if I had my own gym?

My entrepreneurship muscle was twitching. The next time I met up with Diab, I presented the idea. Diab was at the beginning of his real estate journey, continuing to build a remarkable portfolio in the Lehigh Valley that his mother Nawal had begun. I mentioned finding a location for a gym among his properties.

To my surprise, Diab had a suitable space—a four-car garage in Bethlehem that hadn't been rented out yet. He was willing to clean it up and modify it for me. Recognizing that we wouldn't need much equipment to start, he assured me he'd invest the necessary funds if I covered the rent, got a fitness certification, and included him in the profits. I agreed immediately, even though I wasn't sure I could handle the expenses. I was relying on unemployment benefits and uncertain how long they would last. To supplement my income, I applied for the line of duty benefit from the NFL. If approved, it would provide $4500 per month. However, the doctor appointment timeline was uncertain. Nevertheless, I decided to take control of what I could—my actions. I enrolled with NASM to start studying for a personal training certification.

The amusing part was that, besides learning about the fundamental sciences of the body, the personal training certification focused on weightlifting, which was the opposite of how I intended to train my clients. Imagine memorizing a user manual for your job while knowing 65% of it was inapplicable to your work. Despite the irritation, I obtained my CPT in a little over two months, officially becoming a "certified personal trainer." The process was useful. I learned the names of muscles, their divisions, insertion points, and how they collaborate with the skeletal system. I also acquired techniques for designing workout routines tailored to my clients' needs and gained authorization to train in a gym environment, which could prove beneficial.

Around this time, I received an email from my lawyer about my Line of Duty case. An appointment had been set for me to visit a neutral evaluating orthopedic doctor to assess my football injuries. If my rating reached a score of 10, I'd be entitled to 90 months of payments at $4500 per month. I was confident in my case for my wrist and believed I could make a strong case for my shoulder. The doctor's appointment took place in Washington D.C., and I took the opportunity to explore the city, enjoying the electric scooters available for rent.

It was the summer of 2020 when I met my first student. Diab's mom Nawal had a business partner whose son played football. His father was seeking a good trainer for him. When my name was suggested, he was intrigued, and soon after I met Joey, a freshman about to start his first year at Lycoming University on a football scholarship.

Because Joey played running back, I felt a strong urge to propel him towards success in his upcoming season. He was recovering from a Lisfranc injury in his right foot, and he needed to rebuild his leg. He was slightly overweight for his size and position, and his calves had an unsavory jiggle when he walked. He needed a lot of work.

We started with a light workout schedule, three 2-hour sessions per week in a local park. The outdoor environment served as our training battleground. Following the instructions handed down to me by Roy, my esteemed daeqido master, I made a point to bring a large yoga ball to each session, so that Joey could properly stretch his back at the beginning of each workout.

My expertise as a trainer grew with each session and as I honed my skills, I became aware that I was able to decipher the language that Joey's body spoke through movement, color, and coordination. I made crucial adjustments to Joey's training regiment according to his needs and gained a deeper understanding of my own teachings.

Sometimes Joey would hit a wall, where he was unable to do what I instructed. At other times, it was clear that he was ready to move on to more complex movement patterns. I found ways to regress and progress the complexity of the exercises and I made new movements to incorporate more muscles and joints in Joey's kinetic chain. Sometimes I worked out with Joey, sometimes I watched.

One day, while working with Joey in the park, I noticed a woman and her kids observing us intently. After our workout, she approached me with a distinct Spanish accent and asked if I was his trainer. She appeared to be in her 40s. I confirmed, and she expressed interest in hiring me to train her. She asked my rate, and I quoted $25 a session. She was interested and gave me her number, requesting I call her. Her name was Angelice, and just like that, I had a new client.

Having a pretty older lady join my training was a great counter to smelly adolescence. Her goal was to shed some post-baby tummy weight and tone her arms and legs, but she didn't want to "lose her butt." I reassured her that anything lost could be regained, but we needed to break down before rebuilding. She agreed, and we began. She attended faithfully three times a week, and despite her petite frame, she was remarkably strong for her age and size.

Meanwhile, Diab had meticulously cleaned up the garage, creating an impeccable space. He installed AC and heating units, and was working on adding a bathroom and shower, before finishing with paint and tile. The gym was nearly complete, and it looked fantastic.

Diab finished the gym in October 2020, just in time as the cold weather approached, making the park less appealing for workouts. We now had pull-up bars, dip bars, gymnastic rings, warmth, and walls. It was an incredible space, and my brain was working hard on adapting new workouts for the new space. I was having fun.

However, I had a real issue. The gym was built in a residential space, not commercial. Diab and I hadn't discussed this before he started building. I didn't think to ask. Now, there was an issue marketing the space properly. At first, I didn't let it bother me. I knew I had a name and a good product. I just had to open my mouth and build up my clientele.

Paying $800 for rent plus 30% of my revenues wasn't a bad deal, considering I didn't put up a dollar to fit out the space. But $25 per session wasn't sustainable. I wasn't a salesman yet and didn't know how to convey the value of my product. I handicapped myself by selling on price and relied on unemployment to cover rent. I knew I needed to raise prices or market the business discreetly without legal issues. It struck me that I could charge more as I became more confident in my programming skills, but how would I find clients covertly and manage their workout schedules?

I struggled with my secret gym for about a year, continuously striving to attract clients and generate profits. It wasn't always smooth, but I was proud of the transformations I achieved. Joey returned to school and rocked his football season with an impressively shredded physique. Overtime, I did manage to secure more than a handful of clients to my gym. My favorite makeover was a young lady who loved the gym but couldn't complete a single pull-up; in three months, she managed 12 unassisted. I even shocked myself with that one.

Undoubtedly, I had a highly effective product that delivered impressive results, and I learned to program routines for my clients. But my business model was flawed. I'd undervalued my services and lacked a strategic approach to generate leads. My training studio was a secret garage, not a commercial gym; I had legal limitations.

I got good news that November. Dutil contacted me about reopening their stores on a limited schedule. AW was on the shelves in all three stores, and they assured monthly sales reports. This was fantastic news. My brand would debut in its first store, reigniting my fire. My first sales report arrived on December 1st. I opened it to find I had sold just one pair of jeans. It wasn't much, but I was proud.

Despite this small success, my denim business also had major flaws. In my financially weakened state, I couldn't continue frequenting trade shows to acquire more distribution accounts. I relied heavily on Dutil to promote my brand, but their sales associates knew little about the product. I was placing all my eggs in one basket, and there was just one lonely egg.

Chapter 54: Dream Chaser

I cannot overemphasize how crucial Deshonia's support was at this time in our lives. Without her unwavering dedication to maintaining the stability of our home, there would be no dice-rolling of any kind. While I focused on rebuilding our financial foundation and escaping the difficult situation I had led us into, even with both our children, I could pursue my endeavors without worry, knowing De'shonia had everything under control. Moreover, she found part-time employment as a patient care technician at St. Luke's, working nights to generate additional income for us and keep food on the table. I know how blessed I am to have this woman by my side. There is no chance of building a future for your family without a partner who understands the depth and value of your ambitions and believes in your ability to accomplish them.

Now, let's go back to the year 2021. In the months of December and January, I managed to sell my first few pairs of jeans through Dutil. This was a significant achievement for me. However, AW's performance was not impressive to Dutil. The coronavirus pandemic was a black swan event for the retail industry, and Dutil was not spared from its detrimental effects. They were losing confidence in their small consignment deal with a niche American brand; our deal was falling apart.

By spring, Dutil indicated they were ready to terminate the partnership with AW. After five months of activity, my first and only distribution account had failed. I had sold a little more than 10 pairs of jeans.

In a place like Dutil, renowned in Canada for great denim, I couldn't understand why my high-caliber selvedge jeans were having trouble selling to the Canadian denim connoisseur.

☆ After the Last Snap ☆

But then it dawned on me that Dutil's sales associates knew very little about the product. It was undoubtedly hard for them to sell a product they knew nothing about.

On the other hand, I'd spent years merchandising in stores and learning about fabric and product development from Roy. At this point, I knew my jeans were cheap for what they were and I could talk on and on about why that was so. As I was pondering these things, I had a revelation. The only reason I'd pursued a b2b method of selling my jeans in the beginning was because I didn't know enough about what I had or how to sell it. I was content with leaving the selling up to someone else. I was standing on a different footing now after 5 years.

I still didn't understand the psychology of sales, but now I knew intimately the value of my brand. I became convinced that I could sell more AW jeans than anyone else, and it was time to open my own store. Both Roy and I had been collecting and curating content since AW's inception. The previous year, Roy somehow managed to get French Montana to wear a pair of my moto jeans in his music video "straight For the Bag." I followed up with fresh new content captured during my time in Houston with two of my best teammates, Ty Schwab and Nick Holley. I'd even collected professional product shots from Dutil. We had the content necessary to lay a nest on the internet and stay for a while. Losing my distributor account would not be the end of AW; in fact, I was motivated to go harder, keep learning, and build a direct-to-consumer (DTC) business model.

Two major events took place in April 2021. Firstly, a letter was delivered to my father's house by a courier from a New Jersey law firm. They were representing a former teammate of mine from the Giants in a federal lawsuit against me and Roy the Maker seeking repayment of $250,000. Let's refer to this former teammate as Tustin James. Ending the divorce and stepping into a lawsuit was like coming home from war to my wife and kids only to find that some degenerate weasel was trying to break into my house and steal from me my first night back. Tustin James had no idea who he was dealing with. I knew what the court system was. I was a war vet now and as I read into the lawsuit, I saw just how inexperienced Tustin really was. The court was going to devour him.

☆ Andre Williams ☆

His claim stated more or less that Roy the Maker was a fraud, that I knew Roy was a fraud, and that I knowingly defrauded Tustin by encouraging him to invest his money with Roy's company to develop a clothing line that Roy knew would never materialize. Furthermore, the claim stated that Roy and I owned a company together and that squandered Tustin's money for our personal benefit. He was suing us for multiple accounts of fraud & unjust enrichment for the return of the $250,000 he invested.

Tustin was a fool, and he would face an impossible challenge in attempting to prove such an enormous falsehood. Had he opted for a less precise lie, cloaked in ambiguity, perhaps he would have stood a better chance at casting doubt upon my denial of his claim. But instead, Tustin made it easy for me to tell the truth. I would not engage a lawyer; I had no need for one. This male Marilyn monster had mistaken me for prey, but he was wrong and I was prepared for his green attack.

The second significant development came when I received a response from my representatives regarding my Line of Duty application. I amassed a total of 12 points for the sustained injuries to my wrist, shoulder, and fingers, surpassing the required 10 points to qualify. As a result, I would receive a monthly payment of $4,500 for a period of 90 months, with retroactive payments commencing from the date of my application. This equated to a lump sum payment slightly exceeding $32,000.

This was guaranteed basic income and a small bit of freedom to take risks—fantastic news. Of course, there was still a considerable amount of debt to address, but I won't go into detail about that here. The important thing is that I now had options, and paying rent for the gym wouldn't be a problem.

I find myself at a pivotal moment, standing at a crossroads. It was clear that I had a natural talent for training, and a passion for it to match. But the absolute force of my conviction was making its presence felt once again. I knew I would eventually yield to it.

I made the decision to keep the gym open for as long as possible while I worked on my plan to open a store. I was loyal to Diab, and by no means was I intending to abandon the plush training studio he built for me. That was nonsense at this stage of AW's development anyway. But I had a small bit of freedom to take some

☆ After the Last Snap ☆

business risks. I wasn't certain if opening a store was achievable, but I was determined to pursue the possibility. Somewhere in Edison, NJ, there was a warehouse with a half a million dollars in AW jeans sitting on shelves, gathering dust. There was a high climb ahead of me, but I wore hope and faith and took my first steps.

I started searching for potential locations in the Lehigh Valley whenever I had some free time from training my clients. Finding a suitable home for an AW store was crucial. The Lehigh Valley Mall seemed like an obvious choice, but I assumed the rent prices would be high, and I just wasn't ready to ask yet.

Instead, I decided to focus on developing captivating content to sharpen the brand on social media and in the community. I gathered a group of attractive and talented individuals from the area to organize several photo shoots. In total, I successfully conducted three photo shoots across the Lehigh Valley. Two of these shoots took place at the Promenade in Saucon Valley, an outdoor lifestyle mall known for its restaurants, ice cream, and movie theater. Despite being hit hard by the pandemic, with 20 vacant storefronts, it remained an exceptional location for our photo shoots.

After establishing the brand locally through the photoshoots, I gained the confidence to approach the Lehigh Valley Mall. It was owned by the Simon Group, renowned for operating some of the best malls in the country, such as Lennox ATL, Galleria Houston, and South Coast Plaza Sunny Isles. I was pleasantly surprised when two of Simon's leasing agents, Kristen and Allison, reached out to express interest in my brand.

Not only did they offer me a location at the Lehigh Valley Mall, but they also extended an offer for a space at the King of Prussia (KOP) Mall in Philadelphia. The proposals they sent for each location were promising. The Lehigh Valley Mall location, once an old Lady Footlocker, provided a 2000 square feet space at $2500 a month. Meanwhile, the King of Prussia Mall location, a former True Religion store, offered a 2200 square feet space at $4000 a month., The value of my brand had garnered extraordinary opportunity, especially considering that the King of Prussia Mall is the second largest mall on the East Coast, drawing in 20 million visitors annually. The potential for my brand was immense, and yet, despite the incredible opportunities, I found myself feeling apprehensive.

As high as I was on the thrill of opportunity, I realized I had ventured into uncharted territory with a brick-and-mortar store, and even though I was to receive a monthly stipend, my financial situation was still dire. I was still jobless and residing in my father's basement. Either option at the Lehigh Valley Mall would be a high-stakes dice-roll, but I was determined to play my hand. I promised Kristen and Allison that I would provide them with an update soon.

Straightaway, I understood that financing the buildout at KOP Mall was beyond a stretch. I could exhaust every last dollar in my pocket and still fall short, not to mention KOP was over an hour away from my father's house in Schnecksville. Traditional bank financing was out of the question. My $22,000 auto loan with PNC Bank remained in collections, cratering my credit score. I also had other considerable debts to settle with various entities, and now I was embroiled in a federal lawsuit as a defendant for $250,000. I had to navigate the situation with extreme caution.

Chapter 55: Test Everybody

I was required to make monthly payments of $675 for the next 36 months to the lawyer firm that helped me access my Line of Duty money. Because I received a lump sum retroactively from my initial application to the current month, a chunk of that money went to the attorneys. Add to that other financial obligations to various agencies, which required both monthly payments and eventual payoffs, and it was clear I needed more seed money to open the store. I was determined to make it happen.

It had only been a month, but after paying off debts and bills, I had already spent the majority of the $32,000 lump sum. I needed to be strategic with the remaining funds if I wanted to use them to open my store. Clearing my car loan was crucial for improving my credit score and establishing a trustworthy relationship with a bank. In addition, I needed funds for the buildout, which I couldn't count on the bank to front. I needed to find some money.

Roy had taught me many valuable lessons over the years. The importance of setting aside pride and testing everyone was one of them. While I didn't grasp its significance right away, he always said experience was the best teacher. I hadn't realized it then, but "test everybody" was Roy's way of introducing me to the most important lesson for an entrepreneur: salesmanship.

The primary obstacle to opening my store was the $22,000 debt in collections that was dragging down my credit score. I couldn't approach any financial institution with this debt on my record. The problem was the only people I knew who could provide the heavy financial support I needed were also the ones who had hurt me the worst. I knew the Greys could drop five figures without hesitation; I'd just watched them spend six in court.

If I wanted financial assistance from a bank, my first course of action had to be repairing my credit score. I needed money to settle the outstanding balance in collections. $22,000 wouldn't solve all my troubles, but it would open the opportunity to approach potential lenders with a fresh start, free from any visible financial burdens.

I only had one set of people in my network who would consider dropping that much money on my behalf without thinking. I reached out to my one remaining connection with the Grey family that hadn't soured: Cathy-Anne.

Truth be told, Cathy-Anne had made genuine efforts to mediate on behalf of her daughter throughout our relationship. She was fully aware of who I was dealing with and consistently attempted to bring reason to the table during our frequent and irrational arguments.

I was still terribly grieved by the lot of them. The lies they told and the years of abuse I endured to spend time with my son still hurt my heart. But by now, my heart was softening, at least towards Cathy-Anne. I didn't understand what it was that I saw in her at the time, but it appeared to me as remorse. When the divorce concluded, I'd receive pictures of her & Barron regularly, along with gifts and treats around the holidays. In fact, I received more pictures of Barron from her than I did from his own mother.

I could tell that she truly cared about that little boy, and he cared about her too. I couldn't bring myself to maintain a hatred towards someone my son loved, someone who loved my son. The hurt lingered but there was no longer any space for hatred; my heart was healing. De'shonia and Ka'el really were a heavenly heart salve. Regardless of the circumstances we found ourselves in, I was happy with those two around me every day.

Putting emotions aside, I needed money, and the Grey family had it. They were under no obligation to help me, but it was worth a try to test them. Roy's words rung out, test everybody. I would pen Cathy-Anne a handwritten letter. I can't recall the exact words I wrote to her, but I know it was from the heart. Writing it was like passing a kidney stone. There was a painful relief to becoming genuinely vulnerable and forgiving my enemy. It was a turning point for me.

Forgiveness was not an easy road to travel. However, there was one person who bridged the gap between my icy heart and those

☆ After the Last Snap ☆

individuals over there; it was Barron. They loved him, just not in the way that I would love him. But it didn't matter. My role was irreplaceable no matter what they tried.

Barron loved his grandmother, I loved Barron, and if both of those statements were true, then how could I despise who he loved? The Greys were his family too. No amount of ill will could alter that reality. And so, I made the choice to forgive them for the past and open up to Cathy-Anne and the Greys once more.

As I picked up the pen, I leveled my pride, rejected my anger, and I bowed down. I revealed that her warm love for my son had melted my icy heart towards her, and I wanted her to know how much I appreciated it. I told her that I couldn't hold hate for anyone whom my son loved and who obviously loved my son, and that I loved her too. I apologized for everything that had transpired between her and I and our family and expressed that I was sorry for the current state of affairs. It was a painful liberation to let go of it all, like tearing off an old dirty band-aid from a wound that had mostly healed but had yet to be exposed to the air.

After mailing the letter, I awaited a response. A few days later, Cathy-Anne reached out through text, expressing gratitude for my words. It was a small victory, a step forward. I would be picking Barron up soon, and Cathy-Anne informed me she'd be there during the exchange, filling in for Marilyn. I mentioned I had a gift for her and asked for her waist size. She was a size 27. Everything was falling into place. I sent her a pair of the D.K.SHIN moto jeans the following day via priority mail.

When I saw Cathy-Anne in Morristown the next weekend, she looked fantastic in her moto jeans, paired with classy black leather heels, a striped navy blouse, and a sleek leather jacket. The jeans hugged her figure perfectly, and she radiated the chic confidence of a sophisticated woman in her sixties.

Cathy-Anne wasn't just impressed by the style of the jeans; she also fawned over their high quality. Despite knowing that this might be the last time I'd see her wearing them before they were relegated to the old news section of her wardrobe by her stylist, her appreciation was satisfying. Cathay-Anne had more than her fair share of high-end fashion, so her recognition of my brand was everything I was seeking.

☆ Andre Williams ☆

Before parting ways, she mentioned discussing the jeans with Jeff once she returned to Stamford and promised to call me during the upcoming week if I had time to spare.

It was like jumping into a cold pool when I picked up the phone call and heard her voice on the other end. I knew the kind of conversation we were about to have, and I didn't feel ready. But her tone was joyful, and this discussion was necessary.

The conversation veered into the past, though neither of us was ready to delve into the evil we'd wrought against each other. She emphasized that much of the division between us was driven by the lawyers, and the Grey family simply followed their advice to expedite the divorce process. It was a bitter pill to swallow. It was evident she had been heavily invested in the matter, as if she and I were the ones who had been married. Indeed, Cathy-Anne and Jeff had financed the entire campaign. If it had been left solely to Marilyn and me, the divorce would have concluded within a month.

I agreed with Cathy-Anne and disregarded her guilt-ridden excuses because I didn't have the heart to argue, and I needed to stay focused on the task at hand.

I told her I was determined to continue building my denim company from where I left off in 2016, before everything went bad between us. I emphasized that I had invested over $200,000 in the project and was unwilling to simply write it off as a loss. The connections I made to build the brand presented me with the career opportunity of a lifetime, and if I could scale the company, I could recover from the financial setback. I explained, as softly as I could, that the divorce had left me financially exhausted and without the ability to pursue success on the entrepreneurial path. I told her, I had no chance of contributing any meaningful level of financial support to Marilyn and Barron in the near future. I was too torn up. Everything had been exhausted in the divorce. Even my house had been sold at a loss... but the business was still viable because I was sitting on a lot of product. I only needed to clear my credit and align with a bank.

She said she understood that "you can't draw blood from stone" and that I shouldn't worry about financial support for Marilyn and Barron because they were well taken care of. She displayed genuine interest in the project's status and my goals. I disclosed the necessary details about my intention to seek a loan to establish a storefront, requiring assistance in clearing my credit with $22,000. There was a pause.

She assured me she would discuss it with Jeff but believed my request wasn't outrageous. She asked me to write something up, stating what I was looking for, its purpose, and the terms of any potential agreement.

"That won't be a problem," I assured her confidently. I knew I would draft the agreement that same night. My feelings about the situation were mixed because I knew that even if I received this money, $22,000 wouldn't fill the $300,000 hole I had been digging for the past two years. However, I hoped the Greys would help me conquer this short-term business objective. I'd created an opportunity for myself, and the Greys and I had taken a step towards reconciliation.

I prepared an agreement for John and Cathy-Anne to review. I committed to repaying the loan within a year and promised to double the child support I provided to Marilyn once the loan was repaid. I explicitly informed them that the funds would be exclusively used to clear the oppressive collections debt. Alleviating this financial obstacle would enable me to secure a loan to grow my business by investing in a brick-and-mortar location in the Lehigh Valley.

I sent the agreement to Cathy-Anne and awaited her response. My mind was already considering alternative routes if this one was closed. There was no guarantee the Greys would agree to help. A few days later, Cathy-Anne called back. She relayed that after a lengthy discussion, John was willing to assist, under the condition that I wouldn't request further financial help in the future. She explained that lending money to family often led to repeated requests, causing strain on relationships—something they didn't want with me, as Barron's father.

My chest grew hot as beads of sweat formed on my forehead. How much more awkward and uncomfortable could our relationship get? There was a lack of understanding between the Greys and me that was tormenting, but not surprising. John was a socially awkward, intelligent eccentric, and Marilyn inherited her perpetual cringeyness from him. It hurt when John called me family. I couldn't comprehend his definition of the word. In my understanding, family didn't lie, spite, or steal from each other. But that conversation would be forgotten; I was determined to move on.

Cathy-Anne had a personal request too. She asked if I could set aside my differences with Marilyn and establish a relationship like the one she and I had. I told her I would do my best. I acknowledged that Marilyn was her own person, free to care for Barron as she pleased. At the very least, Barron would no longer be a point of contention between us. That seemed to satisfy her.

I assured Cathy-Anne this would be the last time I asked for money. I only needed assistance to clear collections. That would be sufficient to move forward. I explained I had support and a solid plan before everything went wrong, and none of that had changed. She assured me John would write the check and mail it out. I thanked her, and after some more small talk, we hung up.

The check arrived a few days later. I considered if I had asked for too little as I stood staring at the $22,000. It felt like one final game check. There was a time where I could take a game check for granted, knowing another would arrive the following week. Now, I lamented that not a cent of this money would be used for anything other than erasing debt. I wouldn't even be back at square one, just a smaller negative. The money was gone in a week. I fed it to the debt collectors. They devoured it whole, and even swallowed the bones. There was no trace of it.

Chapter 56: Diceroll

It was the summer of 2021, and it was time to make a decision. I was still working at my gym studio, but I knew there was a denim store in my future. I didn't care that I was knee-deep in a federal lawsuit. I didn't care that I was still reeling financially and living with my family in my dad's basement. I didn't even care that we were in a pandemic and people were afraid to breathe each other's air.

Running through the chaos was the only option I could see. I wasn't going to stifle my ambition and back off. I wasn't going to sacrifice my time with my kids, throw away a great business opportunity, and dig my way out of debt with a spoon-sized salary.

Some time after posting the shoot pictures from the Promenade location, I received a message on Facebook from the assistant director at the mall. Her name was Krista, a young and aspiring woman. Without expecting it, she reached out to discuss the possibility of leasing a spot at the Promenade. Until that moment, I had never even considered such an opportunity.

Little did I know, I was about to make my third significant mistake in my business journey. The first mistake was not securing a commercial space for my gym. The second mistake was failing to recognize the immense value of an e-commerce store in the digital age before diving headfirst into brick and mortar. Finally, the third mistake was getting lured into a mall location that already had 20 vacancies.

I expressed my interest to Krista, and she promptly arranged for me to meet the General Manager, the lovely Melissa Napolitano. I met Melissa at her office the following week, and she graciously showed me their available spaces. The mall had a beauty to it in the summertime. As we passed the busy Starbucks at the heart of the mall, I couldn't help but recognize the undeniable allure of an open-air mall setting, especially in the grips of the pandemic. There was potential here if the numbers made sense.

☆ Andre Williams ☆

Melissa took me to a stunning 1500 square foot space that used to be a Journey's shoe store. The interior was beautiful with its studio-like fixtures and natural colors. The backroom had already been perfectly designed with the necessary shelving for my jeans. The floors were adorned with refreshing dark green and burnt orange tiles, creating an invigorating atmosphere, while the sturdy colored plywood walls matched the floor flawlessly and provided an easy mounting surface for anything I needed to hang. The suite was adorned with modern and plentiful light fixtures, making it an ideal setup. I couldn't help but feel inspired.

With anticipation, I asked Melissa about the price of the suite. I was shocked when she informed me that the spot was mine for $1500 per month. I maintained my poker face as I told Melissa that I needed some time to think about it.

That evening, I pondered the possibility of the Promenade. The monthly rent of $1500 seemed manageable, especially considering the minimal buildout required and the perfect storage space in the back. While I knew that the Lehigh Valley Mall was a potentially superior choice, the rent was $1000 more, and the cost intimidated me. I firmly believed that the rent and expenses associated with the buildout would drain me utterly, unless I had some assistance.

It was around this time that an old friend from high school, Sam Pany, reached out to me on Instagram. He didn't play any sports, so we didn't hang out much in high school, but Sam was a businessman like myself. He moved to Florida and started an exotic car rental company. He was extremely smart and already having success with his business. He reached out to ask what I was getting into back home in the Lehigh Valley. I gave him a brief synopsis of where I was with football and with the denim company. He believed in what I was doing. Not only did Sam become one of my first customers, but even more incredibly, Sam became my angel investor. After a few conversations online and over the phone, Sam decided to loan me $14,000 to help with the buildout and setup at the Promenade. A mutual friend of ours, Charles Benedict, visited Sam in Florida, picked up the money, and personally delivered an envelope full of hundred-dollar bills to me in the Lehigh Valley Mall parking lot. Without Sam's help, AW would not have had the seed money for a buildout in the Promenade. Maybe I would have run into the money later, but I would have missed the fall for sure.

I don't recall the exact circumstances, but I established contact with the Small Business Development Center at Lehigh University and met with a man named Darryl Wentz. We discussed my intentions, and he suggested meeting at the Promenade to view the space I was interested in. Our meeting at Starbucks on a Tuesday afternoon was insightful as he elaborated on his role in assisting small businesses in securing funding. We delved into discussions about my business, financing, business plans, and the organization known as the Rising Tide. Ultimately, we proceeded to view the space.

He appreciated the location, nestled among an AMC movie theater, a Red Robin, and a hair salon. Center Valley was known for housing some of the Lehigh Valley's prominent business owners, with the Saucon Valley country club just a 5-minute drive from the mall. It seemed that my price point would resonate well with the area's potential clientele. Darryl suggested setting up a meeting with Chris Hudack from the Rising Tide to explore financing possibilities once I had a solid business plan.

I recognized the immense value in familiarizing myself with the loan-seeking process and appreciated Darryl's guidance through the journey. He sent me a business plan template and told me to make it mine. I had no problem putting it together and Darryl reviewed it once it was completed. He approved it after a couple tweaks before finally setting up a meeting with Chris Hudack from the Rising Tide. I wasn't sure what would come of our meeting, but I was determined to make it happen at the Promenade, regardless. That same night, I emailed Melissa Napolitano expressing my readiness to proceed with the suite at the Promenade. Her joyous response assured me that a lease agreement would be on its way soon.

The proposed deal entailed a short-term lease for 3 months, from August to October, at a rate of $1500 per month. Furthermore, she alerted me that should I choose to continue beyond that period, the months of November and December would be subject to different pricing due to the surge in holiday shopping, coming in at

☆ Andre Williams ☆

$2000 per month. While this was understandable, our immediate focus lay in getting things set up for the grand opening.

She instructed me to begin drafting a floor plan for review and stressed the importance of holding a pre-build meeting with my contractor. Additionally, she advised me to prioritize the creation of my storefront sign, as it would likely take the longest to construct. Suddenly, a laundry list of tasks demanded my attention. The initial excitement of approval quickly transformed into apprehension about impending workloads, deadlines, and the unknown.

We met with Chris Hudack at Starbucks in the Promenade the following week to discuss my venture. Chris was unfamiliar with "selvedge" denim, which was not uncommon. He explained that the Rising Tide was a financial institution that provided loans to businesses in the startup phase, particularly those in underserved communities.

We discussed my plan to open a store at the Promenade and my vision for the business over the next five years. I had the impression that he was verifying that the plan I had given him on paper lined up with what I was telling him. Afterward, we visited the location, and he inspected it before nodding and agreeing that we could proceed with the application for a small loan of $25,000. There would be a variety of new documents to submit along with the business plan. They would require basic financial records for the business, a credit check, and the last few years of tax returns. Darryl assisted me in preparing my first balance sheet.

One of my recent gym clients was a heavy-set chef named Mark Hussett. He was around my age, and although we didn't go to school together, he was good friends with my schoolmate, Matt Eck. During a workout, I mentioned to Mark that I was preparing for a small buildout for my new store in the Promenade, and he recommended Matt, who worked under his uncle's contracting firm. I believed he would be a suitable choice for the job, especially because the main requirements for the store buildout were changing rooms. Besides that, there were only a few other aesthetic changes to complete my setup.

When it came to my storefront sign, printing, and merchandising needs, I knew exactly who to turn to. I had a contact

☆ After the Last Snap ☆

in my network named Ray Rabeh, who owned a printing shop in Allentown, called Project Printed. He was married to another former Parkland classmate of mine, Melanie. He'd become a friend of mine, and he was the clear choice for the task.

The most difficult task on my agenda would be retrieving my inventory from the warehouse in Edison, NJ, owned by a man named David. I knew David through Roy, and they had a history of conducting business together. Owing to the various challenges I was facing at the time, I had fallen behind on the storage fee at the warehouse. Reclaiming my merchandise would require a difficult conversation with David, as well as coming up with the cash I owed him.

As far as I knew, the outstanding bill amounted to just under $8,000. When I arrived at the warehouse, I brought $2000 in cash with me and handed it to David in his office. Seated at his long conference table, I shared with him where I had been for the past four years. He listened with understanding eyes, then proceeded to recount his own painful divorce story. It was evident that his experience had been more challenging, as he and his wife had shared many years together before parting ways. Their children were now grown up, and despite the difficulties, David had managed to move forward. He now had a thriving business, a positive relationship with his children, and was in the process of constructing a retirement home in Belize.

In the end, he agreed to let me take 65% of my goods from the warehouse, while holding the remainder until I returned with the rest of the money. Truly, I found this to be a fair and reasonable arrangement, and I expressed my gratitude. I proceeded to box up my inventory in preparation for the next move, knowing that a large truck would be necessary. Although my inventory was relatively small, it still consisted of well over 3000 units of jeans and a few hundred pairs of shoes, totaling over 70 boxes that needed to be transported.

Amidst all this preparation, the court case with Tustin James was unfolding. It became apparent that his legal representation was far from satisfactory, relying on delay tactics at every filing deadline. It was a tactic I had seen before—delays intended to cause frustration and financial exhaustion. However, I was not

☆ Andre Williams ☆

deterred, as I had chosen not to hire an attorney. My most significant expense was the time I spent getting papers printed at FedEx.

I responded to their complaint promptly, refuting every allegation. It was not difficult for me once I discerned the proper format for my reply. I confided in Diab's mom, Nawal about the situation, and she connected me with her attorney friend in town, who coincidentally happened to be Alana's father, the girl who had informed Ayla about my graduation party hookup in high school. He advised me to get a lawyer to fight the case, but I declined, expressing my only need for proper documentation format to file a reply. After guiding me through the initial steps, he wished me good luck.

Following the filing of the paperwork, Tustin's attorney reached out by email, requesting a phone call. Though I saw no reason to engage, I was intrigued to learn more about their overall strategy. Ultimately, we did speak on the phone, during which he repeatedly inquired about Roy's whereabouts.

I informed him that I had no knowledge of Roy's whereabouts. He attempted to convey that my problems could disappear if I assisted in locating their real target, as they had been unsuccessful in contacting Roy to serve the lawsuit. I maintained that it was not my concern. The phone conversation provided insight; although I was being sued, I realized that they were merely using me to reach Roy. They had targeted the wrong person. I had no intention of aiding them in ensnaring Roy in a legal mess because Tustin was deceitful, and it brought me satisfaction to watch him squander his resources pursuing a futile endeavor. Furthermore, there was no advantage for me if Roy became embroiled in a lawsuit. I was prepared to face Tustin on my own.

Eventually, we had a phone conference with the judge presiding over our case. At that point, the complaint had only been delivered to two out of the three defendants in the case: myself and Roy's company, Shenzhen Designs & Co. Tustin was unable to locate Roy but filed for a default judgment on Shenzhen Designs & Co. since they had managed to serve his company with the lawsuit. The judge wisely chose not to grant the default judgment, as it would open the door for an opportunity to seek double or triple judgment

☆ After the Last Snap ☆

awards against each defendant for Tustin and his team. Instead, the judge decided to initiate the discovery phase between Tustin and me. He set a deadline for its completion three months from the date of initiation of discovery. Furthermore, the judge granted them additional time to locate Roy and serve him with the lawsuit. With these actions, the foundation for our case was solidified.

As the summer of 2021 progressed, I found myself juggling multiple responsibilities, from preparing my store buildout to navigating the federal lawsuit. Despite the challenges, I felt a renewed sense of purpose and determination. Running through the chaos was my only option, and I was ready to roll the dice.

Chapter 57: Grand Opening

We missed our original opening date in August, but by late September, I finally managed to pull it all together. The official opening day was the 23rd. I joined the chamber of commerce and organized a Grand Opening ceremony. We had a ribbon-cutting, took photographs, and made our first sales. Thankfully, Rising Tide approved the $25,000 loan after we opened the store, providing AW with a positive opening balance and cash-on-hand to help with day-to-day expenses.

To my surprise, I generated $2,200 in sales during that last week of September. It was an exciting start to my brick-and-mortar experience. "The Morning Call," our local newspaper, published an engaging story about the opening of my store in the Promenade, which created a good buzz and attracted some early business.

None of it would have been possible without the support of my friend Dan Wynn and my two younger brothers, Tyler and Justice. They helped me transport and unpack over 70 boxes of jeans and shoes from the warehouse. In fact, I decided to hire Tyler as an employee. He was very personable and having him there brought a lighthearted atmosphere to the store. However, Tyler wasn't the best employee, and I ended up spending way too much money keeping him on payroll. A little under $6,000 from the Rising Tide loan went to payroll expenses.

Once I opened up the store and started spending eight hours a day outside the house, six days a week, family dynamics at home changed. Dee was happy for me and supported every move I made, but she had her gripes. The long hours were taking a toll on her, and she was disappointed that I had made a swift decision to invest in the Promenade without considering other possibilities. From my perspective, the only avenue towards possibility was business. We had a denim store in the Promenade, and I had $500,000 worth of

☆ After the Last Snap ☆

inventory in the stockroom. All I had to do was learn and apply an effective marketing strategy and sharpen my salesmanship, and we could earn it all back.

At the end of the day, during my two-year stint in brick-and-mortar, Dee managed her responsibilities at home without causing me any trouble. She truly is my perfect partner, and I owe her a lot.

In our first full month open, AW pulled in over $4,000. It was better than nothing, but it was a stale finish when half of the money made in the month came within the first 10 days. I began to notice things about the mall as the long days went by. For example, the foot traffic was below par. I wondered how long it would take to establish a consistent flow of customers. The first couple of utility bills came as a shock, totaling over $400 for light and gas heat combined. It became clear that I needed to generate more income to make a profit after paying rent and bills.

What made matters even more difficult was that 3 out of 5 customers who walked into the store were women, and I had very little for the plain ladies of Saucon Valley, Pennsylvania. I knew that my revenue potential was limited as long as I carried only men's styles in basic washes, but women desired my product: high-quality jeans in an athletic fit. That much was certain.

I redirected 50% of sales towards an R&D project to develop a ladies' athletic fit. I can't say exactly how we achieved it, but the project eventually produced incredible results. The Chinese R&D team traveled to England to fit and measure the English Women's Volleyball team. It took many measurements on numerous women and fit models to bring it all together, but those athletic bodies served as the foundation for the AW Ladies athletic fit. As of the time of this writing, I have yet to produce a pair of jeans from this development, and I hope that will change in the near future.

Chapter 58: NFL on FOX

November arrived, and it was time to renew the lease for the upcoming holiday months. The rent price jumped to $2,000. Although that was a notable rise, I remained undeterred. I had a strong feeling that things would continue to progress positively, and indeed they did. In November, we saw an increase in revenue, hitting $6,000 for the month, demonstrating consistent improvement. But the most exciting development came in the form of an email from Sara Strauss, a representative from Fox Sports. She extended a partnership opportunity for an in-store commercial feature with QuickBooks during the NFC Championship game.

Sara informed me that, as part of their contract with QuickBooks, NFL on FOX produces a commercial annually to be shown during the pregame show. This commercial serves to highlight how QuickBooks contributes to the success of small businesses. They actively seek out businesses with connections to the NFL, and a committee votes to determine which small business they will partner with. To my astonishment, AW was chosen by unanimous decision. I was absolutely stunned that my business had gained enough visibility to be selected for a commercial alongside QuickBooks. While being a former NFL player certainly played a significant role, I felt a heavy sense of responsibility to present my brand honorably, because this opportunity would expose AW to millions of consumers. They wouldn't have chosen me if my product and brand story weren't strong enough. I felt very proud.

The filming took place in early December. The production crew arrived first to undertake prospecting and logistical work. The director, a man named Paul Canney from Massachusetts, was accompanied by his right-hand man, John South. I had the opportunity to meet and guide them around the property. Additionally, I connected them with Melissa Napolitano to initiate the necessary insurance and liability arrangements.

☆ After the Last Snap ☆

Paul concluded that they would need to rent the vacant suite next door to accommodate the equipment, sound studio, and makeup room. After spending a few hours exploring the mall and engaging in discussions, Paul expressed his gratitude for my hospitality. He assured me he would be in touch within a couple of days to further discuss the storyline he had in mind and any additional requirements.

I was incredibly excited about what I thought would come next. I was certain that this commercial marked the beginning of a new era for my brand, propelling it to new heights. Despite some lament about the limited reach of a "spot" advertisement, given that it would only air once during the game night, I was confident in its potential to reach millions of people. Regardless, this was a pivotal moment for my brand.

Paul promptly responded to my email with a vision that left me inspired. He proposed using selvedge denim to craft a collage showcasing an NFC Championship trophy plaque. The visual would depict me overseeing the store, guiding my staff, and assembling the plaque with scraps of denim. Ultimately, I would complete the plaque and proudly display it in the store window.

He asked if I felt confident in recruiting actors to play customers and staff. He also inquired how I might assist in creating the necessary props. Our goal was to effectively showcase NFL on FOX and QuickBooks through our artwork, my business, and the script. I felt up to the job and knew exactly who to contact for the necessary talent. Just a month earlier, I had met two incredibly talented local artists, Dilean and Kyle. Dilean had a business customizing shoes for NFL players and local sports teams. We had previously collaborated to paint a few Runningman shoes that I showcased in the store. Meanwhile, Kyle, married to a business owner named Gabby, had recently joined the Promenade as well. Gabby owned a lash studio business just three doors down from mine. Kyle was known for creating stunning murals for various businesses across the Lehigh Valley. Although crafting a denim collage was a departure from his usual work, I knew Kyle was more than capable. When I approached him, he was genuinely honored by the opportunity, and Dilean shared the same enthusiasm.

☆ Andre Williams ☆

Hiring staff and customers for the commercial was a breeze. I already had a dedicated group of local photographers and models that I could rely on for content creation, and I knew they would be more than enthusiastic to be part of this production.

Finally, Paul asked if I would consider doing the voiceover for the commercial. He believed it would add an authentic and natural touch to the advertisement if I lent my voice to it. Without hesitation, I agreed, and we immediately began working on crafting a masterpiece. It took us two weeks to prepare and shoot the commercial, commencing filming promptly at 7 am on December 14, 2021, and concluding around 8 pm. The entire process went flawlessly, save for one minor hiccup. My main model, Victoria, tested positive for COVID-19 that morning, requiring that she be sent home, so we had to call a backup. Still, the rest of the day proceeded without a hitch.

Dilean and Kyle both arrived for the filming. Dilean's task was to replicate the QuickBooks logo and apply it onto the Runningman shoe. Although he wished for a more creative opportunity, he was immensely proud to have his work showcased in a commercial. Kyle's job was more challenging as he crafted a denim collage featuring the NFC Championship logo on a plaque, using various selvedge denim fabrics at his disposal. I had over 150 swatches of Japanese fabrics from eight of Japan's top mills. The result was truly incredible and surpassed all expectations. Kyle revealed to me how precise and creative his vision was, and he continues to amaze me with the art he is putting up all over town.

The artists and models were all compensated, and I was gratified to have had such a significant role in bringing forth a professional production and getting everyone paid. Fox reps and the production team even purchased some jeans before departing, which added an extra blessing to the experience. Now, all that remained was to conclude the holiday season and wait for my commercial to air.

Chapter 59: Digital Demons & the Angel of Death

The week before Christmas of 2021, I had a life-altering experience. I was visited by an angel of death, and he nearly took my life. Let me tell you how we met.

I had kept a disciplined exercise routine that year. My goal was to complete 100 push-ups and 50 pull-ups a day. By December, I had accumulated thousands of pull-ups and tens of thousands of push-ups. Though I hadn't played any sports in more than a year, physically, I was still in great shape. But emotionally and spiritually, I was reaching a rebellious peak.

For years, I struggled with my worst vices. At the age of 9, I began grappling with pornography. My first exposure to sexually explicit content was while channel surfing late one night; Cinemax had suddenly transformed into Skinemax. I knew I wasn't supposed to see what I was seeing. It was frightening yet exciting because the response that sexual content elicited from my body was new and pleasurable. I was curious.

As I grew older, curiosity became habit. Interestingly, my first experience with masturbation wasn't a response to pornography but was accidental. I was just a boy, putting lotion on my skin after a shower when I discovered the delight of rubbing the lotion onto my genitals. The pleasure increased as I continued, and after a bout of vigorous strokes, my ejaculate unexpectedly shot across the room. I was shocked, but it clicked—I realized why they put sex on TV.

Decades later, my habit evolved into a kinky fetish, with squirt porn being my genre of choice due to my first real sexual encounter. I knew early on that pornography and masturbation were bad for me. There were multiple incidents in my life that served as clear evidence. In high school, when I couldn't perform for Ayla, she was disappointed and I was embarrassed. It was easy to confess that my fixation on porn was the reason behind my impotence, and I promised her that I would quit. She forgave me, and we moved forward, but I failed to keep my word. Instead, I became more strategic in finding opportunities to engage in self-harm. I had opportunities to learn and do better in each phase of my life, even in my marriage, but pornography was an addiction I could not kick. I would tell myself it would be the last time, but eventually, I always found myself coming back.

As time went on, I began to recognize that it was not only detrimental to my body but also to my mind and spirit. There was one night in college when the compulsion to lust arrested me as I lay in bed. I pulled out my phone and gave in to it. Video after video, my polluted mind fed on the dirty images until I was left with filthy hands. I disregarded the fact that I shared a room with my teammate, who was only three feet away in the top bunk. I convinced myself that I could be completely discreet. No one else was there with me and my pleasure pixels. After I was done, I "cleaned myself up" and drifted off to sleep.

Sleep brought me a nightmare. In my dream, I met a beautiful woman in a red dress as I crossed the street. I knew her because I'd seen her on the internet wearing less clothing. It was fine at first when she began following me around the BC campus. But something was wrong. When anyone came close, her dress would open up like a gaping mouth lined with rows of pointed, bloody teeth. She consumed everyone who came near me and afterward, her dress closed up, and she smiled and stared at me like nothing had happened. She ate my friends and my family, and I couldn't run from her.

This dream was no coincidence, I knew it had deep significance. God was exposing the insidious grip that pornography and masturbation had on me as demonic. The lady in the scarlet gown was a digital demon, and each time I fell into her temptation, when I gave her my eyes and spilled my seed for her, I was committing spiritual adultery with a succubus. I was using my body to worship a digital demon and if I didn't escape her, she would be responsible for the death of all my relationships with people close to me.

I received this warning from God in 2013, and here I was in 2021, still unable to break free from her grip. Pornography wasn't my only vice; I was also a chronic marijuana smoker. Manning the AW storefront got in the way of my habit. If I wanted to smoke, I had to leave the store, but I wasn't willing to miss a sale for a smoke break. I couldn't afford that, so I acquired a vaporizer pen with a delta-8 cartridge, an alternative THC compound. They were readily available anywhere, even the local gas station.

Delta-8 was a poor substitute but served throughout the day. I first discovered it at a local festival called Cannabis-Fest. It was almost odorless, legal, and my first experience with it was pleasant, but by now, you can see I had become very undisciplined, resorting to "temporary fixes" from the gas station. I was caught up in a disgusting habit that ultimately led to hard consequences.

During this same time frame, I stumbled into a salacious app called Reddit. It intrigued me because it had a feature that allowed me to download and store explicit videos onto a hidden folder inside my version of the app. I opened a dark new door with this discovery. I had never really considered keeping any of the explicit content I viewed, because I'd always felt shame after the act of masturbation, and I didn't want to find myself in a situation where my habit could be discovered…"but no one would ever discover my secret reddit folder," I pondered. "But what about my wife? Was this really okay?"

The lady in the red dress responded, "The folder is safe. She doesn't need to find out about us. You don't want to break her heart. She is so good to you and doesn't deserve that kind of mistreatment. Aren't you afraid you could ruin your marriage?" There was a she-devil living in my head, a succubus. I was in a full-blown relationship her and she was convincing me to continue our relationship and take the next step in my unfaithfulness. The woman on the screen was the lady in the red dress, and the lady in the red dress spoke to me in my mind. She was more than a dream now. She was very real and there I was, talking to her and having virtual phone sex with her naked body.

☆ Andre Williams ☆

Reddit's secret folder became her throne. I sat the woman in the red dress on it and stored her away for myself. Every so often, I succumbed to her soft temptatious words and snuck off to visit her throne to meet the lady in the red dress and give the queen my love. She always graced me with her smile or her open mouth and bared herself for my gaze. Allured by her beauty, I worshiped her once more. Afterwards, I stored her away in my secret Reddit folder, knowingly admitting that I would see her again. The lady in the red dress ceased to be a mere fantasy; she became a secret idol that I carried in my pocket. I had become careless. It nearly cost me my life.

A week before Christmas I was by myself in the back of the store, indulging in a few pulls of a strawberry-flavored vape before opening for the morning. A few days prior, I had noticed some fuzzy residue in the pull-hole of my vape. It looked like cotton fibers from my pocket or webbing of some sort. I cleaned it out and continued using it. Soon after, I developed slight chest congestion and a persistent cough, not uncommon for me in the fall, but what caught my attention was the tinge of pink in my phlegm, indicating blood. It was alarming, and I lost an appetite for the vape pen after that.

I returned to the front of the store, enduring a strangely quiet day, which was a blessing because I felt my energy leaving with each passing hour. Now my body was getting cold, and neither my jacket nor the heater was helping. A frigid coldness permeated my body, making me extremely uneasy, not to mention the persistent presence of bloody phlegm.

Finally, a man in a sophisticated peacoat, glasses, and polished Chelsea boots stepped into the store. I immediately recognized him as a potential customer, but my deteriorating health took its toll; I was barely capable of engaging in conversation. Regrettably, the man left without purchasing jeans. I had no power to persuade him. It was then I decided to wrap up my day and head home; there was no doubt that I was very sick.

By that time, I had already let go of Tyler. He refused to appear in my commercial because his girlfriend had issues with one of my models, and Tyler chose to decline the role to spare her feelings. It was a noble gesture, but it was clear he wasn't the right employee for AW. If he couldn't create content, then I was tired of paying for subpar work. I would temporarily close the store until I could recover, even if it meant missing out on the holiday sales.

There were more pressing matters at hand now. I had a serious lung infection, and I was coughing up a mixture of mucus and blood. In addition, I found that I had completely lost my appetite and was experiencing terrible fever spikes every few hours. This was also during the same period when the highly contagious omicron strain of the coronavirus was spreading. I was convinced that I had contracted it, but given that I'd already contracted it before, I was more concerned about the lung infection. I simply hoped that whatever I was going through would pass soon.

I had Barron with me, and I did my best to keep it together, and do my part around the house, but each day worsened. The bloody phlegm continued, the fevers never left, and my appetite wouldn't return. It had been about four days since I left work and I was hurting badly.

I turned to what I knew, honey garlic, an authentic Jamaican cough medicine, but I could hardly manage to swallow a full teaspoon. Instead, I mixed it with hot water and sipped on it throughout the day, taking ibuprofen to battle the fevers. It was the best course of action I could take because there was no way I was going to the hospital.

By the sixth day, it was evident I was losing weight rapidly. My chest ached, my body felt weak, and my energy was at an all-time low. I had never experienced such prolonged sickness before.

The stories circulating at the time about seemingly healthy individuals succumbing to the coronavirus and passing away weighed heavily on my mind. I couldn't help but wonder if I would become one of those statistics. "Unvaccinated former NFL running back dies from coronavirus at age 29." Morbid thoughts had infiltrated my mind.

On the 9th day, there was no change to my health. I was in a terrible state but didn't want to burden De'shonia with the severity of my condition. I didn't want her to worry, especially with the children around. What would she do if I told her I needed to see a doctor? How could she handle it? On the other hand, I hadn't managed to eat anything, not even a single pancake. How much longer could I endure like this? I was questioning myself and I was questioning God too. Was it truly my time to leave this Earth?

Can I make it more clear how terribly sick I was? On an ordinary day, if I was traveling with my family and we encountered a threat to public safety, there is no question in my mind that I would be the person to deal with the threat, because no one is going to compromise the safety of my family if I can help it. I could do so without fear because I know in my bones that it's not my time to die. But now, on the ninth day of sickness, that sense of immortality had abandoned me. I was mortally feeble, and I knew death was closing in. Then, a thought struck me. I lacked the desire for food, smoke, or pornography. Yet, I remembered the woman in the red dress hidden away on her secret throne. Fear gripped me. *Was she the cause of my current condition?* My spirit man posed a question: *If we were to die today, would the woman in the red dress accompany us to the gates of heaven?* Finally, the shame of my behavior returned. The woman in the red dress would not take me up to heaven's gates if we died today. She would be waiting in the depths of hell.

I knew I needed to repent immediately. I went to the bathroom and deleted the Reddit app with the secret folder, vowing never to return. On my knees, head bowed on the toilet, I prayed to God for forgiveness, acknowledging the throne, a disgusting mark of rebellion I'd carried openly before Him. I beseeched God to heal me and spare my life despite my unworthiness.

Day 10 began like the previous nine, but the ending was strikingly different. The clock struck 7 pm, and once again, I felt the fever creeping back. As my body began fighting again, I decided the best plan of action was to bundle up and sleep it off. It was easy to doze off when I hadn't eaten in over a week, and it was a much nicer option than fighting the fever awake. However, as I turned my gaze towards my bed, a peculiar sight caught my attention. There, in the center of the bed, appeared to be a large, mysterious indentation, as if an invisible presence rested there. I was so ready to run from my fever that I didn't care. Nothing would keep me from laying down. I climbed into bed, closed my eyes, and entered another realm. I dreamt about my end.

☆ After the Last Snap ☆

It was silent and very dark as I drifted down toward the center of the dark room. There, someone stood in a hooded cloak. His entire body gave off light. He was the only light in the room. As I approached, the figure became clear. The man was enormous, looming over me, wielding a massive sickle in his left hand. I couldn't see his face, but I knew he was staring at me. I was frozen with terror, unable to move or speak. I knew that this being looking down on me was Death.

Death raised his sickle, and with great force, brought it crashing down on me; I heard it sing through the air. I felt the impact of the blade shattering against my neck. The blade fragments shone against the darkness like pieces of the moon. My heart raced wildly as the death angel lowered his weapon and spoke. "It's better for you to die than to corrupt your family by showing them your lack of self-discipline," he said. "Your relationship with your wife is your relationship with God. There is no distinction between the two - that is the marriage covenant." Finally, he cautioned, "Marijuana is a flower." With that, the figure took a step back and vanished into the darkness.

There was something terribly wrong when I woke up. I didn't feel right at all. I sat up slowly. Dee was seated across the bed, speaking to me, but her words sounded muffled. I couldn't make out anything she said. I looked up to see her face and realized I couldn't; my eyesight was clouded. I was in bad shape. I thought, *if I pass out, the hospital is the next step, and I might not even make it there.* As I tried to steady myself, I braced the edge of the bed and closed my eyes, breathing deep, slow breaths.

My spirit man urged me to take off my hoodie. I obeyed, and as I removed it, my body began to sweat profusely. Within two minutes, I sat in a puddle but had finally broken the fever. I felt better. My vision and hearing returned, and the crisis was averted.

On the 11th day, there were no more fevers, and I began to recover. By the 12th day, my appetite returned. On the 13th day, there was no more bloody phlegm. I was cured. God saw fit to spare my life.

I was still too shaken to articulate what I had witnessed and endured to De'shonia, but I vowed to myself that I would eventually confess the truth to her. For many weeks, I sat alone in the store, writing about Christmas of 2021, playing it over and over in my mind, talking with my spirit man about its implications. I had truly met an angel of death, and he was ready to take my life. I almost died in my own bed, right in front of my family.

It was all because I chose to walk around in open rebellion, hosting a secret relationship with a digital demon, carrying her like a mark of death in my pocket. I was sure that had I not repented and gotten rid of her the day before, the sickle would've made a clean cut. I came that close, only 24 hours away from death.

Finally, everything the angel of death told me was astounding, including the message about marijuana. (My spirit man would have more to say about that subject later.) But what he said about my marriage and the value of my life compared to my family's well-being moved me deeply. I believed that angels had no issue speaking to us in a manner we could understand, but it was still a complete surprise to hear the death angel speak to me so directly.

Regardless of anything the death angel told me, one thing was for certain; the lady in the red dress and I were done. I had been truly frightened. To this day, I run from her shadow because I know that death follows her.

Chapter 60: Famine

2021 ended, and we entered the new year with great hope for 2022. AW fell just short of $10,000 in December. Had I not fallen sick, I know we would have surpassed the 10k mark, so I was optimistic about my brand and its ability to scale.

The commercial was a major win for All Weather Selvedge, but the expected financial windfall didn't materialize. Less than a handful of sales came in online. Upon reflection, it's clear that our weak online presence was to blame. How did I expect to benefit from a national commercial with such a weak digital strategy? At that time, I had yet to grasp the distinction between sales and marketing. I thought that just being open in the mall could be enough to grow. Merely listing the product on a website was not enough—the site lacked optimization for conversions and failed to effectively convey the essence of the brand. Furthermore, I wasn't using paid ads to drive traffic. I did not employ any lead generation strategies to build my email list, nor was I aware of how to nurture customer journeys in an email list. Finally, I was not knowledgeable about how to use social media to build a following and generate sales. I knew that ultimately, a comprehensive digital strategy was needed to drive the business forward. My storefront's ability to attract good marketing material would go to waste without one.

As a result, January arrived, and I faced the predictable decline in sales that accompanies the season. However, the reality turned out to be far worse than I had anticipated, and this downward trend persisted throughout the spring. Not a single month after April saw me earn more than $3,000, with every subsequent month resulting in losses as I had to cover the rent out of my own pocket.

In truth, there was no one to hold accountable but myself. I was utterly unprepared, having failed to devise a strategy to counteract the expected decrease in foot traffic. I had neglected to formulate a plan for online growth or attracting new customers to the store.

☆ Andre Williams ☆

Naively, I had relied solely on word-of-mouth promotion, and this misguided expectation led me astray. Most days, The Promenade was a dead zone. I couldn't expect any other outcome when the mall had 20 vacant storefronts.

Of course, I didn't quit. I decided to conduct an experiment of my own. To attract attention, I placed a noticeable sign in front of my establishment, offering a chance to win a free pair of jeans in exchange for scoring a hole-in-one on my mini-golf game. As a result, I began to witness an occasional influx of enthusiastic players. Occasional victories occurred, prompting a few fortunate individuals to claim their well-deserved prizes. This led to a small number of successful sales, accompanied by some satisfied customers who returned with friends to engage in friendly competition. However, in hindsight, I must admit that I failed to fully comprehend the significance of gathering contact information, such as emails or phone numbers. Had I been more astute, I could have capitalized on this captured traffic and converted it into profitable opportunities.

I invested the last $4,000 from my Rising Tide loan in billboard advertising. However, despite a whole month of promotion, the return was disappointing: I could only directly attribute one sale to the billboard. Shifting my approach, I leveraged the power of local media, securing coverage in Lehigh Valley Style and a feature on a regional PBS production called "Lehigh Valley Rising." This experience allowed me to connect with Larry Holmes and establish a lasting friendship with him and his family. Despite these efforts, the impact on sales was minimal.

However, the most exciting opportunity of the year came from Rich Mar Florist, owned by two passionate sports fans, Rick and Jon Morrissey. My local PR connection asked if I had any interest in attending NASCAR in the Poconos with a client of hers named Jon. Jon, a NASCAR enthusiast, proposed co-branding a car with our business logos and attending the races in the Poconos together. My answer was heck yes. What a genius move on his part. How could I refuse such an opportunity?

The Friday before the race, Jon set up a meet and greet at the Lehigh Valley Grand Prix, where we raced around the track in go-karts with two of the pro racers he sponsored, Jon's family, and

☆ After the Last Snap ☆

some of his close friends. We met later that day at his house for a poolside barbecue. The following day, we met in the Poconos and viewed the race from the DGM Racing pit box with Mario, the team owner. We followed up on Sunday for the Cup race. Our racer, Josh Bilicki, actually crashed out of the race that day, but he was unharmed.

The experience was incredible, providing me with profound insights into how intertwined the sport of NASCAR was with the businesses that backed it. It left me determined to delve deeper. Since then, Jon and I have remained close friends, and he has even become one of my fitness clients. Despite all these great marketing opportunities, AW's sales at the store remained lackluster. It was glaringly obvious that I had a long way to go as a business, and the Promenade had an enduring traffic issue that my marketing efforts alone could not overcome.

In April 2022, the Promenade underwent a change in management. Melissa Napolitano, the GM who brought me into the fold at the Promenade, left her position for a new job elsewhere, and her replacement, Natalia Stezenko, was a poor choice. Her attitude was terrible and shortly after her arrival, she put it on display.

For me, this was a foreboding sign. It harkened back to my first year with the Giants. I had started under Coach Coughlin, who, in my opinion, was an exceptional individual and an outstanding coach. Although old-fashioned, he was a proven winner. However, the leadership decided to make changes and replace Coughlin with Ben McAdoo. He was younger, yes, but unproven and out of shape. McAdoo had his own plans for the team, which did not include me, and after his first season as head coach, I was ousted.

Due to my past experience, I was wary of the new management at the mall. When Natalia started sending aggressive emails about tenants adhering to store hours or risking fines, I became convinced that my time at the Promenade was coming to an end. I began to think that perhaps the Lehigh Valley Mall was the right situation after all.

I contacted the Simon Group again to ensure that the line of communication was still open. They encouraged me to visit an available space, which I did. However, I was still under contract with the Promenade and hadn't made up my mind. The first year in business wouldn't be easy, I knew, but I felt a strong urge to stick with it, double down, and reinvest. I just couldn't decide where I would make that investment. As it turns out, the situation resolved itself. I didn't have to make a difficult decision. It was October, and my lease was set to expire at the end of the month. On the 13th, I received an email from Natalia, the new GM. It read:

> **Good morning, Andre,**
>
> **The term of your license agreement will end on October 31, 2022. Since we have not received any communication from you, we assume that both parties agree that this arrangement may not have been the most suitable, and you will be vacating your space by the end of the month. Kindly get in touch with Krista to arrange a final walkthrough of your space on or before October 31, 2022, to ensure that the space and key are returned in accordance with the terms of your license agreement.**
>
> **Signed, Natalia**

This woman was cold-blooded. It's difficult to describe how I felt at the time. It's like dating someone who I knew was below my standards and as I'm contemplating the breakup, she beats me to the punch and ends the relationship; how dare she.

I couldn't fathom why a mall, already lacking twenty stores, would evict a paying tenant offering a unique, high-end product. I contacted Natalia's superior to voice my dissatisfaction, as I found her email to be impolite and unjust. Even if I had to vacate the mall, there was no way I would leave abruptly in just two weeks.

I received another email from Natalia shortly afterwards, in which she informed me that I had an additional 30 days to vacate the premises. Apparently, I was being evicted due to non-compliance with the mall's operating hours, but Natalia had the audacity to come to my store in person and express her true feelings to my face.

Natalia's own words were, "your target demographic is not here. This mall caters to 80% women. You can either leave voluntarily or we can double your rent." I did not continue the conversation. I told Natalia that I understood exactly what she was saying and that she was welcome to leave my storefront. She was correct. The Promenade did not have the demographic to support a high-end brand like AW because they barely had a demographic at all. It was undoubtedly time for me to make my exit. Consequently, the AW store ceased operations on November 30th. I left with a bad taste in my mouth but was still hungry for another opportunity.

As I mentioned earlier, I had been in ongoing communication with Simon Group about securing a space in the Lehigh Valley Mall. However, my opportunity window had closed, and there were no vacant spots available. Despite this setback, Kristen, the leasing officer, assured me that I should be patient as they were confident that a space would become available in the spring.

AW went dark during the holiday season, and I found myself back home once more. It was comforting to be able to dedicate an entire day to spending time with my family, but the feeling of failure loomed over me. The Promenade experiment had come to an end. Despite the considerable investment, there was nothing to show for it.

One moment stood out to me before I left the mall. During the 13-month stint at the Promenade, I had been exploring a run of banks, applying for credit and loans. In the month leading up to the store's closure, I came across a bank that offered a business credit line. Tabitha Bell, the branch manager for KeyBank in Trexlertown, visited my Promenade location before its closure and was impressed with the quality of my product, my story, and my plan. Through her support, I successfully obtained $25,000 in business credit with KeyBank.

Something special happened for AW when I said I was opening a store. It was as if the brand became real for people. A physical store allowed people to see, touch, and feel the product as well as understand the passion and drive of the owner behind the brand. The combination of these elements signaled KeyBank to extend the hand that AW needed to navigate our next steps in the world of brick and mortar.

I made it a priority to preserve and utilize my business credit until the time came to start anew at the Lehigh Valley Mall.

Chapter 61: Family Feud

December 2022 marked one year since my encounter with the angel of death. I thought about that experience for the entirety of 2023. It was a defining moment when God himself drew a line in the sand and sent a being far beyond my stature, an otherworldly giant, to deliver a strong warning against crossing that line. The encounter left me profoundly sobered. Its ultimate impact was this: I heard God's voice with unprecedented clarity. It was gentle and guiding as ever, but I was far more cautious about defying His guidance.

There was a heaviness weighing on my heart. It was the strained relationship between my siblings and me, and my spirit was urging me not to carry it into 2023. It had been years since I last spoke to any of my siblings, and while I didn't believe I held a grudge, I was certainly angry with them. The years of non-communication as I went through my hardships alone made me distant and indifferent towards them. When Ka'el was born, his arrival went unacknowledged. That was hurtful and I was angry, but it was up to me to express my desire for our kids to have a relationship with each other or they simply would not have one. Krystal had become a mother by this point, and Kareem was expecting a son, totaling six new Williams boys between the four of us.

I made the decision to address all of them at once in a group text. In retrospect, that was a lazy move and it backfired. As I look back at the messages, I can see that I approached them in a raw and condescending manner.

To paraphrase the text message, "I don't care to talk to y'all, but God told me to do it... So, what's up?" There was anger in my words. I was angry because Barron was 6 now and Ka'el was 4, and in all those years not one of them acknowledged their nephew's existences. The petty excuses for why this had persisted for 6 years could not satisfy me. My siblings had no love for me or for my kids. It was easy to see.

This is in spite of the fact that I'd apologized to my sister on multiple occasions. I'd even had a conversation with her face to face, at my father's house in front of her boyfriend (he was there to ask for my sister's hand in marriage), my father, and De'shonia, where we talked through the entire incident. But when I greeted her the next morning, her mood towards me was unchanged. At that point, it was hard for me to feel anything at all towards my siblings, but I still wanted our kids to have a relationship. It was unfair for them to be cut off from their family due to a petty dispute between their aunts and uncles.

As expected, my youngest brother Kareem was the first to respond with combative remarks. I reacted poorly. There was never any real issue or argument between Kareem and me. He was jumping in on beef that had nothing to do with him and that upset me even more. I made it clear that he was fortunate to be a few states away because if he had said the same thing to my face, I would have put him to sleep.

Already, I'd gone too far but I didn't give up. I attempted to make amends, sharing snapshots of Barron and Ka'el sharing ice cream treats at Rita's the previous summer. Inquiring about the well-being of their children, I strived for a reconnection. But my efforts were in vain. Danique rallied to Kareem's defense, stating that Georgia had a "stand your ground" law. Adding fuel to the fire, Krystal added her support, with a resounding nod to Danique's message and an affirmation of her own. Once again, they stood united against me. Their consensus? I was disrespectful and in need of mental help.

I persisted in my efforts because I was determined to make them understand my perspective. It didn't matter if we didn't get along, what mattered was the tarnished legacy we were leaving behind by allowing a divisive separation to exist among the new generation of Williams. I was not proud of that. Unfortunately, reconciliation via group text was a failure.

My mother called me the next day, to chide me about what I said to Kareem. I stood on my remark. I told her that she was wrong for choosing to play her part in defending the divide by not putting

☆ After the Last Snap ☆

her foot down and standing against it. Krystal and Kareem were in the background fuming until finally, they each took their turns to snarl insults at me through the phone. I won't bother repeating what was said. It doesn't matter. It was all bad, and it was all my fault.

I made amends before the year ended by personally calling each of them to apologize and express that my heart was open to them and that I did not hold a grudge. I let them know that it was my wish for our kids to know each other in the future. Although Kareem and Krystal did not pick up or return my call, I left each of them a message from the heart. Fortunately, my oldest brother Danique answered the phone, and we had a conversation. While it didn't lead to much, it was better than nothing.

Chapter 62: Cold Sweat

It was December 2022, and I couldn't help but wonder if we would experience a normal Christmas this year. Unfortunately, that was not the case. As we hunkered down for our third Christmas in Pennsylvania, strange occurrences seemed to be unfolding around us. For starters, we'd entered the vaccine era and there was a morbid sense of security being sold to society regarding the experimental jab that could influence your DNA. When the news came out that vaccinated individuals were still coming down with coronavirus, I knew that something wasn't right. Then they came for the jobs, and De'shonia had to make a choice: would she get vaccinated to keep her job at St. Luke's? Of course not. We would find our own way before we participated in the fear mongering and joined the experiment.

The original plan was to save up credit in order to rebuild the AW store at the LV Mall. However, I found myself faced with a car emergency instead. While returning home from a trip to the laundromat, Dee called me with bad news about our Dodge Durango. The engine light was on, and the engine thermometer was running hot. It was by God's grace that Dee managed to navigate to a nearby Auto Zone. An employee there came to her aid, and after further inspection, he revealed that the coolant tank had cracked, leaving the car running without any coolant. He helped her refill the coolant tank to ensure a safe journey back home. He refused to accept any payment for his assistance.

I took the car to the dealership for repair where they informed me that the necessary fixes would cost several thousand dollars. Determined to get the job done, I used my business credit. With 120,000 miles on the Durango, it was no longer a young car. However, compared to buying a new one, spending a few thousand dollars seemed like a drop in the bucket. Adding to the urgency was the fact that it was our only car; and we needed it to accomplish our shared responsibilities. The first $4000 of business credit went towards fixing the Dodge, and while it was worth it, it was also nerve-wracking. I couldn't help but wonder how reliable our set of wheels truly was.

Barron's prestigious private school, Brunswick Academy, had its annual "Father & Son" breakfast scheduled for December 3rd. I was thankful that the car trouble came before the trip rather than during it. However, I couldn't help questioning whether it made sense to keep subjecting the car to 6-hour round trips, knowing that it was approaching the final stages of its life. We were heavily dependent on the car, and it needed to survive another year or more. But I'd already promised Barron and Marilyn that I would go. I was committed to attending the breakfast.

This was the second time that year I had traveled to Stamford for one of Barron's school events. I attended "Dads and Donuts" earlier that year. Dee and Ka'el took the trip with me so that they could see him too. We stayed at a hotel down the street from Brunswick Academy. It was expensive for us, but that was part of the deal I took. Marilyn dropped Barron off at the hotel so that we could hang out with him for the night. There was a new guy driving her around in her car, which seemed to be her modus operandi.

We splashed around in the pool, and I picked up burgers for dinner. We ate and watched cartoons in the hotel room until his mom arrived to pick him up. The next morning, I met Barron at his school to join him in the classroom with the other dads and their sons. Barron presented me with a wooden frame of a picture he drew of us. It read, "My dad is strong, fast, nice, afletick." After class, we had breakfast and pastries together in the cafeteria and finally, we finished the day in the gym with some fun activities. School let out afterwards and I drove Barron to his flag football practice.

The football practice was held at the residence of a man named Ray Bartosezk. He coached the team with a handful of other dads. The practice itself was awful, but I gave them grace. At least they were taking the time to create a positive experience for their young men. There was a mess of 5 and 6 year old boys and a group of older men standing around and blowing their whistles in Ray's expansive backyard. I helped organize the kids and even set up a couple of drills that made sense for their level, but I wasn't interested in coaching them. I wanted to sit back and observe Barron in his environment.

The football practice ended after an hour and to my surprise, Marilyn informed me that she would be leaving for a "business meeting" but Barron would be heading straight into baseball practice. Ray prepared his yard for baseball practice while Barron hung out at the playground alone. He didn't even have time to eat. I hadn't prepared anything for him and neither did his mother.

It's moments like these that truly broke my heart. If Barron decided not to pursue sports in the future, I would completely understand his decision, and I would be fine with it. The discipline and consistency that it takes to be an athlete is too difficult for most because training and practice aren't always fun. But good athletes can appreciate the process when they are properly groomed with the right combination of food, rest, & healthy competition. But this wasn't proper grooming. There wasn't even a Gatorade cooler with cold water for the kids.

No one sought advice from the former pro. Marilyn and the Greys were convinced that money knew what was best for Barron. Regardless of it all, we had to hit the road and leave him behind. We had already checked out of the hotel, rush hour was approaching, and we faced a 3+ hour trip back to Pennsylvania.

For the father-son breakfast in Stamford, I traveled alone. It was December, Christmas was approaching, and we didn't have the cash to stay at the Stamford Hilton Hotel with the entire family. Cathy-Anne invited me to stay at her house for the trip. It wasn't a bad offer. It would allow me to save money, spend the night with Barron, and drive him to school in the morning.

Marilyn was there when I arrived at the house. She greeted me at the door and invited me inside. She was having a glass of wine with her workmate, another pre-school teacher before heading out for the evening. Marilyn kindly ordered dinner for Barron and myself, and once she and her friend left, I assisted Barron with his shower, helped him into his pajamas, and we enjoyed our dinner together. Afterward, I made sure he brushed his teeth and used the restroom before bedtime.

It was strange indeed to be back at Cathy-Anne and John's home after everything that had transpired. They arrived home late

☆ After the Last Snap ☆

from a trip, and upon Cathy-Anne's entrance, we shared a warm hug. I shook John's hand and expressed my gratitude for letting me stay at their house. I also assisted them in carrying their luggage upstairs. I learned that John, having experienced a back injury before, preferred not to risk it and had left Cathy-Anne to handle the heavy bags.

I was appreciative of the Grey's hospitality, but once I was there in the house, I became uneasy. I realized I didn't want to have to leave my family, travel all the way to Stamford, and stay with the Grey's just to spend time with my son. That's not what I went through 2 years of divorce to accomplish. I was restless in the guest room that night. I was there that night because that is where the Greys chose for me to be. They still had the power to decide how I would live my life with my son. I knew I had to break free from this alternate narrative that the Greys had created for Barron and for myself.

I became friends with Ray Bartoszek at the "Father & Son" breakfast the following day. We had a meaningful conversation about life while our children played in the gym, and we even exchanged numbers. To my surprise, Ray ended up purchasing a pair of jeans from my website that December. To my knowledge, he was my very first billionaire customer. He raved about them to me after he received them. It was undeniable confirmation of the popularity of AW and the quality of my jeans.

Something strange started to occur when I made it home from Stamford. I was not physically unwell that Christmas season, but my sleep resembled that of someone plagued by illness. I began having nightmares that woke me up in the middle of the night, drenched in cold sweat. Night after night, this pattern continued, and each dream seemed to merge into the next, forming a painful montage of my memories. My mind transported me back to every hardship I had experienced with Marilyn: the bitter arguments over money, her breakdown in Miami, even the grim courtroom confrontations. I was relentlessly scrolling through a collage of painful memories until I jolted awake in a pool of perspiration. This unsettling occurrence persisted for over ten consecutive days, occasionally even tormenting me twice in a single night.

☆ Andre Williams ☆

All of a sudden, my past was haunting me, tormenting my mind relentlessly. I couldn't explain it. Years had passed since I'd been liberated from the divorce, and I felt very emotionally secure in this new chapter of my life. Yet, here I was, every night, continually rehashing turmoil from my subconscious. These relentless memories resurfaced, refusing to release their grip on me. The impact extended beyond my sleep; it affected De'shonia as well. She struggled to comprehend the lingering attachment that held me captive each night and disrupted our sleep.

This went on nightly, for well over a week, until one night when I woke up drenched in sweat, and I immediately felt compelled to start writing. My spirit man urged me to write a letter to Cathy-Anne, to be completely open with her and to ask for the same in return. I was beginning to suspect that now that I was finally home, no longer consumed by work or temporary distractions, my emotional scars were throbbing. Something was deeply troubling me after the trip to Stamford. After almost two weeks of reliving my past through these strange dreams, I realized I longed for an exploration of the truth that would lead to closure and allow me to enjoy an unadulterated night of sleep. I needed to move beyond superficial conversations and have a hard talk with the Greys about why they perpetrated such an ugly war with me while we strove to take care of the same child.

A recurring pattern unfolded in each dream: a tug-of-war between myself, the Greys, and the pivotal figure, Barron. He was the linchpin. Without Barron, there would be no grounds for dispute. He had been the bait, the instrument the Greys deployed to ensnare me in the intoxicating drama of the divorce. Peppered with seasonal gifts, and pictures depicting all the fun Barron was having away from me, I became intoxicated on the illusion that my son was being taken from me. I'd sober up with a spot of calculated contact on predetermined schedules that I had no control over, and the cycle would repeat. In the end I found myself leashed to a cycle of debt and emotional turmoil, and the cycle would continue as long as I chose to adhere to the absurdity.

I'd been a fool, focused only on my firstborn above everything else. I recalled how I sabotaged my chances of securing a starting job with the Chargers due to nonstop flights from California to

☆ After the Last Snap ☆

New Jersey, all to exercise my parenting rights under supervision. And even now, I didn't hesitate to close my store in order to journey to Stamford to play my part as "father" during so called, "father-son events." It was time for me to make the difficult decision that I couldn't make in my younger years but first, I would offer the Grey family an opportunity to redeem themselves by putting them to the test.

I would force them to reveal their true intentions. I had one burning question: if they genuinely loved my son as they claimed and truly desired what was best for him, then would they try to rectify the mistakes they made out of spite? Alternatively, if they loved themselves more than they loved Barron, then they would protect their pride and they would tell me everything I already suspected; that Barron was a prize to them that they had won in the divorce, fair or not. I was necessary in his life, but only as a means to maintain their prize, like an occasional auto shop tune-up. They could handle the heavy lifting of raising Barron. They didn't need my input. Their money knew best.

I wanted to know what would happen if I bared my soul for the Grey's to see. Would they take one last opportunity to spit, or would they show compassion and have a real conversation with me about what they had done? Could they actually feel remorse? Here was the letter I wrote to Cathy-Anne.

> **Cathy-Anne,**
>
> **"I married Marilyn on August 29th, 2014. Her parents advised me against it. My parents advised me against it. But we did it anyway because I sincerely thought I was doing the right thing. She was pregnant at the time. I was just drafted into the NFL and I wanted to do right by her and set a good family example.**
>
> **My marriage relationship with Marilyn was mostly 2 years of hell. I've never fought with a man or a woman as fiercely as I did with her, not ever in my life. The one bright spot of the whole thing was Barron's birth. The birth of**

my first son was a spot of light that I won't forget. But it did not improve my relationship with Marilyn. In fact, things got worse... Worse to the point that the relationship started to turn violent. One morning, when Barron was 6 months old, Marilyn kicked me in my back while I was walking down a flight of stairs. She was holding Barron in her arms when she did this. I did not try to fight her, I did not call the police, I left. Even leaving was a battle. In broad daylight, Carolyn sat on the hood of my car with Barron still held to her chest. In the end, I decided it was better to end the marriage than to continue exposing my son to what was going on. Because not only was Marilyn not interested in getting help, but she also began denying that these things even happened.

We filed for divorce weeks later on September 22nd, 2016.

In order for Marilyn to dictate the terms of custody over Barron in the divorce, she used her attorneys to financially break me. They played a dirty game. The first thing they did was send in papers to the court calling me an absentee father who didn't know how to take care of his son. They claimed I had no business taking him out of state to see my mother because it would be dangerous for the child.

This is the ugliest thing anyone has ever said about me in my life. I cannot remember a time where I was more hurt or in more pain about something someone said about me.

The results in court were horrific. I found myself in a situation where I literally had to pay to see my son under supervision. I was to pay her my entire salary that year, all while being locked out of my own home even though Marilyn had effectively moved back to Stamford with you guys.

I will admit that I truly lost my mind during this time. I thought and said and did things that a sane person would not.

In the end, Marilyn got everything she wanted. I was financially broken and essentially homeless. Barron spends the majority of his time with her side of the family & for a handful of days out of the year Barron gets to hang out with his homeless dad in his grandfather's basement. This situation has been unfolding all of Barron's life, with the initial split happening at 6 months old.

There was a time when I was caught up in the emotional drama of the divorce and the loss of sovereignty over my household and my son. I was focused on bettering my feelings rather than bettering myself. I spent too much time being upset about the fact that I live in 2 rooms in my dad's basement with my wife and my kid(s). I used to play pro football, have money, own a home, and now I'm figuring out how to build a business and not be broke.

When Barron turned 6, I realized that he struggles with the darker half of his identity. He doesn't understand why it is worth being proud of just yet. He finds it easier to just identify himself as "mostly white like his mom" even though no one else will see him that way. It is easy to understand the struggle from his point of view. There isn't much I can do at this time except to grow and develop and move on and up in life. There's no conversation that can be digested at his young age that would explain everything he needs to understand about himself. All I can be is an example. I know Barron is me. He probably doesn't see that yet. I know that I did not. I needed examples and time to understand the meaning of legacy.

I have used every legal method and tool to try and extricate myself from this deep valley. I attempted to launch my denim business and I used every ounce of my leverage and network to make a miracle happen for me and my family. I am sorry to say that I've failed. There are limits to what a person can do with a burned foundation and huge debts attached to his name.

Banks do not lend to the homeless. My mental and emotional strength is beginning to wane at this point. My dreams have been deferred. I fear that the struggle to survive will force me into some obscure path. I loathe the idea that my family must continue to suffer alongside me. My heart aches to see Barron turn another year older and I am still here, below ground.

At one time, I was one of the hottest players out of the NCAA, a Heisman finalist, a star pro football player, with a top tier education & great head start on life. Now I am struggling terribly, all because I crossed the Grey's & their daughter. I am beyond sorry.

> Lately, I've been having trouble sleeping. At first I thought I was sick. Full body sweats wake me from my sleep. I begin to perspire each time my mind travels down the dark corridors of my past in the night. Sometimes this happens multiple times a night. I lay in bed wrapped in a towel to keep from soaking the blankets. I am sick.
>
> I don't know what else to do but lay myself low and return to the folks I feel are most responsible for my plight and beg for help. I am begging for help."
>
> All my best,
Andre Williams

I edited and proofread the letter before sending it as a word doc via email. I attached a shorter letter to introduce my letter and offset the raw tone of my disclosure:

> More than anything Cathy-Anne, in 2023 I would really like it if I could sit down with you and your family and establish a genuine understanding. I am glad that we have reached a point where we can finally engage in a meaningful conversation.
>
> I understand that the divorce and its aftermath may appear to be a distant memory for all of you, and perhaps you feel that you've washed your hands of it completely. But for me, the divorce and its consequences continue to dominate my life. Its after effects persist, no matter which path I choose to follow.
>
> You guys may not want to revisit this hard, dark place but what I am trying to get you to understand is that I currently live in this hard, dark place. I haven't left and trust me, I have

tried to do so with all of my might and cunning.

Maybe that isn't your concern, but when Barron comes to me, he also lives in this hard, dark place and that is a painful issue for me. I just wonder how much of a concern that is for you Cathy-Anne.

More pressing than anything else is the fact that in the coming months, I will have to make some decisions about how I am going to move forward because this small stop gap I've been occupying is closing and the choices I make next will directly impact how much time I have to spend with Barron. I have to find a way forward to survive.

I am hopeful that this letter can lay the groundwork for some kind of a meeting with our family. It is important to me to share my perspective on the past and present circumstances especially as it relates to Barron.

I want you to know that I have nothing but love in my heart for you and your entire family. There is no malice or hate whatsoever in regard to what I have endured over the past six years. While I understand that your intentions were not to hurt me, or at least I hope they weren't, you were simply looking out for your daughter and your grandson.

However, in the process of looking out for them, I took some damage. I might be big, strong, and smart but that does not mean I don't feel pain. That does not mean I do not cry. It does not mean I don't need help. I've come to learn that the true weakness of great strength is that everyone assumes you can handle all problems on your own. The worst part is, I am not in this world by myself. I have a small family of my own and they all share in my pain, Barron included.

Cathay-Anne, if you really do consider me to be family, then I would like to continue talking about it. Please read my letter below and get back to me when you have time. Thank you.

All my best,
Andre Williams

The letter wasn't very pleasant to read. If I am being honest, I may not have responded well to such a letter. Yet, I would have reflected on it deeply and considered what I'd done to make someone bold enough to express themselves in such a way to me.

The next day, Cathy-Anne responded via text, "Andre, I have received your letter. My heart goes out to you. I would like to discuss this, but let's wait until the holiday is over."

"Okay, Cathy-Anne," I replied. "Thank you for your response."

Over the holiday, I considered what I was willing to do if Cathy-Anne and John found it in their heart to make amends, apologize, and offer to help in some way. I realize I made the mistake last time of asking for too little assistance when I knew I needed 5 times what I asked for to eliminate all my leftover debts and return to square one at the very least.

I also knew that their request was that I didn't ask for more money for my business and that I hadn't even repaid the original loan yet. But that was all beside the point. I burned well over a quarter million dollars fighting lies in order to be a part of my son's life.

This wasn't about money. It was about being stable enough to be completely available for Barron. Money wasn't the motive, it was the means to a proper end, which was putting Barron's best interests first. Barron didn't need money. He needed what every child needs; 2 loving & available parents, a mom and a dad.

☆ Andre Williams ☆

I decided that if the Grey's really wanted this for Barron and they were willing to walk back all that they had done to break me down, then I would be completely willing to sign over a quarter of my business to Marilyn. She could collect her money monthly, for life. Even if they could just help me eliminate my debt, without any additional assistance, I'd be prepared to make the same offer.

Of course I came clean to De'shonia about what I was proposing, and she was incensed. I thought it was funny that my business had no real value on paper apart from the physical product I held, and the manufacturing network behind it, and yet I was sure that it would be a success and De'shonia did too. That is why I loved her. She was mad but she went with the plan. She always went with the plan.

Chapter 63:
A Time to Mend Deferred

I never reached the big sit-down with the Greys. They jumped the gun. Cathy-Anne got back to me after the holiday with a letter from John Grey.

> Here is John's response. Let's examine it and proceed with our discussion.
>
> - Cathy-Anne Grey

John's response was concise and clear:

> I appreciate that Andre is looking for investment in his business and assistance at this point in his life, but we are the wrong ones to provide either.
>
> Andre's jeans business has been a dream that he has pursued since roughly 2016 and despite the best of intentions from Andre, the business has not demonstrated the ability to scale its revenue and grow into a self-sustaining profitable entity. I do not know whether it is due to the product, its pricing, the channel distribution strategy, or any of many other factors. But what I do see is a lack of traction after 6 years.
>
> I feel had he taken his career in a different direction and worked for a Nike, Adidas, Under Armour, Reebok, etc., he would have

☆ Andre Williams ☆

gained the business acumen to ultimately start his own retail business in a successful manner (I started my own business after 16 years polishing my healthcare investing skills for others at Canaan Partners and JH Whitney & Co.). I think the best path for Andre is to go work in a business where he can learn as well as leverage his skills and experiences to develop a career that enables him to support his family and grow professionally.

- John Grey

His response was short and lacked any attention to the emotional or historical relevance of the matter he was speaking on, but I didn't expect anything less from John Grey. The conversation with Cathy-Anne the next day was hard. I knew the Greys were unwilling to help me any further. I was not entitled to receive anything from them. But I was opening the door for the Greys to acknowledge the harm they had caused and understand the impact their actions had on both me and Barron, and to take responsibility for it. Even if they didn't believe in the business, I just wanted them to be honest and try to make things right. I won't forget the words Cathy-Anne spoke to me on the phone that day.

"First of all, John and I felt like you were pointing the finger very strongly and we didn't appreciate that. I don't feel one ounce of blame for your circumstances. The first time we gave you the money, it wasn't because we believed in your business, it's because we felt bad for you. But you were exactly right. We told you in the beginning not to marry Marilyn. When the divorce broke out, we did our best not to make it an ugly battle, but we were only defending ourselves from your vicious attacks and you were filing for full custody.

You don't have to worry about that little boy. He will never have to worry about money ever in his life. We will make sure of that, and we will take the best care of Barron. You are smart and charismatic. You have a great education. You can bounce back from this. You will be okay. Carry on. That divorce probably took years

☆ After the Last Snap ☆

off of all of our lives. It was hard on all of us, and we spent a small fortune, but I would die for Barron."

I ended the phone call by telling Cathy-Anne that I love her and her family and that I forgive them for everything that they did. It was all I could do. I'd met an angel of death a winter ago and almost lost my life. It was beyond me at this point to hold on to what I'd been through with them, but it was far beyond me to allow them to dictate my future by sticking to their plan for my son and me. I told her that it wasn't money that allowed them to control my circumstances, it was my own weakness, which was my love for my kids. I let her know that I would be hiding my weakness from them because I needed to get up on my own now.

When I told Cathy-Anne that I forgive the Greys for everything, I truly meant it. I do forgive them. I mean it every time I say it. But forgiveness does not mean that I forget. I don't feel the pain anymore, but I haven't forgotten it, and when I remember, I have a chance to forgive again, and I take the chance every time. Because forgiveness is what is necessary to heal. It is what is necessary for God to move in our lives. It removes us from the mental prison that we've created in our trauma. Forgiveness is the key. However, forgiveness does very little for the person who has been forgiven. They have their own journey to walk.

Now my eyes were open. I could now see the Greys for who they truly were. Their gifts and holiday cards were not gestures of love, but rather tactics of control.

The Greys refused to accept blame or take responsibility for the situation I found myself in. They claimed I begged poorly, and instead of making amends or offering apologies, they chose to defend their pride and hide behind bold lies, refusing to wash the blood from their hands.

Cathy-Anne pushed the facts of the past to the side. She spun her own narrative because she could afford to do so. It didn't matter that the court paperwork called me an absentee father and a danger to my own child. It didn't matter that the divorce dragged on for 25 months as I hemorrhaged all my money and tried to work a high-pressure job in a high-pressure environment. It didn't matter that I had to pay to see my own son under supervision. It didn't matter that I lost my house or that all the equity in it was eaten up by Marilyn and by the lawyers. None of these things mattered.

They were not in the business of helping me take care of Barron. Why would they do that? Maybe they feared that with even a small opportunity, I might achieve more than their own daughter. If I fell on hard times, that was great. Indeed, that outcome had been their agenda ever since I decided to leave their daughter.

I'm certain that a vain question lingered in their minds: what if Barron could experience a life of abundance with his dad and his paternal family? When would he begin to question which parent he preferred to spend his time with? They were not going to allow it. The Greys wanted the control that their wealth afforded them.

These Greys were incredibly rich, and yet they stole from a kid in distress, eroded my foundation, wrestled away custody of my child. All this to save face for their troubled daughter. At least then, she could walk around town with the boy and say that they had won. They were thieves. They were kidnappers. They were proud of it, and according to them it was up to me to carry on in my circumstances and somehow manage to keep up with them and with Barron in Stamford for my "Father & son" time.

He was their trophy, their spoils of divorce. They had taken him and had no intention of giving him back. It gave them great joy to lavish Barron with all the privileges money could buy: private school education, tennis lessons, ski trips in Aspen. They would send me photos and mocking messages about how wonderful he was and how beloved. They had no intention of supporting me as I tried to stand on my own feet. It wasn't hatred; it was a deep resentment for what they perceived as my abandonment of their daughter. She was now "used goods." Most men of their kind would not give her a second glance. Perhaps the worst part for them was that I had moved on and found true love. I did not suffer the shame of loneliness as their daughter did. When I had my time with Barron, we took care of him together, even before he turned one. I know it hurt Marilyn, Cathy-Anne, and John to see Barron with his other family.

But they knew my value as a father to Barron was irreplaceable. They didn't mind keeping me close. Barron could have me in doses, he must. It was good for him. And it was good for them too. Marilyn couldn't do it by herself.

We'd moved in with my dad in the summer of 2020. He gave us time to get back on our feet. But we needed to figure it out, and quickly, because my dad was on his way out too. He needed to sell the house and move back to NJ. The back and forth driving every day between Pennsylvania and New Jersey was a slow killer.

This was a line in the sand, drawn by me. It was time to stand up. I knew who I was at this point, what I was capable of, the principles I stood for, and how far I was willing to go to defend them. I acknowledged my mistakes in the past and I was prepared to pay for my sins. I would not deny myself in order to "make a living" when I knew my value was much greater than the dollar sum in my bank account.

I would withdraw from the Greys and do what was absolutely necessary to accomplish my goals and generate the lifestyle I knew I was capable of achieving for myself and my family. I would stop stretching myself to complete the Grey's narrative.

It was now or never. I made a vow that day that I would give AW my complete focus and attention. I would not treat this opportunity like I did the Chargers in San Diego. Either it would succeed, or it would fail. If it succeeded, great. I could pay my debts and have my freedom to choose again. I could show my son his value the way that it pleased me to do so.

If the business failed, then so be it. It wasn't meant to be. I'd find a way to let it go. I'd get a job. I would defer my ambition as an entrepreneur and seek whatever else the Lord had in store. But first, I was going to push my business. I would push until it hit a land mine and blew up, or until it fell off a cliff and died. This was my last chance to do so.

I was running out of time either way. My father vowed that this would be his last winter in the house. It would be our last winter in the house then. I wasn't going to waste more time bringing Barron back here. The next time I received him, we would be in our own house. That was my vow. I told Marilyn that she could keep him for his New Year's break.

Chapter 64: New Year, New Me

One of the final clients I acquired prior to closing the Promenade location was a gentleman named Eric Bartosz. He approached me with a request for his book *Bar40: Achieving Personal Excellence*, a self-help guide designed to help individuals achieve their best year ever. He asked me for a quote for the testimonial section of the book's 2023 edition.

Rather than just spout out some random quote, I bought a copy on Amazon and gave it a read. It was a great book about setting intentions daily in the most important aspects of life, to accomplish attainable goals that you set for yourself. I came up with a quote to describe it:

> "In a world that monetizes our distraction, *BAR40* seeks to expose the value we can find in focus. It is a daily reminder that a significant portion of our success in this life is 100% up to us!"

When I shared this quote with Eric, he was so impressed that he also felt compelled to showcase it prominently for all to see by placing it on the front cover. Now I was the one who was impressed. I felt honored that he thought that much of my writing to place the quote on the cover. On the other hand, I couldn't help but be inspired by *Bar40: Achieving Personal Excellence* to embark on the journey of writing my own book. Why couldn't I have my best year ever and write a book? I came across a quote by Stephen King, stating that a well-crafted book was like completing a season in sports. Anything beyond three to four months was a manifestation of procrastination. This was all the motivation I needed. Determined, I made a vow to finish my book in the year

2023. Now, on December 29th, I find myself reaching the conclusion of the final chapters.

Simon Group reached out to me in late February with an offer at Lehigh Valley Mall. Surprisingly, it turned out to be the exact same location they had presented to me over a year ago. However, this time it had been leased by a women's shoe and accessories boutique. Kris, the leasing officer, greeted me warmly and showed me the space. The storefront was located on the second floor, just across from Footlocker, one of the most trafficked areas in the mall. This location was a true gem that far surpassed the old Journey's I had been in. Spanning 2,000 square feet, the buildout had been meticulously designed with built-in changing rooms, ample shelving racks adorned with rolling ladders, and an abundance of fixtures that left me awe inspired. With perseverance, I managed to negotiate the monthly rent down to $2,100, with an additional flat fee of $350 for utilities, bringing the grand total to $2,450. March brought the excitement of receiving the keys, and without wasting a moment, I began the process of setting up the store in preparation for a cold opening on April 1st.

I was sensitive to God's voice at this time, and as I was setting up the store, I heard the Holy Spirit speak to me about my marijuana use. He was ready to clarify for me what the angel of death had said. He emphasized that regardless of if it's in its flower form or not, I had to let go of it. It was an idol in my life—a habit that I performed religiously. Some days I smoked marijuana more times than I read the Bible. Surely, I was committing an offensive sin. He assured me that He would assist me in this journey if I was willing to heed His guidance. His instructions were unequivocal: abstain from smoking on weekends, refraining from indulging on Fridays, Saturdays, and Sundays, as well as on the final Monday of every month.

"That wasn't so bad," I thought. God was willing to work with me, and I was ready to heed the call. I kept the smoke-free weekend pattern up smoothly for about two months before I missed on a Monday. I didn't worry about it; I knew I had been consistent and I would continue to be. I decided I would make up for the miss the following Monday. Tuesday came and I was setting up the store until finally, it was time for the late morning toke. I took the path out to the back, near the dumpsters, to prepare my bowl and enjoy a smoke. Something strange occurred. Despite smoking an entire bowl, I didn't feel high at all. I walked back inside feeling disappointed and disgusted. I thought to myself, I smell and taste like smoke and I am not even high. My conviction hit me at that moment and I took all my weed and paraphernalia and threw them into the dumpster.

God spoke again, "Don't buy it, and don't bring it home." Through the gentle whispers of His Holy Spirit, God continues to work on me, and I am proud to say, I can count on one hand the number of times I have smoked in 2023. I kept God's words and I continue to strive to be obedient. Obedience to God's voice is hard at times, but the thought of the angel of death beginning our meeting by swinging his sickle at the right of my neck helps to keep me sober.

The second time around, building out the store was much easier because I had already gone through the process once. I was able to set up the store using the business credit that I obtained from KeyBank. The project cost a little over $8,000 in part because of the abundance of high-quality fixtures the store already had, which I put to good use. I used bars and s-hooks to hang all the jeans on the wall, and with the existing shelving, I organized the shoes on the wall in an artful way. With only 17 separate styles in my inventory at the time, I utilized the wall space to design a creative display, maintaining an open floor design. For added flair, I had my friend Ray from Project Printed wrap all my tables with lifestyle imagery featuring local people in my jeans. Additionally, I placed a TV on the back wall behind the register table and played lo-fi music all day, creating an inviting, calming ambiance. I capped off the space with a new storefront sign and on April 1st, 2023, we were officially back in business.

I didn't have any grand marketing strategy in mind initially. My objective was to gauge the level of business based on the standard foot traffic during that specific time of the year. With a cold open, I managed to generate nearly $6,000 in sales during the first month of operation. This was encouraging, and while the foot traffic may not have been extraordinary, it was still a major improvement compared to the Promenade.

☆ After the Last Snap ☆

Unfortunately, my luck took a downturn in the following month. Our sales plummeted to $2,500. I was aware that as the weather became warmer, sales were likely to decline. So, in that regard, I wasn't completely caught off guard. However, it was becoming apparent that there was a bigger issue than poor sales that my business was facing. I was having trouble understanding how I could save money for a new denim order with my large overhead and inconsistent sales. I had a supply issue.

Because my manufacturer was based overseas and unable to accommodate small orders, the minimum amount of money I would need to create a new denim order was $150,000. This left me unable to replenish old styles or introduce new styles without a substantial investment. This was a major hindrance to my growth as well as daily sales because I was beginning to run low on my larger sizes. This troubling issue trickled down into all other parts of my business. Without a consistent monthly revenue of $10,000–$20,000, securing external investment for my next denim order was unlikely, and despite having around $400,000 worth of goods, sales were too slow to make any substantial savings. It was clear that some sort of pivot was essential.

As I strolled the mall looking for inspiration, I recognized that some of the stores with the most traffic had a great number of accessories in their stores. My experience at the Promenade wasn't lost on me. I knew that I needed to expand my marketing efforts and establish a strong online presence, but I believed a line of easily replenishable accessory items that could be created in smaller volumes, at a cheaper cost, and sold at more inclusive prices might be able to generate steady revenue in the mall environment.

Before I could explore this line of thought further, I received some troubling news from Kris, the general manager. She visited my store and sheepishly handed me a notice. It explained that a permanent tenant had signed a long-term lease for my space, and I had 30 days to vacate the space from the end of June. I knew that this was a possibility as per the lease agreement, but I didn't expect it to materialize after only three months in the space. After thanking Kris, I retreated to the back room of the store. Dee was actually in the store with me that day when I gave her the news. We were not new to adversity. I knew what to do this time. I took her to the back, held her hands, and prayed with her, just to ask God for peace and to thank Him for whatever move He was making in our lives. I knew it was for good and to prosper us, not to harm us.

A thought came to my mind after we prayed and returned to the front of the room. Why was I continuing to allow these realty corporations to take advantage of me when I could be growing my business online? Roy's old website had died a while ago with the onset of the Tustin James lawsuit, which was still dragging on, and that was just some place my products were posted anyway. It wasn't a real e-commerce business. I hadn't gotten in the weeds yet to understand what it took to sell online.

This was not the time to wallow in regret, feel discouraged, or give up on my business. At this point, I knew more about retail, clothing, and entrepreneurship than anything else. I had access to a manufacturing network that produced goods for the world's top brands. I had the ability to source the highest quality materials and craftsmanship available. It would be counterintuitive to forgo the pursuit of the fruit of all my potential just for the sake of a closed door.

Furthermore, the satisfaction I received from building something that people loved and willingly exchanged money for was reward enough to keep going because I knew I had a product that people wanted. Quitting is simply not an option. My choice was clear—I would continue to grow, learn, and build upon my achievements. All Weather Selvedge would dive headfirst into the realm of e-commerce.

Two important events took place in December of 2022. Firstly, Tustin James' lawsuit against me entered arbitration. My opponent and I were scheduled to present our cases in front of an arbitrator, and the proceedings were conducted online. We spent approximately five hours examining and cross-examining each other using the evidence we each collected during the discovery phase. I was able to outmaneuver Tustin and his legal team with relative ease.

First, I presented pictures of some of the clothing samples he had produced with Roy, despite his claim that no work had been completed after he made his payment. I possessed these images because Tustin had created nearly 400 clothing samples, and many of them were stored in Roy's office in Fort Lee, where I held creative sessions with his designer during my time in New Jersey. Tustin actually had a number of decent pieces, and I'd taken pictures of them. Methodically, I presented the images one by one in front of the arbitrator, and he ultimately admitted to still having many of them in his possession.

Secondly, Tustin eventually presented the contract he claimed I signed along with Roy the Maker for the work on his clothing brand and to no surprise at all, the only signatures on the contract belonged to Roy and Tustin. Moreover, the subpoena issued by Tustin's attorney to Chase Bank provided evidence that his investment had been received there to a business account that belonged to Roy's company. The subpoena also revealed that there were no other signatories on the business account apart from Roy and that neither my name nor any payments to me were recorded in the company account.

Finally, his testimony conclusively demonstrated that his professional connection with Roy revolved solely around rehabilitation sessions for his ACL injury, completely unrelated to me, as Roy was also an excellent trainer. I was never involved in any aspect of their transactions. In fact, during the period he claims to have interacted with Roy, I was physically located in a different state altogether.

His attorney made a weak attempt to hold me accountable for his financial losses by arguing that my tweets promoting the website, where my product was featured on Roy's previous platform, somehow "pierced the corporate veil," even though they failed to prove that I was a member of Roy's company.

The arbitrator ultimately rejected his narrative, dismissing his complaint. I emerged victorious in the case. Approximately a month later, Tustin's lawyers submitted a "trial de novo," an effective legal maneuver that nullifies the arbitration's findings and calls for a full-fledged trial. Taking action, I promptly filed a motion for summary judgment, a strategic legal move that circumvents the arduous litigation process by asserting that a particular fact is irrefutable based on the case's documented evidence.

☆ Andre Williams ☆

After submitting our paperwork for the motion, the case was left in a state of limbo for several months. There was no update on the case until the end of the summer, when a letter from the court finally arrived. To my disappointment, it revealed that our paperwork had been incorrectly filed due to the omission of the exhibits attached directly to the motion. Realizing the mistake, I promptly resubmitted the necessary documents as instructed. Another period of limbo ensued for several more months before I received an answer from the judge. Without the help of an attorney, I was not able to effectively kill all four of their legal accusations, but I did manage to shoot down their most obvious lie, which was that we had a contract together. There was no way to refute that we did not. Although I cannot definitively state that the case is 100% closed, it is clear that Tustin has financially exhausted himself with this federal lawsuit, which has been dragging on for well over three years without yielding any positive outcome. I don't feel bad for him at all, and it was fun helping him waste his money on a crooked court case.

The most important financial development of 2023 was a workers' compensation case that I filed against the Chargers in either November of 2022. It all started when I stumbled upon a compelling advertisement on LinkedIn by a sports injury lawyer named Thomas Betts. Little did I know, California law allows injury victims a generous 10-year window to pursue rightful compensation. With Tom's expertise, he skillfully opened the case on my behalf, focusing on my wrist injury. After months of anticipation, I was finally granted an assessment with a highly regarded doctor in June of 2023. In fact, the day I received the news that I was being booted from Lehigh Valley Mall, I'd just returned from my appointment in Santa Ana, California with this orthopedic doctor.

Several months later, we received the medical report, which indicated a remarkable overall permanent disability rating worth over $90,000. Additionally, it outlined the need for future care and surgical procedures, the costs of which were yet to be determined. It was clear that the Chargers' insurance company would have to honor their responsibilities. Eventually, we reached a favorable settlement agreement out of court in December 2023, totaling a

☆ After the Last Snap ☆

generous sum of $140,000. After compensating attorney fees, I was left with about $119,000. Finally, it was time to leave the basement.

The money I received from my wrist injury was not enough for a happily-ever-after ending, but it did allow me to pay down some of my debts, invest in my business, and afford us a new place to live. We found a townhouse for rent in Whitehall that provided the space needed for me to store my inventory, run my business, and give my family the room we need to live and grow. After four tough years, we are able to start fresh. As I write these final chapters, we are in the process of slowly moving out. I am grateful to have fulfilled my promises I made to my dad to move out by winter as well as the vow I made to myself to be in a house of our own the next time I received my son.

I spent the last four months of 2023 successfully transitioning my entire business to an online platform, utilizing Shopify at *awselvedge.com*. The first thing I did was immerse myself in learning by buying into various business groups that specialize in helping first-timers master the most important aspects of e-commerce and paid advertising. While some of these investments may have been costly, the knowledge and experience I gained have been invaluable.

I learned that there are many things needed beyond a physical website that go into making sales and running a successful e-commerce business. For example, I learned the intricacies of designing a website that converts by focusing on the psychology of the user experience, such as ease of navigation, creating a sense of urgency for the buyer, and creating an appealing offer that is hard for the buyer to pass up. I came to understand how powerful Facebook was as a marketing tool for seeking out my ideal buyers, creating an intent to buy, and directing those potential buyers to my website to shop. Lastly, I discovered that making a sale was less important than beginning new customer journeys and forming relationships with customers that lasted far beyond the first sale, because on average repeat buyers brought more value to the business than new customers. I found that creating those customer journeys had a lot to do with effectively capturing emails and automating weekly and sometimes daily contact with my email list.

☆ Andre Williams ☆

Through experimentation, trial and error, and sound guidance, I managed to find some consistency in my sales pace on a small testing budget, generating a sale every three to four days. There is no question in my mind that I can successfully drive sales with my online platform. However, I eventually arrived at the same deep supply and demand issue that I identified while at the Lehigh Valley Mall. Despite the large value of my stock on hand, without the ability to make small re-orders to my manufacturer to replenish sizes, there was no way my sales pace could effectively outgrow my expenses before my inventory was depleted. Running traffic to my website is a losing game in my current business model.

The unfortunate consequence of the Tustin James lawsuit was that it caused a strain in my relationship with Roy the Maker. While it did not directly affect my ability to do business, it is my belief that Roy disappeared from view to avoid being entangled in an unnecessary lawsuit, and that did make it harder for me to deal with my Chinese manufacturing base. I did manage to use them to produce an accessories collection to complement my denim, which included some essential clothing items like boxers, socks, belts, and wallets. However, these new items did nothing to address my real issue, and without the automatic traffic that a mall location afforded me, producing those accessories didn't make a lot of sense for my business. However, those accessories led me to an unexpected solution.

The underwear model I used for the AW boxers photo content was more than just a good-looking face; he was a conduit to something bigger. His name is Troy Parton, and he happened to work for Vidalia Mills, the sole selvedge denim manufacturer in the US. Through Troy, I got introduced to Dan Feibus, the CEO of the mill. Dan not only became a customer of mine but also a fan of the AW brand. Since that fateful introduction, I've been in regular contact with Dan and his team about creating a Made in the USA line of AW denim. Partnering with a US-based selvedge manufacturer like Vidalia Mills could revolutionize my business, open new marketing avenues, and solve my supply issues completely.

"There are no guarantees in life except for death and taxes." That's what people say, but those words don't bother me. My faith lies in the promises of God, and He is a faithful God that doesn't lie. Psalm 34:19 says, "The righteous face many hardships and perplexing circumstances, but the Lord delivers them from them all." I hold onto that promise with everything I've got. To me, it's simple: my business is bound for success.

History has shown us that even the most successful entrepreneurs faced immense difficulties before achieving greatness. Look at Jeff Bezos and Elon Musk. They both experienced financial struggles for a decade before finally breaking through. What set them apart was their refusal to quit and their unwavering belief in their visions. This is the mindset of a true entrepreneur.

Consider this: Elon Musk constantly battles for the title of the world's richest man with Bernard Arnault, the owner of the LVMH conglomerate. The only thing Bernard sells is nice clothes and alcohol. Jeff Bezos once asked, "What would you rather do? Spend the 10k and risk losing it all? Or save the 10k and continue doing what you're doing now for the rest of your life?" For me, there's no question. I have to roll the dice one more time.

There's a market share waiting for me. Why else would God consistently provide me with the "right-on-time" fuel to keep pursuing my ambitions and scaling my obstacles? I know He orchestrates the circumstances I need to overcome in order to grow. With faith, persistence, and a burning ambition, I will conquer those challenges. I refuse to settle for a comfortable, mediocre life. I will always choose the harder path because, as long as I keep my head up, I can see that success is within reach. Victory lies just beyond the horizon.

Chapter 65: Closing Remarks

This past December was another special one. The Lord spoke again, mysteriously but still unlike the last two Christmases. This time, He encouraged me to engage in a 3-day water fast to consecrate myself for the New Year. My wife and I undertook the fast together, and we're on the final day as I write these words.

My mother-in-law had gifted us a night's stay at Great Wolf Lodge in the Poconos for Christmas. It was just one night, but it was all we needed. We had a day to relax, drink, eat, and zone out to the sounds of falling water and the joy of many children. I even made a new friend at the water park—a financial advisor from New Jersey. We engaged in a deep conversation about athletes, discipline, fitness, and business. He even bought a pair of raw denim later that week.

There's an old African proverb that goes, "the strength of the crocodile is in the water." It means you'll have the upper hand in your natural environment. I know that my athleticism and aptitude for fitness are among my greatest gifts. These things come easier to me than anything else in life. Through my encounters and studies under the guidance of Master Shen, I've acquired skills and knowledge that uniquely set me apart in this field. In 2024, I aspire to use my unique gifts and the lessons I learned in my entrepreneurial journey about digital marketing to open up a new revenue stream. By this point, I understand that everything takes time to grow, but I am committed to unlocking this gift because I know I can use it to build the nest egg I am putting away for the "Made in the USA" denim project. Fortunately for me, I don't see many faith-fashion-fitness influencers on the internet. I believe I can occupy this niche and grow out of it. I pray that this direction

☆ After the Last Snap ☆

is within God's will for my life and that the work I do brings Him glory.

A few weeks ago, I had a conversation with Marilyn that blew my mind. I asked her if she would consider releasing me from child support, but she declined. However, two days later, she called me back and made me an offer. She said she would remove me from child support and provide enough financial assistance to help my family overcome whatever hardship we were facing, but in return, she wanted me to sign over legal guardianship of Barron to her. She was essentially asking me to sell my child for money.

Her rationale was that in case she died, she wanted to ensure that Barron could continue his education at Brunswick, as she doubted my ability to provide him with the lifestyle to which he'd grown accustomed. She assured me that nothing about the current structure would change if I accepted the deal because, "I wasn't involved in making decisions for Barron anyway."

I knew a devil had sent her on an assignment to torment me. Marilyn felt like her money made her free, but she was actually a slave to it, which is why she approached me with the devil's work. Even though she deserved it, I made a very strong effort not to cuss Marilyn out. Instead, I declined her offer as gently as I could, explaining that if achieving fame and wealth was my desire, I could have easily sought it from Satan himself. I'm certain he would have granted my wishes in exchange for my child's life or the life of someone else I cared about. I didn't need to accept a deal from a lesser devil.

Marilyn responded with a threat. She warned me that she would take legal action to change Barron's name to Grey when he turned 13, and that I would face a lawsuit if I ever attempted to remove Barron from Brunswick Academy. She routinely communicates nonsense like that from time to time, but I won't unpack anymore of it because it is a pointless waste of space in my book. I've come to realize that there is no power in meditating on what Marilyn or anyone else thinks of me. It is an egregious waste of time.

Obviously, Marilyn is incredibly upset that I chose to focus on rebuilding myself and my family this year rather than driving back and forth to Stamford for the few "father & son" moments they afford me. I missed his Brunswick breakfast this year; he went with his grandfather instead. Before it came around, I told Barron that he had the option to come and spend some quality time with me during the break. If he wanted to do so, he should tell his mom to bring him to me. I'm not sure what his thoughts were, but Marilyn wouldn't entertain it. I know I will be seeing Barron soon enough. I miss him tremendously, but this year has been well spent, and Barron knows who his father is. I made sure of that years ago.

Now, let me share something about my wife De'shonia.

Apart from establishing his relationship with God, the single most important decision a man will make in his life is the woman he chooses to marry. The woman a man marries will either amplify his potential or diminish it. She will either support his legacy or undermine it. I heard Steve Harvey say this once, and it resonated with me because every word of this saying is true. I have the receipts to prove it. I have been broken down by a woman and I have also been built up and supported by another. But my relationship with my wife is secondary to my relationship with the Creator. My relationship with God shapes my ability to love and serve my wife. That is why the angel of death told me that, in the context of marriage, my relationship with my wife is my relationship with God. A man's relationship with God is fundamental because God is love, and we can only love and love others because He first loved us.

To love is to live, and to live is to serve. I must learn how to live and serve my wife so that she can live well and submit to her husband. A man who cannot serve and a woman who refuses to submit will never see each other as equals, and they will always have conflict and discord between them.

It's work for De'shonia and me to get it right each day, but the relationship I have with my wife is the most fulfilling, refining, and satisfying connection I have ever experienced with another person. She understands who I am, supports me through challenges, and inspires me to strive for greatness. I cannot overstate how crucial she has been for my peace of mind, emotional well-being, and for the stability of our family unit. I am committed to protecting our bond and crafting our legacy together.

Now, let me shift the focus to business and entrepreneurship.

☆ After the Last Snap ☆

It is a complete surprise to me that I am chasing the apparel business in my 30s. My 20-year-old self would not have guessed that outcome. I do possess a keen sense of style, but I am certainly not a fashionista. This is a good thing in my eyes because, from what I have learned thus far, only a small portion of success in this business has much to do with "fashion sense."

Doing good business means understanding people, empathizing with them, and genuinely caring about them enough to understand their hopes, fears, and struggles. This goes for your customers, your partners, and your employees alike. Good business is about building enduring relationships over time. Each person involved in your business has intrinsic value, which is extracted over time with good products and services, and a nurtured sense of community, relationship, or connection.

My goal isn't only to dress people well and make money. I want to create a good business that can stand on its own and push into the future with innovation and partnership. I want to be a business that creates opportunities, community, and prosperity for everyone that chooses to do business with me.

The primary objective of AW Selvedge at this current time is to re-align with Vidalia Mills for a made in USA denim collaboration. That will take cash flow to begin a project of that size, but Vidalia doesn't seem to be in a rush. In the meantime, I will become the crocodile in the water. It is time to rebuild the AW FITNESS CLUB. As of June 2024, I've partnered with the Sports Factory of the Lehigh Valley to host my fitness club. I created the GENERAL FITNESS QUEST for my club members, a collection of 44 workout routines that I will take you through personally to achieve level 1, superior fitness. I endeavor to digitize the quest and enhance my ability to monetize my product.

I know I will be here in the Lehigh Valley with my family for a while. What is the long-term play I see for the LV? I want to create a Sports Agency and give some of these exceptional student-athletes a pro-style training and mentorship experience. I want to build a structure that can prepare them to dominate in their sport, build their brands, and capitalize on the value of their talent. It's an exciting idea that I am actively exploring.

I'd like to finish up with a few statements on God and my faith.

☆ Andre Williams ☆

Jesus was the divinity of God wrapped in human flesh, and He came to Earth the first time as a servant. He served mankind in three ways: first, by laying down His life on the cross to atone for the sins of the world; second, by healing the sick, delivering those captive to demons, and revealing the power of faith and of the Holy Spirit; and third, by bringing the good news of eternal life in Christ. He did not come as a powerful king, but as a humble carpenter, washing the feet of His disciples. I met Jesus by diving into His word, and He helped me to accept my own circumstances. If Jesus, the blameless and deserving Son of God, lived a simple life and died like a dog, why should I feel entitled to something more grandiose?

In my early 20s, I found myself on a promising path, but my failure to heed God's guidance and my indulgence in sin led me down a spiral of hard consequences. But the story is far from over for me. Because of God's grace and mercy, I have another chance.

I heard those terms explained best by my good friend and college teammate Dominique Williams. He said that grace is receiving the things that we don't deserve, and mercy is not receiving the things that we do deserve. I thank God for His grace and mercy!

I've encountered four types of people in the world.

The first individual chooses to deny the existence of the spirit and claims that we are only flesh, a smart animal. I've observed that this kind of person doesn't ask deep questions and is okay with a surface-level existence where their only concerns are feelings and experiences.

On the other hand, there are those who hold the belief in a higher power. This belief manifests as a deep spiritual longing, compelling them to embark on a quest to find God or something akin to God. There is a challenge here because those who thirst for spiritual fulfillment without a solid foundation tend to latch onto anything that tickles their souls, especially those things that stroke the ego.

There are many personalities in the realm of the spirit claiming to be God or aiming to convince you that you are God. It might start out as innocently as a horoscope or reiki healing for a sore back, but dive deeper into this realm, and you might encounter a

☆ After the Last Snap ☆

dark spiritual force that will entice you with lavish promises in exchange for something of great worth, sealed in blood. Some might dismiss this claim as nonsense, but those who know the truth understand what I am articulating. When Jesus Christ was fasting in the desert, Satan came to Him with temptation. He will come to tempt you as well.

The amazing thing about God is that He has never hidden Himself from me. He has been right here with me, and when I began to seek Him earnestly, I found Him. The scary part was that when He revealed Himself to me, I was confronted with a choice to either listen to His words or not. That is the third kind of person—the one who is contemplating whether or not to heed the words of God.

I was intimidated at first because I believed that I was sacrificing something by surrendering to the Creator of the Universe. And to some extent, this is true. I gave up my former self (the version of me that chose his own way and satisfied his own desires) so that I could understand God's will for my life and move down the path that He set for me. I am okay with this because I know that the freedom I will achieve by accepting my assignment from God is greater than any goal that I could create on my own.

That is the fourth kind of person—the one actively living out their assignment from God. They are building the kingdom and stacking their heavenly treasures. They possess the kind of faith that moves mountains, claims territories, heals the sick, and casts out demons. It doesn't matter which category you find yourself in today because as long as we still have breath in our lungs, we have time.

There came a point in my faith walk where I learned and understood who God is and what He doesn't like, but much more important than that, I came to learn and understand what God likes and what He asks of me. God likes spiritual discipline, and He wants to see me practice it because it draws me closer to Him. Practicing spiritual discipline is much easier than trying to avoid the things God doesn't like. I've naturally retreated away from those things because I practice spiritual discipline by reading my Bible daily, tithing, praying, fasting, and sharing my faith.

☆ Andre Williams ☆

Many claim that there are various paths to God, but the truth is that only one God created the Earth and everything in it, and He is the only one returning to claim all. I could write another book about matters of the spirit I've discovered throughout my life's journey. That world is fascinating when you accept that it is true—topics such as fallen angels, giants, demons, aliens, religion and spirituality, and the end times. But none of it matters without a genuine relationship with God. No one can persuade me that He is not present, loving us, and patiently waiting for us to seek Him. He is not hidden; rather, just waiting for a humbled heart and a prayer.

Man is made up of three essential parts: the physical body that we can perceive, the soul as the center of emotions and intellect, and the spirit as the divine breath of life, our direct connection to God. No matter how hard we try to deny it, our purpose remains unchanged. We were created to worship and give glory to God. Some may resist this truth because they refuse to bow a knee, but the reality is that we are all worshiping something already. I appreciate all of you for taking the time to read my story. I love you, and I hope that my message blesses your life!

www.ingramcontent.com/pod-product-compliance
Lightning Source LLC
Chambersburg PA
CBHW060516080526
44586CB00012B/506